Mountain Commandos
at War
in the Falklands

The M&AW Cadre after weapon training on RFA *Resource*. There are only thirty-five men present: Sgt Derek 'Tug the Tourist' Wilson was absent for some reason!

Back row, left to right: CSgt E. Young, CSgt P. Montgomery, Cpl J. White, Cpl J. Meade, Cpl J. McGregor, Sgt J. Mitchell, Sgt J. Martin, Cpl G. Heeney, Cpl M. Barnacle, Cpl S. Groves, Cpl J. O'Connor, Cpl R. Sharp.

Middle row: Cpl M. O'Donnell, Lt C. Murray, Cpl N. Devenish, Cpl G. Bickett, Cpl S. Nicoll, Cpl A. Heward, Sgt J. Rowe, Cpl S. Last, Sgt M. Mclean, Sgt D. Wassall, Sgt C. Stone, Cpl T. Holleran.

Front row: Capt. R. Boswell, Cpl G. Foster, Cpl A. Boyle, Lt F. Haddow, Sgt K. Mahon, CSgt W. Wright, Sgt T. Doyle, Cpl S. Healey, Cpl N. West, Cpl R. Sey, Cpl K. Blackmore.

Mountain Commandos at War in the Falklands

The Royal Marines Mountain and Arctic Warfare Cadre in Action during the 1982 Conflict

Rod Boswell

Foreword by
Major General Julian Thompson

Pen & Sword
MILITARY

AN IMPRINT OF PEN & SWORD BOOKS LTD
YORKSHIRE – PHILADELPHIA

First published in Great Britain in 2021 by
PEN & SWORD MILITARY
An imprint of Pen & Sword Books Ltd
Yorkshire – Philadelphia

Copyright © Rod Boswell, 2021

ISBN 978-1-52679-162-7

A CIP catalogue record for this book is available from the British Library.

Typeset by Concept, Huddersfield, West Yorkshire, HD4 5JL
Printed and bound by CPI Group (UK) Ltd, Croydon, CR0 4YY

Pen & Sword Books Ltd incorporates the Imprints of Aviation, Atlas, Family
History, Fiction, Maritime, Military, Discovery, Politics, History, Archaeology,
Select, Wharncliffe Local History, Wharncliffe True Crime, Military Classics,
Wharncliffe Transport, Leo Cooper, The Praetorian Press, Remember When,
White Owl, Seaforth Publishing and Frontline Publishing.

For a complete list of Pen & Sword titles please contact
PEN & SWORD BOOKS LTD
47 Church Street, Barnsley, South Yorkshire, S70 2AS, England
E-mail: enquiries@pen-and-sword.co.uk
Website: www.pen-and-sword.co.uk
or
PEN & SWORD BOOKS
1950 Lawrence Rd, Havertown, PA 19083, USA
E-mail: uspen-and-sword@casematepublishers.com
Website: www.penandswordbooks.com

Dedication

This book is dedicated to all Cliff Leaders, Reconnaissance Leaders and Mountain Leaders of the Royal Marines who served with distinction throughout their time in the service.

From the early days in 1942 they trained commandos for their role in breaking into Europe in the Second World War. In the 1970s they were required to prepare the Royal Marines Commando Brigade for operations in the Arctic and in mountainous terrain. They provided a service that is second to none.

In the 1970s the Mountain and Arctic Warfare Cadre acquired the epithet of a 'climbing club' from poorly educated members of other parts of the Royal Marines. This rather insulting name was effectively riposted by the events chronicled in this book and by further operational efforts by MLs in Northern Ireland, Kuwait, Eastern Turkey, Sierra Leone, Iraq and Afghanistan.

It is to all those qualified to be called CL, RL or ML that this book is dedicated by a man who is proud to consider himself a member of this very small, exclusive and effective club.

Contents

List of Plates

Like herding cats! A Cadre staff photo at Arbroath, 2 April 1982.

Climbing on the ML2 course at Sennen Cove in Cornwall.

An ML2 course on their first ski patrol training exercise.

Introduction of an ML2 course to ice climbing on a glacier in the Lyngen Alps in North Norway.

ML2 course 1/81 on the summit of a mountain in the Alps, northern Italy.

Ice-breaking drills in Norway in February!

The anchorage at Ascension Island.

Ascension Island. Members of the M&AW Cadre returning to RFA *Sir Tristram* from English Bay after three days on ops guarding the airfield at Wideawake against potential Argentine raiders.

HMS *Ardent* carrying out a morale-improving firepower demonstration a few days before she was sunk by the Argentine Air Force.

RFA *Sir Tristram* deep in the south Atlantic, only a few days before the landings at San Carlos Water.

HMS *Ardent* passing *Canberra* at speed in mid-May.

San Carlos Water.

Sergeants Mahon and Doyle watching aircraft attacking over the ships but missing the two Skyhawks just above the hill to their rear!

San Carlos Settlement.

View of the full camouflaged Brigade HQ in San Carlos Water.

Brigadier Thompson with his bodyguard and Air Commodore Pedroza, the Argentine commander of the Goose Green garrison, who formally surrendered his troops to 3 Commando Brigade.

Top Malo House after the raid on 31 May. Mount Simon can be clearly seen in the background.

The Top Malo house area with prisoners under guard by Sergeant Mclean and Corporal Sey, 31 May.

Corporal Boyle manning the radio and guarding the Argentine weapons and equipment.

Argentine prisoners in Teal Inlet awaiting interrogation by the Brigade HQ intelligence section.

The Brigade HQ location at Teal Inlet on 1 June, taken from the M&AW Cadre HQ.

The M&AW Cadre HQ building, the closest building to Brigade HQ.

A Wessex 5 helicopter taking off at dawn from Teal Inlet.

A Sea King at the Teal Inlet landing site coming in at dawn.

Moving forward in two BV202 vehicles and crossing the Malo river en route to setting up the brigade patrol control HQ, 3 June.

The brigade patrol base camouflaged in a rock formation to the southeast of Mount Kent, 3–5 June.

Forward Cadre HQ near Brigade HQ, north of Mount Kent, 11 June.

The new improved Cadre HQ location, better camouflaged and closer to the Brigade HQ location, 11 June.

Gazelle helicopter flying a white flag on 14 June to signify to the Argentines that hostilities were over.

Government House photographed just before sunset on 14 June after Juliet Company of 42 Commando RM had replaced the Argentine flag with the Union Flag of Great Britain.

Sunset over Port Stanley, looking west towards the mountains, 14 June.

Two dead Argentine soldiers on the coast road on the outskirts of Port Stanley.

The full length of the runway at Port Stanley Airfield showing no damage from bombs whatsoever, 15 June.

Ajax Bay on 17 June, showing the 500-plus senior Argentine prisoners.

The graveyard at Ajax Bay, photographed from the Gazelle, 17 June.

The final shot of *Canberra* leaving San Carlos Water on 25 June.

HMS *Hermes* pictured on 26 June with all the Sea Harriers on deck.

RFA *Resource* turning to drop anchor.

List of Maps

Acknowledgements

This book only came about as a result of the courage, professionalism and dedication of the other thirty-five members of the Mountain and Arctic Warfare Cadre Royal Marines who participated in the Falklands conflict of 1982 as the 3 Cdo Bde Recce Tp. It is these men about whom this book is written and I am extremely grateful to them all. Those who have died since 1982 all contributed before their demise and their words are included within the book. The others have all supported this project, and their participation has made this book possible.

I start with the 'famous five', who have provided me with help as I struggled through the writing of this book with unremitting support, suggestions and encouragement. First, Major General Julian Thompson RM for his sage-like help and always sensible suggestions for the way forward; Major Mark Bentinck RM (retired Corps Historian) for his sagacity and knowledge of the Corps' history and for his total support for the project; and Clive Richards, another Royal Marine, whom I thank for his knowledge of the English language, his beautiful artwork and his unconditional patience and support. Steve Nicoll, who served with me in 1982 as a corporal and retired as a major many years later, I thank for several reasons. First, for his guile in provoking me to write a book that I had no intention of writing (and am astonished that I have actually done it) and secondly, for his support, suggestions and general help and motivational skills. The fifth member of this group is Keith Clarke, who has nothing to do with the Royal Marines but is one of the best salmon fishermen I know and a kind and helpful companion (with his wife Ros) on many expeditions chasing salmon all over the world. His clear perspective, unspoilt by any time in the military, helped me change an 'after-action' report into a readable book. He remains a good and trusted friend and I am very grateful to him for his patience and kind support.

In addition, Hector Gullan has also provided me with support and the confidence to keep going. He is a man whom I respect as a thorough and very competent soldier and a true friend, and I thank him for that.

Obviously a big thank you goes to the serving MLs within the Corps for their assistance, especially the modern Cadre (now under a more professional name) who have given me a great deal of assistance in completing this book. Both Major Gaz Veacock and WO1 Craig McMillan (whose father completed the ML2 course during my time as OC Cadre in 1980) gave of their time and expertise in support.

Rupert Harding of Pen & Sword Books, who has taken on the project and provided me with the confidence to keep going, gets a very big vote of thanks. His gentle guidance that both challenged me and encouraged me to keep at it is the real reason that the book is now finished. I would also like to thank Sarah Cook, my editor, for her hard work in converting my text into a much more readable and more easily digestible book.

Finally, I would like to thank my wife Sarah. Having been a GP for many years in York, she took on the role of GP ('Grammar Policewoman') for this project. She has laboured through every single word of this document, including all the rewrites and alterations, and has continued to put up with my tantrums with a patience that is almost saintly! To say that it would not have been completed without her support is not overstating her involvement, and I remain in awe and one of her biggest fans, obviously!

Foreword

by Major General Julian Thompson

The Falklands War of 1982 marked the first occasion that the 3rd Commando Brigade had its own dedicated reconnaissance force. How this force was created is explained by the man responsible for its existence in an operational form (with emphasis on the word 'operational') – the author of this book: Rod Boswell. In the opening chapters the reader will learn how Rod transformed what was purely a training organisation, the Mountain and Arctic Warfare Cadre (M&AW Cadre, or the Cadre for short), into what became the Commando Brigade Reconnaissance Troop, and took it to war in the Falklands.

As Rod explains, the forebears of the Cadre were the specialist cliff leaders of the Second World War commandos. Their name describes their role: to lead commandos up cliffs on raids and assaults in the Second World War; that and nothing more. After that war the Cliff Climbing Wing continued to train cliff climbers, and after a while some of the instructors became more ambitious and, dare one say it, perhaps because it was more fun than climbing cliffs in Cornwall, ventured into the mountains: first in Britain, then Norway, the Alps and the Himalayas – indeed any place where there was a mountain to climb. The connection with a military role sometimes became so tenuous as to be almost invisible, at least to those of a cynical turn of mind serving at the time. As a young lieutenant leading a training team on the Commando course in the latter half of the 1950s, I had a stand-up row with the then officer commanding the Cliff Climbing Wing, a well known mountaineer, when I introduced a 'battle' on the cliff top into the final night's climbing exercise for the young recruits in my troop. This, he implied, was a distraction, almost amounting to sacrilege, to sully the purity of rock climbing with anything so sordid as a battle.

In due course the Climbing Wing became the M&AW Cadre as part of the Royal Marines' commitment to NATO contingency plans for operating in Arctic North Norway. The Mountain Leaders of the Cadre trained and provided skilled instructors in the skills required to live, move and fight in the Arctic and mountain environment of North Norway.

Rod commanded the reconnaissance troop (Recce Tp) in 40 Commando when I was the commanding officer, a period which included an operational tour in the 'bandit country' of South Armagh. He held similar views to mine on what the priority was: top-quality soldiering was the first requirement for a reconnaissance outfit. His troop, which contained some mountain leaders, was so successful and highly regarded that the SAS squadron based in our operational 'patch' subcontracted some of its tasks to Rod's troop. One of several such operations involved maintaining a four-man observation post in the attic of the Sinn Fein office in the border town of Crossmaglen for several weeks.

So when, some three years later, I was chief of staff at Commando Forces in Plymouth and Rod came up with the proposition that the Cadre should have a wartime role as the Commando Brigade Recce Tp, it took about three seconds to realise he was on to a winner. The rest, as they say, is history – or to be more precise it leads in to the story of the Cadre's achievements in the first – but by no means last – of their wars, first as the brigade Recce Tp described in these pages, then as the brigade reconnaissance force, and now as part of the brigade's information-gathering specialists in 30 Commando Royal Marines.

The Cadre that I knew in the Falklands set standards of excellence in soldiering skills that were never bettered by anyone, including the SAS and SBS. This professionalism included never making map-reading errors; the skilful use of ground; excellent tactics in engagements; dexterity in calling for and adjusting supporting fire; and the ingenious siting of observation posts close to the enemy. The Cadre performed these and other tasks without hubris of the kind that led others to near, and sometimes actual, disaster, through ignoring advice or as the result of incompetence or second-rate soldiering.

The Cadre carried out a number of brilliant operations, but to me the *pièce de résistance* was their action at Top Malo house, fully described in Rod's book. The outcome was to eliminate the Argentine Special Forces' observation posts from the high ground overlooking 3 Commando Brigade's approach to Mount Kent and its adjoining features, the jumping-off place for the brigade's battles for Stanley. So the Argentines remained unaware of our approach by this route, and the direction of our initial attacks came as a surprise. The Top Malo battle is a demonstration of how a small body of men can have an influence on the course of one phase of a campaign.

The Cadre was an elite within an elite, for the Royal Marines as a whole are an elite in their own right. The training regime undergone by every Royal Marine is recognised as being one of the most testing in the world. The result is a force that is world class, along with a handful of others, including the French Foreign Legion and the United States Marine Corps. The Cadre and its lineal successors have built on that bedrock of superlative soldiering skills while adding their specialist expertise to produce a reconnaissance force which is second to none.

This book benefits because it is written by a recce man of considerable experience, and one whose judgement and skill I have valued in two very different campaigns.

Glossary

3 Cdo Bde – 3 Commando Brigade. The brigade responsible for all Royal Marines operations other than those of the Royal Marines Special Forces. In 1982 the major units within the brigade were 40, 41, 42 and 45 Commandos, each commanded by a lieutenant colonel. 41 Cdo RM was disbanded by defence reductions in 1981.

81mm MOR HE – 81mm mortar high explosive ammunition. The basic ammunition for the British 81mm mortar.

ADC – Aide-de-Camp. A junior officer who acts as aide to a senior officer and is his personal staff officer, ensuring that he is in the right place in the right rig at the right time.

AMF(L) – Allied Command Europe Mobile Force (Land). The NATO 'fire brigade', made up of personnel from all sixteen NATO nations and designed to operate on NATO's flanks. Thus an attack on the AMF(L) would be seen as an attack on the whole of NATO and a reason for all nations of NATO to become involved under the NATO Charter.

AO – Administrative Officer. Responsible for the provision of all administrative support to the Cadre. As a unit with two vehicles and only one driver, we always had a shortfall of transport. We spent most of our time operating away from our base and thus always needed the support of chefs for feeding and also had a permanent requirement for medical cover from medical attendants (MA) and occasionally from a medical officer (MO).

APWT – Annual Personal Weapons Test. The annual test that all RM personnel have to take and pass on their personal weapon.

AR15 – US Armalite rifle of 5.56mm calibre. The first-choice weapon for MLs as it had two advantages over the SLR: first, it offered automatic fire capability, and secondly, it was shorter and lighter than the SLR, which made it more manageable when climbing.

BARV – Beach Armoured Recovery Vehicle. A recovery vehicle used to recover any broken or damaged vehicles in a beach assault and under enemy fire.

Blue on blue – An incident that involve troops of the same side firing on or attacking each other.

Bofors – Second World War-era 40mm anti-aircraft weapons that provided the main shipboard anti-aircraft capability for the conflict.

Bootneck – Nickname for Royal Marines as used by the Corps and by the Royal Navy. It refers to the days under sail when Royal Marines wore queues (pony-tails) and tarred them to manage them, thus making their necks black, the colour of their boots, hence bootneck.

C130 – An RAF supply aircraft used to deploy parachute troops. Also known as the Hercules.

Cadre – The definition of a cadre is: 'The permanent nucleus of an organisation (especially military), to be expanded when the need arises.' Most cadres in the military are set up for short periods to provide a pool of experts for a particular training or operational task. This definition has been the cause of much confusion where the M&AW Cadre is concerned as it was actually a full-time complemented organisation within the Corps.

Camp – Term used in the Falkland Islands to describe anywhere other than Port Stanley. It even had a time difference from Port Stanley of one hour.

Capt – Captain.

Casevac – Casualty evacuation. Means of removing casualties for further medical treatment.

Casevac Helo – Helicopter used for casualty evacuation.

Cdo – Commando. A fully trained Royal Marine is a RM Cdo. Cdo is also the name given to Royal Marine Commando units (such as 45 Cdo RM).

Chacon – Chatham Container. A medium to large container used for storage and transportation of stores and other equipment by land or sea.

CL – Cliff Leader. Forerunner of the RL and ML branch within the Royal Marines.

CO – Commanding Officer. Title given to officers in command of larger and more important units within the military.

Corps – The Corps of Royal Marines, reduced simply to the Corps for simplicity.

COS – Chief of Staff. A major in HQ 3 Cdo Bde and a colonel in HQ Cdo Forces.

Cpl – Corporal.

CSgt – Colour Sergeant.

CSM – Company Sergeant Major or in the M&AW Cadre the Cadre Sergeant Major. An experienced SNCO who was effectively the disciplinarian and immediate second in command to the OC. He is the most experienced ML within the Cadre and the Corps.

CTCRM – Commando Training Centre Royal Marines, usually referred to as CTC. Based on the river Exe in east Devon, it has been the main training base of the Corps since April 1970, although it was originally known as the Infantry Training Centre Royal Marines (ITCRM).

Dhobi – Indian (probably Urdu) word for washing. Used by the military to include clothing, equipment and bodies.

DPM – Disrupted Pattern Material, the standard camouflaged material used for British wear on operations. It is a mixture of black-, green- and brown-coloured patches of material.

DRORM – Drafting and Records Office Royal Marines. The administrative heart of the Royal Marines for management of drafting, paying and personnel administration for all Royal Marines.

FEBA – Forward Edge of the Battle Area. In simple terms the front line.

FLUB – 'Fat lazy useless bastard': Recce Tp epithet referring to those members of the Corps who do not maintain the required physical fitness levels.

GMT – Greenwich Mean Time: London time or the time used to set all the world's clocks. Every 15 degrees of longitude to the east or west of London means an hour added or subtracted from GMT. Thus, GMT runs from 7 degrees 30 minutes east to 7 degrees 30 minutes west, and then add 15 degrees for every other time zone.

GPMG – General Purpose Machine Gun. A 7.62mm medium/heavy machine gun used by British forces.

Gucci/Gucci Kit – A RM comment about kit and equipment that owes more to appearance than to its relevance for war.

HE – High Explosive.

Helo – Helicopter

HF – High Frequency radio. A type of radio frequency used for longer distance signals work.

Huey – American-manufactured helicopter deployed by the Argentine Air Force during the conflict. Hueys saw heavy war service with the USA during the Vietnam War.

ISTAR – Intelligence, Surveillance, Target Acquisition and Reconnaissance: the full description of the task of Recce Tps.

IWS – Individual Weapon Sight. In 1982 this referred to a first-generation image intensifier that allowed us to see in the dark. It was very heavy, bulky and not a great help, but it had proved very useful on operations in Northern Ireland. It was less successful during Operation Corporate, where weight was a much more important factor.

JNCO – Junior Non-Commissioned Officer (corporal or lance corporal).

LAW – Light Anti-tank Weapon. The 66mm LAW was a very effective American weapon that we found very useful for a variety of different tasks during Operation Corporate.

LC – Landing Craft.

LCpl – Lance Corporal.

LCU – Landing Craft Utility. Designed for heavy loads, including a tank or multiple personnel over medium distances in all weathers.

LCVP – Landing Craft Vehicles and Personnel. Designed to carry up to thirty troops or two Landrovers and ancillaries over relatively short distances.

LSL – Landing Ship Logistic. The primary assistance vessels for the RM, used for carrying stores and personnel for operations away from UK shores. Manned by RFA personnel, they are the backbone of all amphibious operations.

Lt – Lieutenant.

MA – Medical Assistant.

M&AW – Mountain and Arctic Warfare: the role of the Royal Marines, specifically for the northern flank of NATO.

M&AW Cadre – The permanent cadre of specialist ML instructors instigated in 1970 to provide the Royal Marines with an expert base of personnel to train others for operations on the northern and southern flanks of NATO.

Mexefloats – Powered barges carried on each LSL and provided as heavy goods carriers for long operations. Manned by RCT crews, they are a very necessary part of the equipment needed for beach landings.

MGRM – Major General Royal Marines.

MGRM Cdo Forces – Major General Royal Marines Commando Forces. The general officer responsible for all of the Royal Marines Commando Forces (the operational majority of the Royal Marines).

ML – Mountain Leader. The current iteration of the branch within the Royal Marines responsible for providing specialist instructors to train the Corps for operations in mountains and in the Arctic. It is the specialisation that provides leaders for the specialist brigade troops that provide the Commando Brigade with ISTAR as required.

ML1 – Mountain Leader First Class. A SNCO RM who has completed his ML training and is a fully trained expert in operations and training in mountain and Arctic environments.

ML2 – Mountain Leader Second Class. A JNCO RM who has completed his ML2 course and is a qualified instructor in M&AW warfare.

MLO – Mountain Leader Officer. Any officer who has completed and passed the ML2 course.

MO – Medical Officer.

Mooning – The baring of one's behind as a show of defiance or outright rudeness.

NATO – North Atlantic Treaty Organisation. A political and military alliance formed in 1948 from the sixteen nations that abutted the Soviet Union and still at this size in 1982. The alliance ensured that the Soviet Union was unable to expand her borders through military force, and guaranteed the freedom and security of its members through political and military means. Its motto is: a strike against one is a strike against all.

NP8901 – Naval Party 8901 is the permanent party of Royal Marines stationed in the Falkland Islands.

OC – Officer Commanding. Title given to the commanding officers of smaller units within the military.

OP – Observation Post. A small semi-permanent patrol forward of the FEBA used to provide early notice of enemy movements and intentions. Usually provided by Recce Tps within a Commando unit.

Op role – Operational Role. The wartime fighting role for any organisation within the Royal Marines. Not to be confused with OP (Observation Post) task, which is a patrol for observing enemy operations or intentions.

Operation Corporate – The codename given to the operation to recover the Falkland Islands after the invasion by Argentine forces in 1982.

ORBAT – Order of Battle. The operational organisation of any fighting part of the Royal Marines or any other military organisations.

Phys – Physical training.

PInfo – Public Information. The title given to Royal Marine staff officers who are responsible for the public face of the Royal Marines. Their primary role is to ensure that any adverse publicity involving Royal Marines is reported upon accurately and honestly and to ensure that no poorly researched information is published without full approval by the relevant staff HQ.

Pongo – Historical nickname used by the Royal Navy and the Royal Air Force for the British army.

PRC 320 – The HF radio set used by the M&AW Cadre in 1982.

PRIC – Photo Reconnaissance Interpretation Centre (RAF)

PT – Physical Training.

PT&SO – Physical Training and Sports Officer. An officer trained as a PTI who provides leadership and guidance to PT personnel.

PTI – Physical Training Instructor. The PT coordinators within the RM.

Pulk – Norwegian name for a sled used to carry heavy infantry weapons and equipment on snow. It is usually towed by two skiers and is often assisted by a further two, particular when travelling downhill.

PWO – 1st Battalion, Prince of Wales' Own Regiment of Yorkshire. The UK AMF(L) battalion from 1978 to 1984. I served with them as their operations officer from July 1978 until April 1980.

RAF – Royal Air Force.

RCT – Royal Corps of Transport. The unsung heroes of any beach landing operation. They manned the mexefloats and were an intrepid, dedicated and brave band of warriors whose true worth only became apparent on arrival in San Carlos Water.

Recce Tp – Reconnaissance troop. These troops are an integral part of every Royal Marine Commando unit. They are usually commanded by an ML officer and most of the NCOs are ML personnel. They provide their CO with specialist patrolling and OP skills for relatively short distances in front of the FEBA.

REMF – Rear Echelon Mother F**ker. USMC epithet adopted by the Royal Marines for personnel who are not part of the front-line fighting troops.

RFA – Royal Fleet Auxiliary. The RFA's superb fleet of tankers, store ships and ammunition carriers that enable the Royal Navy to stay at sea for long periods of time.

Rigid Raider – A small high-powered motorboat designed to take up to eight passengers at speed over a relatively short distance.

RL – Reconnaissance Leader. Part of the evolution of the specialist branch within the Royal Marines now known as the ML branch.

RM – Royal Marines.

RN – Royal Navy. Host service that includes the Royal Marines.

RSM – Regimental Sergeant Major. A WO1. The most senior NCO within the RM.

R to I – Resistance to Interrogation. Type of training for 'prone to capture' troops; MLs, pilots and SBS members are among those in the RM who go through this training.

Russian Bear – Very large maritime aircraft used by the Russians for a multiplicity of tasks including intelligence gathering.

RV – Rendezvous. A location known to all team members as a join-up location should the patrol be split up for any reason. An emergency rendezvous (ERV) is a place known to all patrol members as the final place to withdraw to in an emergency situation.

SAS – Special Air Service. Army Special Forces.

SBS – Special Boat Service. Royal Marines Special Forces.

SF – Special Forces. Specialist troops of the three services whose role is strategic rather than tactical in nature.

Sgt – Sergeant.

SLJ – Shitty Little Job. Thus, SLJO is a SLJ Officer and SSLJO is a Senior SLJO. The latter term is used for a middle seniority staff job that is mundane but unfortunately necessary.

SNCO – Senior Non-Commissioned Officer. Ranks include sergeant, colour sergeant, warrant officer second class and warrant officer first class.

SOPs – Standard Operating Procedures. Small to large-scale unit standing orders for certain tactical operations when on active service. SOPs are particularly relevant in small team work, and may include OP routines, break from action drills and the management of radio and cypher use drills.

Swift Scope – A short but very powerful telescope used by snipers and Recce Tps for increasing their visual scan area.

Tab – Tactical advance to battle. Parachute Regiment expression used for moving as fast as possible across country.

Time – One of the constant problems we faced after Operation Corporate was trying to remember what time anything happened. All the ships worked on GMT (London time) but the Falklands Islands were 60 degrees west of London putting them four hours behind London time. To make matters worse, the Argentines decided to set Stanley Time to that of Argentina (three hours behind GMT), thus putting the whole of the islands on two time zones. This was patently ridiculous so the entire time down south we operated on GMT but lived in 'local' time. I have written this book in 'local' time, where first light was about 0600 and last light about 1600 every day.

TQ – Tactical Quartermaster. The title for the second most SNCO in the Cadre who was responsible for all stores and store-related duties. It was a very busy and important role in a small organisation with a global reach.

USMC – United States Marines Corps: the American equivalent to the Royal Marines.

USSR – The Union of Soviet Socialist Republics.

Wet/Wets – Any drink taken in the field. Commonly heard in comments like 'stopping for a wet'.

WO1 – Warrant Officer First Class.

WO2 – Warrant Officer Second Class.

WP – White phosphorous. White phosphorous grenades are very fast-acting smokescreen grenades that proved very useful during Operation Corporate.

WW2 – The Second World War.

Yomp – RM term for moving across country usually encumbered with as much kit as each man is capable of carrying on his back. In the Falklands campaign this could be anything up to weights of 150lb per man.

Introduction

Shortly after sunset on 8 June 1982 two of the eight four-man teams of the Royal Marines Mountain & Arctic Warfare Cadre* (M&AW Cadre) infiltrated into Goat Ridge, a long rocky ridge between Mount Harriet and Two Sisters. Each mountain was occupied by a 600-strong battalion of Argentine infantry soldiers dug-in in well established defensive positions. These men were prepared to defend their locations against the soon-to-arrive British troops aiming to restore the Falklands Islands to their rightful owners after the Argentine invasion of 2 April 1982. The task for the two patrols was to gain as much intelligence as they could about the enemy positions on the two mountains and to provide battlefield sketches, in as much detail as possible, of any and all enemy locations on the relevant sides of the two features.

After a very difficult move through wet and dangerously slippery terrain, they established an observation post (OP) location at the eastern end of Goat Ridge. The OP consisted of the two team leaders seated back to back in a concealed position and supported (about 15m away) by the remaining six members of the two teams, who were prepared to provide any fire support and assistance needed should either location be compromised by the enemy. The joint patrol stayed put throughout the daylight hours of 9 June and then exfiltrated after sunset and withdrew to the west to return to safer ground free of the enemy, carrying the details of their highly successful patrol with them.

---

*The term 'cadre' when used by military personnel refers to an organisation of 'experts' put together for a short-term solution either to an operational requirement or to a specific change of training. On completion of the operation or training, the 'cadre' is shut down and all ranks involved return to their home units. The Royal Marines M&AW Cadre was established as a permanent unit in order to maintain a core of experts to assist with training for operations in mountains and in the Arctic climate of northern Norway. It was and remains to this day a permanent part of the Royal Marines chain of command and is not just a temporary solution to a short-term training requirement. (It is not to be confused with the term 'cadre' as used by Communist-inspired guerrillas and terrorists. They use the term in its original manner but adapt it to mean the core of special groups of terrorists almost anywhere in the world.)

On their return the two team leaders went immediately to see the commanding officers of 42 Commando (Lieutenant Colonel Nick Vaux) and 45 Commando (Lieutenant Colonel Andrew Whitehead) to debrief and to pass on the field sketches they had produced. The information they provided would prove vital in the plans made by both COs for the successful assaults made on those features on 11 June 1982.

This very professional and courageous patrol will be described in more detail later in the book but is introduced here to demonstrate the extent of the work carried out by the thirty-six men of the M&AW Cadre during Operation Corporate, the recovery of the Falkland Islands in the summer (in the UK) of 1982. This book also tells the wider story of the M&AW Cadre on operations in the South Atlantic in 1982, and covers in detail the period from September 1979 until September 1982.

The M&AW Cadre is an organisation within the Royal Marines that can trace its history back to the birth of the commandos early in the Second World War and the establishment of the Commando Snow and Mountain Training Centre in Braemar, Scotland, in 1942. The Cadre existed throughout the war. After the war the Royal Marines retained the commando role, and the Commando Cliff Assault Centre Royal Marines was opened in St Ives in Cornwall in 1946.

Since those early days there was a growing need within the Corps for a specialist group of climbers within the commandos, as described in Mark Bentinck's book *Vertical Assault – The story of the Royal Marines Mountain Leaders Branch*.* It would be both unnecessary and fatuous to do anything other than praise Mark's accurate and knowledgeable publication and I do not intend to do so. Suffice to say that it is a clear and detailed history of the evolution of Royal Marines climbing qualifications from cliff leaders through reconnaissance leaders to the mountain leaders of today, and covers the entire history from 1942 until its publication in 2007.

This book tells of the period immediately before and during Operation Corporate in 1982 and introduces the team of MLs serving within the M&AW Cadre at that time, providing a record of the efforts they made to produce the 3 Cdo Bde Recce Tp that was so successful during operations in the South Atlantic.

The gestation period of this book has been a long one and it has come about for two main reasons. The first and most obvious is that we are not getting any younger and, at the time of writing, six of our number from 1982 have already died. The pool of accurate and clear memories is thus

---

* Special Publication 34 by the Royal Marines Historical Society.

reducing, so the book needs to be written now whilst a majority are still hale and hearty. Secondly, other people and organisations are seeking to take the credit for work carried out by the M&AW Cadre in 1982 and this must be corrected.

The Argentine Special Forces in particular have attempted to rewrite history to the extent that the raid on Top Malo House, which was a successful patrol action by the Cadre in 1982, has now become accepted by the Argentines as almost being a victory for them, despite the actual outcome. This book aims to illustrate how the Cadre was prepared for its role in 1982 and the operations it accomplished, and to ensure the truth is told. The story is told largely in the words of those who took part; I am simply the editor of their reports and collator of the details. It is not a task I would have chosen, but as their OC in 1982 I see this as my final responsibility to all those who participated in the period 1979 to 1982.

In August 1979 I was appointed to take over as OC M&AW Cadre in April 1980. I had gained a 'just' pass on my ML course in 1974. I felt at the time that it was an exceptional mobility course designed to teach people how to move and survive in very difficult terrain. The mix of latitude, altitude and the transition from sea to land required specialist training and a group of very fit and dedicated men who were totally at ease in those difficult climatic and geographic locations and conditions. I also came to the view that it had become more of a physical fitness climbing course than a military training course for specialist reconnaissance operators. I decided therefore that when I finished my course I would try to return and change the syllabus with the intention of increasing the operational emphasis without reducing the climbing component at all.

My first thought when I received my posting order was to make an appointment with Colonel Julian Thompson RM, the chief of staff at HQ Commando Forces in Plymouth. The senior instructor at the Officers' Training Wing (OTW)* when I went through training, he had also been my commanding officer at 40 Commando Royal Marines when I had commanded his Recce Tp for two years. Colonel Julian and I had very similar thoughts about the future of the M&AW Cadre and agreed that a detailed and specifically operational war role would be the way ahead for the ML branch and for Commando Forces as a whole. I was reasonably sure that Colonel Julian would be the next commander of 3 Cdo Bde and I wanted to be sure that he would ask for M&AW Cadre assistance should

*Officers' Training Wing, Commando Training Centre Royal Marines, Lympstone, Devon.

some future conflict occur. With this mindset, he and I agreed that we would seek to find a way to prepare for that eventuality. We kept our meeting very close to our chests and I then set about preparing to take over the Cadre on completion of the 1980 winter deployment to Norway.

At that time the M&AW Cadre had no formal wartime role apart from a poorly recorded option that they would provide four four-man teams to ski from the Norwegian border to Murmansk to provide assistance and terminal control of air raids directed at the USSR's largest military complex at that time. The physical aspect of this task was well within the ability of the M&AW Cadre. The lack of any cover en route, however, and the amount of Soviet radio intelligence around Murmansk ensured that it was an almost certain death sentence for any troops who attempted it. I for one was very glad that I was never called upon to carry out this suicide mission.

The programme of the Cadre at that time was an annual circuit beginning in September, with the start of the ML1 and ML2 courses in west Cornwall for rock climbing and cliff assault training. In October it moved to North Wales, where the emphasis was on longer climbs, long mountain marches and the development of higher altitude mountain skills. The final ten days consisted of survival training in the Inner Hebrides, followed by resistance to interrogation training. November was a mix of ski courses in Norway for novice Arctic personnel and the mountain training of 45 Commando Royal Marines for the remainder. December revolved around consolidation of personnel and preparation for the winter deployment to Norway with the brigade, plus Christmas leave. January to March was spent on the full winter warfare training course, with the emphasis on training the trainers to prepare the ML2 personnel for their next appointments within commando units. In late March the courses went to northern Norway to climb in the Lyngen Alps, where Norway's highest mountains are located, and to participate in the relevant NATO exercises in the years they were held. Returning to the UK in late March, the Cadre moved to Fort William and the Ben Nevis area for final climbing assessments and snow and ice climbing in the region. The courses then finished just before Easter and personnel went on leave before posting to their next units. Qualified ML2s were physically fit and strong climbers who could operate in all weathers in the harshest climates in the world.

From late April to early June the Cadre staff worked on administrative duties in Arbroath and undertook a small amount of military training, which included annual range courses and parachute training if possible. June and July were spent in preparation for and participation in Exercise

Ice Flip, the annual high-altitude training in the European Alps. This was also available for Commando Recce Tps if they were not otherwise engaged and participation significantly improved the knowledge and ability of the MLs to operate at altitudes in excess of 10,000ft above sea level. (It was argued that ML course volunteers were mostly from the Corps Recce Tps and thus were already well-trained soldiers who did not need further military training. I disagreed, feeling that the type of skills needed for long-range patrolling work required learning in the right military and geographical context and being completely at ease in the environment was not enough.)

This annual programme had evolved since the early 1970s when the Cadre was established in Arbroath. In my opinion, since then the training programme had increasingly emphasised the climbing aspect whilst slowly reducing the military skills levels. I wished to change that approach and knew that the only way to do so was to become the OC and work from within. At the time I rejoined the Cadre it was nineteen men strong, of whom seventeen were MLs, plus the storeman and the driver. What follows is the story of how the required changes to the M&AW Cadre were made, the people who made them and how the Cadre rose to the ultimate test of modern warfare during the Falklands conflict. I trust it will withstand scrutiny by all those who were involved and certainly by those who seek to write their own version of history.

Note that ranks used in the book are those held by the participants in 1982 and do not reflect the promotions subsequently earned by all participants during their careers.

Chapter 1

M&AW Cadre
(April 1980–April 1982)

After completing the winter deployment of 1980, I finished my time with the Allied Command Europe Mobile Force (AMF) where I had been the tame Royal Marine officer on exchange. I left the Prince of Wales's Own Regiment of Yorkshire (PWO) where I had been the operations officer for two years and drove to Arbroath to take over as OC M&AW Cadre (known as the Cadre) from Captain David Nicholls. David had been the OC for the previous three years and was a very professional ML and skilled infantry soldier with a lot of combat experience, so I knew I was taking over a well-oiled machine. My new sergeant major was Warrant Officer 2 (WO2) Brian Snowdon, a man I knew by reputation as a fine professional, capable and knowledgeable ML. He had been the Recce Tp sergeant in 41 Cdo when I was in 40 Cdo. In his own words,

> Sitting in my office in May 1980, a figure appeared at the office door dressed in civvies. I said 'Who the hell are you?' The reply came, 'I'm the new OC' and from that moment onwards we forged a tremendous working relationship and friendship with the same aim to create an operational unit. The OC, myself and TQ [Tactical Quartermaster, Colour Sergeant Everett Young] formed a great working relationship, that is, apart from the OC's driving.

I received a tremendous handover from David Nicholls. The sting in the tail (and the last snippet he passed on) was that the Corps was very short of ML2s and it had been decided that in 1980 the Cadre would run two ML2 courses, the first starting in May and the second at the normal time in September. This was a double blow for me, meaning that my initial plan to start changing the Cadre's courses and preparing for an operational role would have to be delayed because of the requirement for the entire Cadre to be involved in ML2 training. It also meant that my intention to start the build-up of ancillary skills required for the new role would have to be delayed. The NCOs needed to attend the courses would all be involved in the ML2 course training until at least April 1981.

I learned very early on that I had joined a group of MLs whose attitude towards a future operational role was very close to mine. They mostly fully agreed with my future plans for the Cadre. This was a great boost to me as I had not been at all sure how my ideas would be taken. But I should have expected the quality of the ML personnel to shine through and, of course, it did. Brian Snowdon again:

> Having rejoined the Cadre in May 1979 as sergeant major it was without doubt the pinnacle of my career. However, I believed the Cadre was perceived as a 'private climbing club' and had lost the vast military potential it was capable of. After all, the Commando Recce Troops were largely made up of ML officers and NCOs and most of the Marines went on from Recce Troops to either become MLs or to join the SBS (Special Boat Service) or other specialist recce organisations. My ambition was to change this perception and introduce the operational role as I believed in the Cadre having a military capability as the brigade Recce Troop.

Very early on in our working relationship I called a meeting of all the SNCOs within the Cadre and laid out my intentions for my time as the OC. I was absolutely delighted that my plans were given unanimous support by those in attendance. Unfortunately, my immediate plan to begin altering the content of the ML2 and ML1 courses had to be put on the back-burner because of the need for an additional ML2 course. However, we were able to spend valuable time pooling knowledge and contacts for when we would start fully on the preparations which we intended to begin in April 1981.

At that time Major General Jeremy Moore MC and Bar was commanding Commando Forces. He had taken me through training when he was OC of the Officers' Training Wing and he was also the brigade commander when I had been the Recce Tp commander in 40 Cdo RM. After my meeting in October 1979 with his chief of staff Colonel Julian Thompson, General Moore and Colonel Thompson had discussed the future operational role for the Cadre. As a result, the Cadre was included within the final NATO exercise at the end of the winter deployment to the Arctic, where they carried out a number of patrol and observation tasks that put all their skills to the test. As usual during the winter deployment the Cadre was sent to all the units of the brigade to provide the expert skills for them to perform well in Arctic conditions. Again, quoting Brian Snowdon,

> Most importantly, at the end of the Clockwork training [winter deployment] the Cadre began involvement in the final brigade/ NATO exercises providing long-range patrols and having a presence within the command and control at Brigade HQ. This was a major turning-point in the Cadre's future as we had the capability to carry out long-range deep penetration patrols. During Clockwork 80 I was deployed to train the Royal Engineers. During training we had a visit from General Moore, who was having lunch 'in the field' with a group of NATO VIPs. I was informed by his aide-de-camp* (ADC) that I was requested to attend and to sit next to the general. Moments before I sat down the ADC said, 'This is your chance to put your case for an official operational role directly to the general', and he would be taking notes of the meeting. Shortly after [I sat] down, the general quite casually turned to me and said 'I believe you have some suggestions about the future of the Cadre?' I believe from that moment on his staff officers were taking what we were trying to achieve seriously.

Although in May 1980 I was unable to progress my plans because of the additional workload, I started showing our intention to alter the perceived opinions within the Corps that we were just a 'bunch of professional climbers'. This perception I always found rather odd but put it down to the fact that the majority of non-climbers considered that people who liked to climb must be short of common sense and thus were not true soldiers! This was so far from the truth that it required considerable patience when dealing with some of my contemporaries. I remember on one occasion, when we were preparing to go to the Alps for our annual high altitude training period, telephoning the relevant staff officer in London to ask his permission to purchase glacier cream and glacier glasses for use in the snow in order to protect our faces and eyes from the glare and reflection. His response was extraordinary. He told me that he was 'not going to pay for sunglasses and sun-cream for our holiday in the Alps and if we needed such kit, we should pay for it ourselves'. I could not explain the need for the kit in any way that he could comprehend so I had

---

* The ADC (aide-de-camp) is the personal staff officer for his senior officer, and all senior officers in the military as a whole have an ADC for this purpose. The ADC ensures that the senior officers' programmes are properly organised and that there are no clashes within the programmes, among other important administrative tasks.

to be a little creative and got the stores through the medical squadron, who did at least understand the medical need for eye and skin protection at high altitudes with full snow cover. This may seem rather petty, but it was the sort of problem that I had to deal with almost daily.

Having taken over command and set the wheels in motion for a very busy year, I started to plan the requirements of the year ahead (1981 and onwards). My first thought was that if we were to become a part of the brigade order of battle, then we needed to be close to Brigade HQ. Being stationed in Arbroath and reporting to a general in Portsmouth for the training side of the job and to a brigadier in Plymouth for the operational side of the job was not going to work as we needed to be 'in plain sight'. I sent a formal letter to HQ Commando Forces requesting relocation of the Cadre from Arbroath to Plymouth, and explained the need to reduce travel costs and accommodation requirements as well as gaining easier access to air transport for both Norway and the European Alps. My suggestion was rejected out of hand on the grounds that Arbroath was closer to the mountains of Scotland and Norway and thus we were in the best possible location and should remain there. I was flabbergasted but realised that it was just the sort of ill-educated response that I should have expected from the current beliefs of the more senior officers of the Corps at that time. Fortunately, one of the members of the 3 Cdo Bde staff was a very old friend, Captain Phil Wilson, who telephoned me before I had a chance to do something I would later regret; he told me to wind my neck in, and gave me some outstanding advice. He told me that he knew what I was trying to achieve but the best way to do it was to let him have a go from his end first and await developments. Phil was (and is) a great student of the human condition. He said that the best thing to do was for him to send an order for the Cadre to reconsider its geographical location and consider a move further south and nearer the main part of the operational Corps in Plymouth. I should sit on this for a month or two, then send back a casual response stating that we were very happy in Arbroath and had no desire whatsoever to move south. Phil had realised that my early request had been dealt with by the administrative/logistic part of HQ Commando Forces and not the operational side. There was no way therefore that the exchange of letters had 'crossed the floor', as it were. In due course I received the formal letter. I waited about six weeks and sent a very casual reply saying that we were very happy in Arbroath and had no desire to leave there at all. The order to prepare to move to Plymouth returned at great speed, signed by the brigade chief of staff! I bought Phil a few beers on the strength of that bit of advice. At last the wheels were rolling and more importantly I knew I had friends in the right places to help with our plans.

At the first Cadre future operations role planning meeting I held we discussed a range of topics, especially the future operational role. I realised that we had to produce a *fait accompli*. We had to be able at some stage to say to Brigade HQ that we were able to put several fully prepared and trained operational teams in the field. These teams had to be able to get anywhere we were asked to put them (mobility skills), to stay covert through practice and knowledge of the terrain (actual fighting skills) and, more importantly, to report everything we were able to observe (signals skills). Each team needed to be independent and self-sufficient, so additional and superior medical skills would also be necessary. In addition, we had to ensure that all MLs were fully combat ready as prone-to-capture troops and were all given proper resistance to interrogation training.

I knew that I could not arrange for some of these requirements without help from friends within the various services. During my last tour in Northern Ireland I had worked very closely with some of the special Recce Tps and I contacted one or two of them and asked if there was any way I could get places on the Special Forces (SF) signals courses. I had to call in a few favours but was able to negotiate a swap: a couple of places on the ML2 courses in return for up to six of my corporals being sent on the SF signals course. My attempts to achieve medical training were less successful. I ended up dealing with the Medical Squadron, whose staff could not have been more helpful but they were unable to get us on the full SF medical course on the grounds that we were not SF. Fair enough!

By the spring of 1981 we were back to the normal routine for the Cadre. We had also begun to prepare for the operational role in much more detail. I tasked Sergeant Des Wassall, who had just joined the staff, to set up a study team to arrange a six-week long-range patrol course for Cadre staff. It was to begin in early May and be completed by mid-June, before we started our preparations for the Alps. This he did, and we then started the preparations for coordinating the operational role within the ML2 and ML1 courses for late 1981. The plan was that the two courses would finish at the end of March 1982 with a formal operational readiness exercise. The ML1 students would act as team commanders to ML2 students and the exercise would involve a classic long-range patrol exercise across the Highlands of Scotland, culminating in a raid and tactical withdrawal by aircraft back to base. We had already altered the Inner Hebrides survival phase to include resistance to interrogation training, and proper patrol exercises in Norway now included longer distance skiing and actual obser-vation post (OP) tasks along the routes. Reporting and planning were within the exercise briefs so that the ML2s who qualified in April 1981 were far better prepared for this role than any graduates from previous courses.

By Easter 1981 it was my belief that the Cadre was ready to go to Brigade HQ and offer the ability to provide four operational teams plus a unit HQ. This would give the brigade commander the ability to stretch beyond the immediate tactical reach of his Commando Recce Tps, while remaining well inside the strategic reach of SF. At no time was there any suggestion that we wished to interfere with the SF role, nor was there any feeling in the Cadre that the way ahead was to become SF. Our best efforts were aimed at providing a Parachute Brigade-type brigade patrol troop (BPT), giving the brigade commander additional competent and capable troops for operations only.

During the period April 1980 to April 1981 I was mostly employed running the ML1 and two ML2 courses whilst laying the groundwork for offering the brigade commander the option as above. By April 1981 Brigade HQ was seriously considering the proposal to move the Cadre to the south coast and the decision was made that we would move to Plymouth after Easter leave in 1982. I went to Plymouth to carry out a recce of a new location in late May 1981. Brigadier Julian Thompson had taken over command of the brigade and he was entirely on side. I was able to see a more relevant way ahead for the Cadre, with a more significant future for the branch as a whole. In periods where money was dominating all aspects of planning, it was totally unacceptable to have a training unit in the brigade, however specialised and well trained, with no operational role. Forming a specialist operational unit at very little cost to the brigade was clearly the way ahead.

Easter 1981 was also a significant time for me personally. Immediately after Easter leave my new administrative officer (AO) arrived. His presence immediately reduced my workload by about a third and my CSM's work-load by about a half. My predecessor, Captain David Nicholls, had for-warded a formal request for an AO and it had been approved. We had discussed it in our handover but neither of us was very optimistic about how soon it would happen. The arrival of Lieutenant Jon Young was a godsend, and it could not have happened at a more appropriate time. Jon was a Special Duties officer who had been a signaller when he was an NCO. His skills in that area were priceless. He was also an intelligent, competent and able administrator and very quickly became an important cog in the Cadre's wheel. He found many of our ways very strange and an early misunderstanding caused us to cross swords. He asked if there was any reason why he should climb as part of his job. I explained that his job was to drive the office and to be our 'base commander' in my absences, which were many. If he wished to climb, he was very welcome to do so, as that was what we did. From this he inferred that it was somehow a test of his resolve, and so at the very first opportunity he insisted on joining a climb. There are many people to whom climbing is the staff of life. Jon is not one of them. When we started the night climbing phase, he came to me and asked if he really had to night climb. I was horrified because I then realised that we were not working off the same sheet, and he was working up to asking for a transfer. He did not perceive that he was already providing the service he was employed to provide. We had a proper 'clear the air' session and agreed that if he wished to climb for pleasure, he could at any time, but he did not need to climb for work at all. From that moment on we got on like a house on fire. He became a very good friend and served the Cadre with distinction for his entire tour.

Shortly after Jon's arrival I had more time for my real job of commanding the Cadre rather than administering it. This gave me more opportunities to work on my plan for a proper operational role and things began moving ahead rather well.

It was at about this time that a new staff officer arrived at Brigade HQ. Major Hector Gullan was a Parachute Regiment officer seconded to the Royal Marines for a two-year tour. He had served with the SAS and was a very competent soldier. He had heard of the Cadre and visited us early on to get a feel for our capabilities. He and I became good friends, and remain so. His keenness to help was an important part in the next phase of the Cadre's growth into an operational role. Hector was a proper soldier and a serious volunteer to work in Commando Forces. He believed that all the soldiers serving in the Royal Marines or the Parachute Brigade were from the same stock and he very much wished to experience working with them all. Once he had visited us in Norway, he became a steadfast supporter of both the Cadre and its need for a proper operational role. It was largely due to Hector's influence that we were able to get students on the SF signals courses in exchange for seats on the ML2 courses. The first SF student sent to the ML2 course in 1980 was superb and came very close to being selected top student. However, it was to Hector that I went when I realised I would have to remove one of the two SF students from the next ML2 course because he was not up for the challenge. The first student on that course had taken a serious fall and broken his leg whilst climbing in

North Wales and had to be released. However, the second student was coasting and taking every opportunity to avoid getting fully involved in the course, so I needed him to be removed. Had he been a Royal Marine it would have been an easy decision but I was worried about the politics and called Hector for advice. His response was exactly what was needed. He asked one question: 'If he was a Royal Marine would you get rid of him?' My answer was 'Yes, absolutely.' He replied, 'In which case send him home but I wish to speak to him first.' Hector attended the orderly room where I gave the soldier his marching orders. This was greeted with some contempt, to the extent that Hector asked me to allow him to speak to the student in private. After this discussion the student was returned to the UK (we were in Norway at the time) the next day. I found out subsequently that his service in the SAS was also terminated on his return to the regiment.

By September 1981 the preparations for the modified ML1 and ML2 courses were complete and we started them with the twin aims of providing ML qualified personnel who were also properly prepared soldiers to fit into a brigade patrol troop organisation. I was hoping that I could get interest from on high towards the end of the two courses so that I could then go ahead and formally propose an operational role for the Cadre and for that role to be as brigade patrol troops. However, circumstances intervened – as will become clear in later chapters.

The final exercise at the end of the ML1 and ML2 courses took place over three weeks in March 1982. The plan was to parachute into the Cairngorms and then to transit by various means across the country to the northern end of the Mull of Kintyre. From there they would move down the length of the Mull and complete the exercise by assaulting RAF Machrihanish before making an operational withdrawal by RAF Hercules transport aircraft (C130). The exercise had taken a very long time to set up and the weather was not kind. The 'parachute insertion' was made by 4-ton vehicle as the conditions were not acceptable for parachuting. From then the patrols moved through a series of checkpoints, which included crossing Loch Lomond in rigid raiders provided by the Landing Craft Squadron. Next they moved from the west coast by fishing vessel to the insertion landing at the north end of the Mull of Kintyre, followed by a transit on foot down the length of the Mull to establish OPs around RAF Machrihanish. Finally came the raid on the control tower and then withdrawal by C130 in darkness, using red lights to guide in the aircraft. This worked splendidly, especially for the secret agent (also known as the OC) who joined the patrols at Machrihanish for the final phase and got a ride in the C130 as a result. Unfortunately, our plans to parachute back into Arbroath were again thwarted by the weather but we arrived back to barracks feeling that it was a job very well done.

The final week of the ML1 and ML2 courses was spent at Arbroath in the last week of March 1982. Problems with Argentine 'scrap metal collectors' in South Georgia were being reported in the news. There seemed to be a lot of over-reaction to these strange activities and I had a few conversations with various MLs who had served in the Falkland Islands. The consensus was that the Argentines did this sort of thing fairly often, but it was nothing to worry about and it would soon blow over. How wrong we were!

Chapter 2

Preparing to Sail South
(Arbroath, 26 March–5 April)

On completion of the final exercise we returned to Arbroath to finish the final week of the ML1 and ML2 courses. It was essentially a week of writing course reports, resolving the postings of students, and returning, repairing and replenishing stores following an eight-month training programme. In addition, we had to complete the packing of all the stores and equipment before the move to Plymouth. In order to take advantage of the availability of additional personnel from the ML1 and ML2 courses we decided to finish the packing before we all went on Easter leave on Friday, 2 April 1982. The annual Cadre dinner dance was planned for Saturday, 3 April and finalising those details was a high priority. This event celebrated the end of the Cadre's working year and served as a fond farewell to all those ML1 and ML2 students who were to be posted away from Arbroath at the end of Easter leave.

The news of the Argentine 'scrap metal merchants' in South Georgia was noted but not treated with any real interest. The Argentines had often made aggressive noises in the past about the 'Malvinas', as they liked to call the Falkland Islands, but had never progressed beyond rhetoric apart from a few silly flights onto the racetrack at Stanley. Consequently, we believed that they lacked both the ability and the motivation to do anything other than rattle their sabres and bleat to the world's press. Furthermore, veterans of Naval Party 8901 (the permanent party of Royal Marines stationed in the Falkland Islands), of whom there were a few among the ML personnel, assured us that this was just another case of the Argentines whinging to the UN and the press and it would go nowhere.

I was very pleased with the way that the new ML courses had worked but felt confident that I could make a few improvements to both of them before the 1983 deployment. Not all the students fully agreed with that plan but the overall belief within the Cadre and the ML branch in general was that we had made a significant step towards acquiring a proper operational role. The move to Plymouth would give me a better chance of convincing the brigade commander of the merits of my concept, and he would then sell it to the Corps. The final parade of the two courses was to be held at 0900 on Friday, 2 April.

On that morning I walked into the officers' mess at about 0745 for breakfast to find that it was full of 45 Commando RM officers. I was greeted with some derision and mickey taking, as they had been called into the unit nearly four hours earlier following the Argentine invasion of the Falkland Islands, of which I was unaware! As the company commanders were mostly senior to me, I had to endure some rude comments – 'Don't worry, you can go back to bed – you REMFs will not be required and it's only the proper troops who will be called forward!' (REMF is United States Marine Corps slang for a non-fighting member of a fighting organisation.) Not best pleased with this abuse, straight after breakfast I headed for my office and the Cadre HQ.

I spoke to Brian Snowdon and suggested that we postpone the pass out parade until I could find out what was happening. I asked Brian to call in all the SNCOs and held an impromptu meeting to confirm that they, like me, were all completely certain that they wished to participate in whatever lay in store as a result of the invasion. Having confirmed my belief in their commitment, I immediately made a call to the brigade commander in Plymouth. I was quite surprised when he answered the call himself, and perhaps spoke rather out of turn, remarking 'You cannot go without the Cadre. We are properly prepared for whatever task you have for us.' In true fashion, Brigadier Julian – who was and is a perfect gentleman – replied to the effect, 'Don't worry, Rod. We won't leave you behind and John Chester has you on his list to contact as soon as possible.' Major John Chester was a man I knew well. The Cadre had shared a location in Norway with his rifle company on the previous year's winter deployment before he was appointed to be brigade major (or chief of staff) at HQ 3 Cdo Bde.

Straight after coming off the phone I called in Brian Snowdon and my administrative officer Jon Young and we held a mini planning meeting. I advised them of the phone call and that we would be included within the brigade order of battle and that we should cancel all plans for leave and prepare for a very swift move somewhere in order to head to the South Atlantic. I also checked in with the Corps drafting officer at the Drafting and Records Office Royal Marines (DRORM), who was an old friend, to confirm my thinking that the ML1 and ML2 students were not to go to their next postings until at least 20 April and would remain under command of the Cadre until then, or until hostilities were over. He told me that no decision had been made in that respect but he would assume that since I had them, and possession was nine points of the law, I should keep them! With this gem of news, I sat down and started to look into the new Cadre ORBAT for this forthcoming operation. My first thought was to get the entire Cadre to Arbroath.

Two of my corporals (Heward and Meade) had gone on early Easter leave as they were expecting to join a British Army climbing expedition to the Andes in late April. I needed that to be cancelled and required them back in Arbroath soonest. I got hold of the leave book and confirmed that they would be at Corporal Heward's family home, so I phoned that number. Corporal Heward's mother answered the phone and I asked to speak to him. 'I am afraid they're not here,' was her reply. 'They set off yesterday to spend a long weekend in Brighton with an old friend and I am expecting them back on Monday.' I asked her for a contact number, but she was unable to help so I asked her to tell them if they contacted her to call me in Arbroath immediately, regardless of the time, as I really needed to talk to them. I asked the telephone exchange to get me the number of Brighton police so that I could talk to the duty inspector. When I got hold of them I asked the duty Inspector if he could help me, telling him that I was unable to explain why but as a Royal Marines officer I needed to contact two of my men who were currently on leave in Brighton. I also suggested that he might get an idea of the reason if he listened to the news on the BBC. He asked for confirmation of my location, my job and my commanding officer. I explained that I worked for the commando brigade in Plymouth but was based in Arbroath and I was the CO of the M&AW Cadre. He told me that he would verify my identity and then get back to me. He phoned back about 20 minutes later and asked two questions: where they were staying and what car were they using? For the former I had no idea, but I knew they were in Corporal Meade's car and gave him the details. He finished the conversation by confirming the number they were to call and wishing me luck with whatever it was I was about to get involved in. His final words were 'Remember to keep your head down!' I assumed it would take them all day but my phone rang within the hour and it was Corporal Meade asking, 'What's up Boss?!' The rest of the tale is best told in his own words:

> Obviously having made the call we were excited to set off back to Scotland but unfortunately, we had both left gear that we would need at our respective parents' houses, so we would need to call in at Hampstead and Beverley again on the journey north. This we did,

departing my parents' house in Beverley in the early hours, with me – as the only driving licence holder – becoming increasingly tired. Eventually, north of Newcastle, I told Al that he would have to drive as I was no longer able to do so safely. At this point I should say that Al did have a provisional licence and had been receiving high-quality driving lessons, from me, around Condor Airfield (Arbroath)! I knew that he was a good driver, if a little short on the experience front. So, for Queen and Country, and knowing that there wasn't much chance of [being reimbursed] if we spent the night in a nice country hotel, Al agreed. The truth of it was he was rather chuffed to be driving my car through the night on a bit of an adventure!

My car was a Toyota Celica which was a decent car and quite quick and I cannot recall Al being too shy with the throttle. After satisfying myself that we might survive the night, I got my head down, only to be woken up by a huge bang (exceeded only by the sound of the 29 Commando Regiment Royal Artillery shells landing just by us on Goat Ridge). Al declared he had just converted a bouncing bunny to roadkill. As there was nothing I could find to discount his account I accepted that this was probably the case and we continued north. Only now we were no longer stealthily making our way north to Arbroath: owing to a hole the size of a 120mm shell hole in my exhaust, we were broadcasting our imminent arrival about 500m ahead. This did nothing to aid slumber but I let Al carry on driving as he seemed to be far more alert than I felt. We arrived at Condor* shortly before 0700 on Saturday, 3 April, loudly driving to G Block to park up there. We had made good time.

When the whole adventure was over and we returned to Scotland, I had to take my car to a garage in Dundee to get a new exhaust fitted before I could drive home to Beverley in time to watch the ships on TV coming into Southampton from the South Atlantic. To this day, Al has not offered to split the cost, which, as a Yorkshire lad, is very painful to me.

This was just one of several stories of individual initiative shown by members of the Cadre over that weekend.

Major Chester, the chief of staff, called me mid-afternoon on Friday, 2 April to tell me how many spaces I had for the trip south. He had originally asked me how many vacancies I needed, and I had told him

---

* Condor base. The home location of the Cadre near Arbroath.

forty-six all ranks. He was surprised at this number, but when I explained that it included the entire Cadre plus the ML1 and ML2 courses he realised I was not exaggerating. He told me I had been allocated thirty-six places on RFA *Resource*, which was to sail from Rosyth Dockyard at first light on Monday, 5th April. This gave us about forty hours to get everything ready, loaded and embarked.

I immediately gave Brian Snowdon and Jon Young this news and clarified that I would very quickly decide who should make up our total of thirty-six. I needed two troops of four sections, plus an HQ for controlling them, and each section would be four strong. We had trained eight signallers, so they were first on my list. We also had two officers, two colour sergeants and four senior ML1 sergeants to fulfil the role of team leaders. This meant that I needed a further sixteen MLs to make up the four-man sections. Then I was left with the task of deciding the final four names for the HQ. Interestingly, we had thirty-two qualified ML NCOs within the Cadre staff and ML course personnel, although a few of them were not fully fit thanks to injuries suffered on the course. I thought therefore that I had a little leeway by leaving the injured behind. Little did I know that once I had explained this to the CSM, he passed the news directly to the troops. As a result, I started getting visitors to my office, selling their cases for travelling and fighting with us. First in were three walking wounded, Sergeant 'Mac' Mclean and Corporals Steve Groves and Matt Barnacle. All three had been fitted with plaster casts (two to legs and one to his arm/elbow) and they had assumed that I would automatically dispense with them straight away. They had therefore removed their plaster casts and marched into my office declaring that they were fit to travel and fight and that I could not go without them. I was getting a little tired, so I called them to attention and then ordered them to mark time (marching on the spot) and marched myself out of the office. This order was not well received by Mclean and Groves, who had removed casts from their legs, but Barnacle was laughing as his problem was with his arm! I went into my CSM's office and told him what I had done. He chuckled and said, 'Let's go in and see how they are doing.' Suffice to say, they were all a bit pasty faced but determined to make their point. I stopped them and told them that I would not dream of leaving them behind but only because it was going to take us a few weeks to get to the Falklands and by then they would be fit and well. I also decided that all three of them would be in the HQ team in case they had not fully recovered in time for the action.

I was now left with a serious morale problem and a difficult dilemma. Brian Snowdon was not a man I wanted to leave behind, for a whole variety of reasons. His knowledge, competence and experience made him worth his weight in gold. We had worked hand in glove together for two years, had developed a mutual understanding and knew exactly how to get the best from each other, and had become very good friends. It was largely due to his loyalty and commitment that we had achieved our progress on the route towards a proper operational role, and under normal circumstances he would be the first name on my list.

However, three weeks earlier his wife Gail had given birth to their third child, a lovely girl, but unfortunately she was born with a cleft larynx and it was taking all their time to keep the little mite fed. I had watched Brian becoming more and more tired as the days passed. I had not even considered leaving him behind until given the numbers by the chief of staff. I was trying to make a fair and proper decision, and I realised that leaving Brian behind would save his family considerable grief and enable him to help Gail with their beautiful baby. I also believed that there was a huge chance that a diplomatic solution would be found to the problem in the South Atlantic. I rationalised that nobody in their right mind would risk an all-out war in order to distract from their incompetence in governing a country, and that the Argentines would have to stand down and remove their troops from the Falkland Islands before our arrival. Obviously, I am a better soldier than a diplomat, but at that time I truly believed we would sail to a point somewhere off West Africa and steam around for a while, and then return home once the Argentines had come to their senses. This was part of my thinking with respect to the three NCOs and their plasters, and I levelled it directly with my CSM.

Rather than mess around I spoke immediately to Brian. He was not best pleased but I explained my argument, making it absolutely clear that had he not got a fragile child to look after, the situation would be a no-brainer and I would not dream of sailing without him. To say that he took the order well is inaccurate and we did not re-establish full diplomatic relations for about ten years.

My next problem was with my administration officer. Jon Young had become indispensable during his two years in post and was a full member of the team. I respected his judgement and liked his company. In a job where the 'buck' stopped with me, it was good to have a mature fellow officer with whom to discuss certain matters in private and with no holds barred. It was something I had grown used to and relied upon. Jon, however, was not an ML and if I took him, I would have to leave an ML behind in the UK. I could not do that, so explained to Jon that he would not be travelling with us. I needed men who could do all jobs and his lack of climbing skills was a limitation I was not prepared to accept. He was devastated and I was sympathetic, but my mind was made up. In true Royal Marine fashion he accepted the order and got on with the job in hand. My final problem was resolved. I now had a full team of thirty-five and needed one more. I needed a replacement CSM and an operations officer who could also manage all the stores. Colour Sergeant Bill Wright magically appeared in my office as I was mulling over the final name and, hey presto! – the list was complete.

I had known Bill for ten years. I first encountered him at CTCRM Lympstone when, as a corporal, he was in HQ Company awaiting his promotion to sergeant and a posting to his ML1 course. I had just learned that I was to go on the next ML2 course, and met him when I visited the ML section office to ask for some advice on what I needed to do to prepare myself for the course. He was drinking coffee and looked immaculate. I was surprised at his turnout. He would have impressed a drill instructor and I wondered what job he was doing at CTC at that time. He replied that he was a spare corporal in HQ Company and to avoid getting stuck with a whole bunch of 'shitty little jobs' (SLJs), he had acquired a clipboard and every morning on parade, when his CSM asked if anyone had any jobs to do, he raised his hand and was dismissed from the parade to get on with whatever that job was. It was a licence to visit various mates around CTC and spend his days drinking coffee, doing physical training in the gym and generally anything other than the SLJs for which he expected to be pinged. I thought him a man of considerable enterprise and no shortage of confidence, and made a mental note to keep a look out for him in the future. I got to know Bill much better during our respective courses and was delighted when we were both posted to 40 Commando RM as Recce Tp commander and Recce Tp sergeant in April 1975.

We joined the unit in South Belfast, only to find that the Recce Tp had been disbanded. It was a 'ceasefire' tour as the IRA needed to recruit and retrain. They had called for the ceasefire, which had been leapt upon by the politicians. The CO had been ordered not to carry out any aggressive or sensitive operations during the ceasefire and as a result had taken the Recce Tp from the ORBAT. Instead, I was appointed as a watchkeeping officer in the Commando HQ with the promise from the CO that the Recce Tp would reform on our return to Plymouth in four months' time. Bill Wright was made tp sergeant/tp commander of 'Thirteen Troop', consisting of the Recce Tp corporals commanding a complete recruit troop that had been posted into the unit before the deployment.

I found my job particularly dull and was not best pleased but managed to keep my sanity by going out on foot patrols with the mortar troop until I was caught at an incident by the CO, who very quickly put me back in my box! Meanwhile, both my and Bill's predecessors had been posted out of the unit and we had to prepare our takeover of stores and equipment that had been left behind in Plymouth. I was concerned that we would be signing for a lot of kit unseen but was immediately reassured by Sergeant Wright that it was his job as troop sergeant to manage and control stores and he would sort it out, whatever the state of the stores we found when we returned to Plymouth. He must have had an inkling of what lay ahead as we found when we got back that we effectively had no stores. All the shelves were empty. I was absolutely horrified, but Sergeant Wright faced the problem with complete aplomb. 'Don't worry, Boss', he said. 'I'll sort this out and it won't take me very long.' Without going into any details, we were back to a full stores list, complete with spares, within a month. I then realised what a stroke of good luck it was to have him as my new troop sergeant. I never discovered how he did it because we were never called to task. I can only assume it was legal and I never asked too many searching questions. Since then, Sergeant Wright had been promoted to colour sergeant and rejoined the Cadre in that rank in September 1981. He was a man I trusted, and I found him to be completely reliable, especially on operations, which were his forte.

After my discussions with both the CSM and the AO, I needed to talk to Colour Sergeant Wright. He had come to the office to discuss a contact he had at the RAF's Photo Reconnaissance Interpretation Centre. The contact had been made during our last operational tour with 40 Commando Recce Tp in South Armagh in 1976. We had made extensive use of their ability to provide aerial photographs of just about anywhere in the world for use in patrol and OP planning. He confirmed that I was happy for him to call in a favour and see what aerial photos he could get of the Falkland Islands. I gave him the go ahead and told him to get whatever he could from the PRIC and to put it as an operational request. I also shared with him my decisions concerning Brian Snowdon and Jon Young and asked him to start thinking about the duties of CSM/TQ/Ops Officer for the forthcoming operation. He was initially surprised until I explained the limited numbers available to me for travel and also the family difficulties for the CSM, but his response was, as always, very positive and so off he went to talk to the CSM and to organise as many photos as he could acquire. Colour Sergeant Wright was the second most senior ML in the Cadre and the use of him for this role was both obvious and correct once the decision to release Brian Snowdon had been made.

Two days later I received a telephone call from the guardroom telling me that my PRIC delivery had arrived. I told them to send it to the Cadre lines and waited for what I thought would be a Landrover with a bag of photographs. It was actually four 4-ton vehicles each carrying two pallets of boxed photographs! The PRIC had pulled out all the stops and made ten copies of every aerial photo of East Falkland Island that they held at their HQ. Amazed, I left the guys to reduce the number of photos down to two copies of each and to offer the rest to 45 Commando RM who were also packing stores.

Late on Friday afternoon I received a call from Brigade HQ asking me to give them a list of our immediate operational stores requirements for the forthcoming conflict. I requested a little time to think about it but was told it had to be forwarded to them by 1200 the next day. I called a meeting of the senior team and gave them an hour to talk to all the guys in light of this instruction. I explained that it was not a free giveaway. Everything we asked for had to be necessary, suitable to be added to our already heavy burden of stores, and not 'Gucci' (that is, kit asked for because it looked good or was really expensive). Everything we took with us had to seriously enhance our fighting ability and power. The resulting list presented to me for consideration was really interesting. We were short of PRC 320 radios (a high-frequency radio perfect for the task) and were also short of firepower, but M79 40mm grenade launchers would resolve that shortfall. We also had a need for automatic fire capability in the form of GPMGs. In addition, there was a small list of items such as stereo-photograph readers, lightweight cookers and some items of clothing that would help. I rejected items such as lightweight duvet sleeping bags and specialist down outer clothing as I felt that, although the idea was sound, it was way too Gucci! The heavyweight GPMGs and the ammunition required for them were also far too heavy to be considered for the four-man teams, but the 40mm grenade launchers were a serious force multiplier and were right at the top of the list. Once everything was agreed I contacted Brigade HQ in Plymouth and passed on my shopping list. I thought no more of it as I was convinced that we would be way down the list of priorities but I am happy to say I was proved completely wrong.

At about 1700 on Friday afternoon I received a telephone call from Kay Babbington. Kay is the wife of Peter, OC K Company, 42 Commando RM, and a very good friend. She said, 'I suppose you are going too?'

I replied, 'I don't know what you mean but Yes!' She then said, quite seriously, 'Make sure you keep your head down and also make sure that you bring Peter back in one piece.' I told her I would do my very best, and wished her a good Easter holidays; I was aware that I would have absolutely no chance to watch out for Peter but I also knew that Kay would feel better if she believed one of his friends was keeping an eye out for him. This conversation would return to me on the day the Argentines surrendered.

An example of how things were seen by the teams is well covered by Sergeant Chris Stone in his recollections, as follows:

> I don't remember at what stage we became aware that the islands had been invaded but it was bloody soon after our return to Arbroath. That was the signal for frantic preparations to begin for what was to be the biggest operation since the Second World War. The greatest responsibility by far at this stage fell on the shoulders of the newly and rapidly appointed Sergeant Major/TQ, Shiner Wright. Shiner wasn't nicknamed 'Brackets Rackets' for nothing. There wasn't anything Shiner couldn't beg, steal or borrow (mostly steal!) and all of us who deployed owe a debt of gratitude to his 'wide boy' talents throughout the campaign!
>
> Suddenly a WW2 blitz spirit was apparent, and wives turned up to make coffee and sarnies for the lads as they worked through the night loading Chacons. As for the 'grunts', there wasn't a lot we could do, but in the interests of being seen to be doing something, we decided that we ought to zero our weapons. Looking back on it, it was absurdly early to be thinking of this, but everybody was getting caught up in the operational spirit. There was no transport available, so a gang of us loaded my car with our weapons and ammunition (can't remember how we got the ammo, but Shiner was probably behind it!) and headed off to Barry Budden Ranges. On the drive there I put my cassette of 'The Ride of the Valkyries' on at full volume, just to get us really in the mood, and we arrived on the ranges to the bewilderment of some Pongos who were firing their APWT [annual platoon weapons test]. We explained politely that we were highly operational and had priority, and they, equally politely, made way for us.

On Saturday night our planned Cadre dinner dance took place in Arbroath. Everyone was stood down at about 1800 and we took the night off. I and most of the other guys have little recollection of the party. It was a good night, though not a late one, and it was a chance to talk to most of the guys and their wives/girlfriends, but I do not remember the details. I had a relatively early night and slept like a baby.

I took a little time out on Sunday afternoon to pack my own kit for the trip. It was a strange experience. After I had packed my rucksack, webbing and suitcase, I realised that I might not be coming back for some time, if at all. I decided therefore to pack all my belongings. I had rather a lot of stuff including my parachuting gear and climbing kit. In addition, I had previously decided that I should purchase a house and had been buying items for the new place once I returned to the UK. Denbyware china/pottery, Le Creuset pans and pots, bed linen and towels as well as glassware and other kitchen items were on my list of 'Things for Setting up Home'. It felt strange but I marked all my cases and boxes with the names and addresses of my parents, my sisters and my brother and a few friends just in case someone other than me had to sort out my kit later on. This was something that I had never previously considered but it felt important should it come to a shooting war down south.

By late on the Sunday afternoon we had been through several evolutions of stores preparation and packing. My TQ, Colour Sergeant Everett Young, had loaded and unloaded the three Chacons we had been allowed to take as the requirements for the trip evolved over the weekend. By Sunday afternoon we had one Chacon filled with cold weather equipment (skis, snowshoes, pulks and Arctic shelters, topped up with ski waxes and Arctic rations, plus various small items for use above the snowline) should we be tasked to go to South Georgia. A second Chacon was filled with cliff assault equipment including a good supply of ropes, bipod and roller haulage systems, a wide variety of climbing safety kit to be used for cliff assaults, harnesses, safety helmets, ropes and belaying equipment. The third Chacon was loaded with all the equipment we needed for conventional warfare. This included weapons, some 5.56mm ammunition (we would be the only people in the brigade using that calibre), spare compasses, maps, a supply of emergency rations and, lastly, safety kit for harsh conditions. Colour Sergeant Young had made a herculean effort to ensure that we had every possible contingency covered and that effort proved completely successful once we got stuck in down south.

By Sunday evening we were in all respects ready to go. The kit was prepared, rucksacks and webbing were ready and the ORBAT was agreed. Transport was ordered for the Chacons and other stores and we arranged to parade on the main parade ground at 0400 on Monday morning to embark on the coach to Rosyth, where we would board RFA *Resource*.

A parade ground at 0400 is not the best time to be confronted with a problem I should have sorted out 48 hours previously. One of our injured was Corporal Kev ('Doc') Doughty, who had very seriously hurt himself in a fall at Tremadoc in north Wales the previous October. His injuries had been life-threatening but he had made a remarkable recovery. His right arm, however, was still in need of considerable repair work before he would be able to serve as a Royal Marine once more. In fact, he never fully recovered fitness and was later invalided out of the Corps. I had not thought about Corporal Doughty over the weekend as I had a lot on my plate. I was not prepared to be confronted by him with all his kit ready to go. I consequently had a most distressing (for both of us) few minutes when I told him he could not travel. He was absolutely devastated. It was an experience I will never forget. He was a tough and hard man and to take away from him the opportunity to participate was something nobody should have to do. He was not a qualified ML because of his injury but he was a fine soldier and would definitely have been included had he been fit – but he was not.

On our arrival at Rosyth, it was a wet, cold and miserable day, which seemed particularly apt for what was ahead. We off-loaded from the transport and I checked in with Captain Mike Cole, the OC Zulu Company, 45 Commando RM, with whom we would be travelling. We both embarked and checked in with the chief officer and then left the guys to sort themselves out. No time was wasted at Rosyth and very soon after our arrival the ship set sail. Sergeant Chris Stone again:

> After what seemed indecent haste the Cadre, along with various odds and sods, embarked on RFA *Resource* and snuck out of Rosyth on a grey, cold and wet morning. It really was beginning to seem that my comforting words to my family may have been premature. It is a horrible fact that as a Royal Marine Commando, saying goodbye to wives and children for long, and sometimes open-ended periods, became almost routine, but there was no doubt in any of our minds that we were going to give those cheeky dagos a damn good spanking, unless horror of horrors, the Navy might sort it out first.

We were on our way, but at that stage we had no idea of our destination.

Chapter 3

Rosyth to Ascension Island and Beyond

(5 April–21 May)

Embarking early in the morning of Monday, 5 April, Zulu Company of 45 Commando RM and the M&AW Cadre RM were the first of the Operation Corporate land forces to set sail from the UK to the Falkland Islands. It did not feel so momentous to us and it was a particularly dreich day, showing northeast Scotland at its meteorological worst. Dark and grey with heavy rain, it seemed fitting to be setting off for the southern hemisphere after such a hard-working weekend with no idea what the future held for us. I remember going on deck as we passed under the Forth road and rail bridges and thinking that this might be my last view of England – and then realising that it would actually be my last view of Scotland as I had already missed my last view of England months before!

The first few days were spent settling in. We still had a lot of kit to be sorted out as we needed to be prepared for whatever lay ahead. The Cadre split into its eight four-man sections and each section sorted out its own standard operating procedures (SOPs) so that all possible contingencies could be anticipated. In many ways it was rather amusing to watch 'small groups of determined men' (Churchill's definition of the Commandos in 1942) acting out various drills all over the ship for the first five or six days.

Our reception from RFA *Resource* was outstanding. The crew could not have been more accommodating. Conditions were not up to passenger ship quality but the food was excellent and the accommodation was certainly adequate. I did not receive a single complaint about *Resource* at any time. She was one of the largest of the RFA supply ships and carried everything a Royal Navy ship needed, including fuel, food, ammunition and a large supply of spares needed to keep ships fighting fit at sea. Captain Bruce Seymour was in command of *Resource* and he led an outstanding crew. They were flexible and very hard-working, and the ship functioned as a well-oiled machine.

It was particularly interesting for me as my only experience of the RFA had been as a child in Singapore. My father, one of the naval base pilots, used to take me with him when piloting the big ships into and out of the base. I have great memories of enjoying VIP status as a young child and being supplied with large quantities of ice cream whenever I was on board! I joined P&O as an apprentice when I was 17 and with my subsequent five years' experience at sea, I understood what it was like to work on board a large cargo vessel and so found settling on *Resource* quite easy.

A couple of days after setting sail I was invited to the captain's quarters for morning coffee, along with Captain Mike Cole RM who commanded Zulu Company. Captain Seymour could not have been more hospitable and after a general chat he admitted that he had an ulterior motive for issuing the invitation. He asked if one of us would act as interpreter to translate the large number of military signals he was now receiving. Being a supply ship master, he had little experience of the military in general and the Royal Marines in particular. He was, obviously, fully conversant with naval procedures but he was finding the jargon used in the military messages a little confusing. I offered to help for two reasons. I was closer to understanding his mindset, having been at sea for five years, and, because he was receiving messages that were not available to Mike and me, it gave me a chance to find out what was going on away from the ship. Mike was happy for me to take it on and we kept in touch after every meeting I had with Captain Seymour. What amazed me was the enormous quantity of signals traffic he was receiving daily. Most of my translation work involved filtering out the wheat from the chaff. Most of it was about the consolidation of the significant quantity of stores that needed to be carried out to Ascension Island.

All the ships had been told to fill up with stores and set sail as soon as possible but no plans had been made for the inevitable off-load once we arrived in the Falkland Islands. The decision was made that the quartermaster staff officers of HQ 3 Cdo Bde would construct a detailed loading plan between the UK and Ascension Island, and that all the stores would be moved to comply with that plan upon arrival. The amount of work this entailed was huge and I remain in awe of the very successful efforts made in Ascension Island by all involved in the transhipment of personnel and stores. Suffice to say that after the fleet sailed from Ascension it was in all respects ready for the offload at San Carlos Water, even though at that time no decision had been made about where the troops were to be landed. A tremendous amount of very clever and sensible staff work was carried out by Brigade HQ. Their plans worked more or less seamlessly once we arrived in San Carlos Water, in spite of interference from the Argentine Air Force.

As far as the Cadre was concerned, the trip south became increasingly balmy as the temperature rose and the seas stayed calm. We spent our days taking as much physical exercise as we could in order to keep fit and the sections spent a good part of each day working out their SOPs and ensuring that all their kit was ready for war. There was also plenty of time to relax. By the time we arrived at the equator I was convinced that we were as prepared as we could be for what lay ahead.

As we moved further south our need to undertake more strenuous exercise became apparent and we all increased our efforts. Unfortunately for me, Mike Cole suggested that he and I should exercise together and I agreed. What I had forgotten was that Mike was a qualified physical training and sports officer and his idea of hard PT sessions was very different from mine! I thought I was pretty fit but it soon became a survival session for me as Mike raised my level of fitness to the highest it had ever been in my life. My relentless competitive nature meant that I had to keep up with him and our daily battles on the flight deck gained quite an audience. Both his and my guys sat and watched their bosses battle it out. I still remember the pain of the grid sprints with which we always ended and I like to think that Mike felt it as well. Joking aside, working out with him made me physically better equipped for what was ahead and more importantly gave us both a lot of fun – but my main memory remains the pain of it!

The day before we got to the equator Bill Wright, now the de facto CSM of the Cadre for the operation, told me that the 'crossing the line ceremony' would be taking place the next day and I would be the first victim of Lord Neptune when he came aboard. I was less than enthusiastic, having spent half my five years at sea in the southern hemisphere and particularly the South Pacific. This carried no weight with Bill, who explained that it was my first crossing as a Royal Marine and so I would have to be 'done' with the rest. His argument carried little weight but we both needed a break, so I sacrificed myself for the ceremony. Suffice to say it was pretty disgusting, and it took me a long time to get the oil, mud, grease, paint and whatever else off my body before I was clean enough to return to the real world.

The next day was a momentous one for one of my crew. Corporal Nigel Devenish was due to be married on Saturday, 17 April. Clearly, it was not going to happen but the Cadre decided that the next best thing would be to hold a dress rehearsal for his wedding on board *Resource* on the day in question. This turned out to be an historic event enjoyed by all. All the relevant officials were found and the 'wedding' duly took place. Corporal Al Heward became the stand-in wife and Corporal Steve Nicoll the vicar, with Corporal Ray Sey acting as the father of the bride. An indication of how seriously it was taken can be seen from the set of orders produced prior to the wedding service, as shown here:

ORDERS FOR THE WEDDING OF NIGEL DEVENISH

GROUND
Atlantic Ocean. An area noted for its amount of water with the occasional outcrop of land. On this ocean sails RFA Resource.

SITUATION ENEMY FORCES
A couple of thousand duff Argentinian troops plus the odd rusty frigate and let us not forget the mother-in-law.

FRIENDLY FORCES
M.A.W. Cadre, Z Company SBS and the remainder of the British Task Force; also, the future bride the lovely Miss Alana Heward.

ATTS & DETS
John White: Best Man
Rey Sey: Bride's Father
Steve Nicoll: Vicar

MISSION
To carry out mock wedding ceremony of Nigel Devenish and Miss Alana Heward.

EXECUTION GENERAL OUTLINE
All members of the M&AW Cadre will muster in the corporals' accommodation (officers smoke room) at 1800 17th August for the mock ceremony. On completion of the ceremony a procession to the NAAFI will follow, where cake cutting and telegram reading will take place. The remainder of the evening will be taken up with a celebration of this glorious occasion.

ACTION ON CAMERAS
Smile

ACTION ON RUDE WEDDING JOKES
Blush

ACTION ON SPEECHES
Cheer

ACTION ON TELEGRAMS
Cries of 'Hear Hear'

ACTION ON BEING BOUGHT A DRINK BY
TIM HOLLERAN
Faint (Drink pint first though!)

ACTION ON THINKING KEV MAHON IS WEARING
A CRASH HELMET
Think again!

ACTION ON LIGHTS
Turn them off

CO-ORDINATION INSTRUCTIONS – TIMINGS
Muster in the Corporals accommodation 18:00, 17th April 1982
Ceremony   18:10
Procession   18:20
Speeches, etc.   18:25
Drinkies   18:40 Onwards

SERVICE SUPPORT – DRESS
Bride All in White
Groom, best man, bride's father Suits or paper gash bags
Vicar Jesus rig
Remainder Optional, the smart but casual, Billy Bernard's look (see
   Shiner Wright)

EQUIPMENT
Corporal Devenish to ENSURE that wedding tackle is TAKEN and
in WORKING ORDER

RATIONS
A wedding cake is being provided for the reception

TRANSPORT
Foot

COMMAND AND SIGNALS
Nigel will be in command until 23:00; after 23:00 Alana will assume
the dominant position

SIGNALS
All telegrams to M&AW Cadre, RFA Resource

A very good time was had by all and we arrived at Ascension Island the
next day. Ours was one of the first half dozen ships to get there. Colour

Sergeant Wright's memories were very similar to mine, so I include them in his own words:

On RFA *Resource* as we proceeded south, and presumably because we were at sea, we started to get stacks of signals regarding our role and possible missions. This sparked a need to get extra bits of kit and it is where I first heard of '01 Demands'. There was a section of SBS on board and I took my lead from them in ordering kit and put in the most outlandish signal for kit thinking that we'd never get it. As the ship passed through the Straits of Dover, we were informed that a Wessex helicopter would be dropping an underslung load and then landing to offload more kit (and I think a couple of people).

The load was mostly our stuff in the form of thirty-six 9mm pistols, nine L42 sniper rifles and a few (but not our whole request) AR15s, umpteen holk* abseil kits and much, much more. I was totally astounded at the request being fulfilled and the lack of accountability. No signatures were required, nor even a signal acknowledgement.

We proceeded south and engaged in stacks of training, signals, weapon handling, fitness training, etc. In the quiet hours, myself and [Corporal] Tony Boyle hit on the idea to raise money for the Cadre fund by making jack-knife holders out of real leather (which came gratis from the *Resource* stores) and selling them to the members of Zulu Company who were aboard. They were hand stitched, and the off-cuts were sold off as 'lucky Cadre bookmarks'. Maybe they were! I managed to get hold of a hand-operated sewing machine from the ship's QM and did a roaring trade tailoring the ship's officers' shorts for when we entered the tropics. The Cadre fund did well. Matt Barnacle also ran a very busy side-line in leather pistol holsters complete with webbing straps. We had been issued with 9mm pistols as secondary weapons but with no means of carriage, hence Matt's 'Heath Robinson' solution.

One day, whilst we and Zulu were on deck doing phys, we were buzzed at very low level by a couple of Russian Bears. Quick as a flash, there was a mass 'moon' from all on deck. That must have gone down a storm in the Kremlin!

Shortly after our arrival at Ascension, Zulu Company was told to prepare to be transferred so we kept out of the way and watched them leave *Resource* for another ship. I was awaiting the arrival of HMS *Fearless*

---

*A specialist piece of equipment designed to make abseiling safer and faster.

carrying the Brigade HQ and hoping to get an indication of our forth-coming tasks. One of the RFA LSLs, RFA *Sir Tristram*, had arrived from the Caribbean virtually empty and was to be used as a transit ship for moving people and stores around until the final load plan was completed. I was expecting that at some stage I would be told whether to move the Cadre or to stay where we were. On the morning of 18 April I received a call from the captain of *Resource* who told me he had orders to sail imme-diately and that we were to disembark to *Sir Tristram* as fast as possible as the SAS were being taken on board and she was off down south. In a mood of 'ours not to reason why', I told the Cadre and we set about getting off the ship on the same helicopters that were bringing the SAS on board. I do not remember any conversations or meetings with the SAS, but I was not expecting any. The whole thing went reasonably well, except that our last Chacon was lifted off *Resource* about 50km south of Ascension as the final piece of kit from the transfer. This was an impressive feat of flying by the Navy helicopter pilots and one to which we were to become accustomed.

Shortly after our arrival on *Sir Tristram* I was told we were to stay there until further notice. RFA *Resource* and the SAS had already departed southwards to participate in the recovery of the South Georgia Islands. I must admit that I breathed a sigh of relief when I was given that infor-mation as I had been worried that someone would think of sending us there. If that happened, we would miss the main event. But I need not have worried. As history has shown, it was the SAS involvement there that con-fused the issue. Their efforts on Fortuna Glacier caused the crashing of two helicopters and had anybody died on the glacier the naysayers in the UK would have made it very hard for Prime Minister Margaret Thatcher to continue with Operation Corporate. The inability of the SAS to operate with other forces was further strained on the Falkland Islands, largely caused by their failure to participate in the core activities without going off on their own. Their refusal to give credibility to others with more knowledge and experience became their modus operandi and caused more problems than it solved. Suffice to say that they did assist M Com-pany of 42 Commando, who actually carried out the operation on South Georgia. M Company then had to remain on the islands until the end of the war. We, on the other hand, had work to do on Ascension Island.

Once we had settled on *Sir Tristram* we started looking for the remain-ing kit that we had ordered before sailing from Rosyth. We had asked for nine M79 40mm grenade launchers to be used as force multipliers for the teams. We had all used this weapon in Northern Ireland for setting off gas grenades during riots. We were well aware of the potential benefit that accurate HE grenade fire out to about 300m could add to our protection against assaulting enemy troops. Colour Sergeant Wright went ashore with a small team to look for these stores and found to his astonishment that the runway at Wideawake Airfield held many tons of stores. The staff at Wideawake had put all the stores pallets in three rows alongside the runway for its entire length of about 2.5km. Wright was told by the RAF staff that all the stores had been put in this pile and that his team should sort through it all and find their own stores and then let the stores personnel know what they had taken. A long time later they found our stores, but the M79 grenade launchers had gone. Even though they were clearly marked for the M&AW Cadre, they had been found by the SAS who had opted to take them for themselves. They obviously felt, as we did, that the weapons would be very useful. Although very irritated by this, we immediately put in for a further set of nine M79s which arrived within three days, further illustrating that the supply system was working well. But this would not be the last time that we would have problems with army personnel and our kit.

I found myself sharing a cabin on *Sir Tristram* with Captain Jeff Niblett, who was one of the senior pilots of the brigade air squadron. He was one intake behind me in officer training and we had known each other for a number of years, so it was an easy move for me. All RFAs have a single cabin available for the senior embarked officer, and that was occupied by an army major, the commander of the battery from 29 Commando Regiment RA which was loaded on board. After a couple of days in Ascension the battery was transferred elsewhere and Jeff and I discussed who should take the cabin. It suffered from a major problem: it had a telephone. With my experience on RFA *Resource*, I realised that the only person immediately contactable to help translate messages as we travelled further south would be the person on the end of that telephone. Jeff and I agreed to hope that an officer senior to us would come on board so that we could stay where we were whilst he could take all the calls! Fortunately, the gunner major was replaced by the lieutenant commander commanding the fleet clearance diving team. Jeff and I needn't have worried. He immediately checked both our seniorities with the Naval List and as we both reduced our seniority dates by a couple of years, we knew he would declare himself to be the senior officer and should have the cabin. We were both delighted when he explained that we should stay where we were, and he would become the senior embarked officer. This suited us both well and it took him only about four days to realise that he had been had. He tried to change the accommodation, taking himself away from the phone, but we were not for moving and he remained the 'boss' until we landed! Jeff is a man with a very dry sense of humour and he's incredibly good company. We were to see each other a few times during the conflict, where he performed well above and beyond the call of duty on several occasions. He was to be awarded the Distinguished Flying Cross for his outstanding courage.

Shortly after most of the fleet had arrived in Ascension a report was issued that an Argentine submarine had been sighted on the eastern side of the island, possibly intending to disembark Special Forces. The anchorage and the ships were all on the western side. It was decided, in collusion with the RAF staff at Wideawake Airfield, that the Cadre should provide OPs around the coast of the island in order to look out for and, if necessary, engage with and prevent any Argentine forces gaining intelligence or attacking the fleet in the harbour.

We very quickly prepared to go ashore. Orders were given and we set out to provide a complete screen around the island, especially at Wide-awake Airfield. The Cadre was now on its first operational task, and it was one for which we were completely prepared. What we were not prepared for were the problems we instantly faced from land crabs. These feisty crustaceans saw us as invading their territory and for two days we fought off many of these not-so-little raiders. After two days of this, and with no obvious sightings nor any potential of Argentine forces having travelled 8,000km to harass us at Ascension, I called the brigade commander and asked for permission to withdraw. I explained that our cover of the island was adequate and no troops could have penetrated our screen with-out being seen. Had any Argentines landed three days earlier they would certainly have been seen by then. He agreed and ordered me to bring the Cadre back to Wideawake Airfield and return to *Sir Tristram*. We traipsed back to the airfield and waited near the control tower until we were all complete and then I requested a helicopter ride back to *Sir Tristram*. We were very tired and none too pleased with the island's wildlife. However, I was delighted with the ease with which we had set up and run a proper OP screen and I knew that we were in all respects ready for action.

Whilst waiting for our helicopter, I was accosted by an RAF group captain (who, I assumed, was the CO of Wideawake Airfield), who asked under whose authority I had withdrawn from my role of protecting his airfield. I said the brigade commander, but he then ordered me to return to my guard positions. I refused. I was under command of the commando brigade and if he wanted troops to guard his airfield, he should look to the RAF Regiment, whose responsibility it should be. As things started to get a little heated the CO of 45 Commando, Lieutenant Colonel Andrew Whitehead, spotted the commotion. He immediately supported me and told the RAF officer that if the brigade commander felt they were safe then they were safe. I thanked Colonel Whitehead and we got out of there as quickly as possible.

About two days later I was again called to the Brigade HQ and asked to go ashore with the Cadre and find the Vaux beer delivery. I was amused by this order but apparently Vaux Breweries had sent enough beer to give two cans to every person in the fleet. The beer had definitely left the UK but nobody knew where it had gone. We went ashore to find it. After searching the entire airfield one of my guys came across several RAF personnel drinking beer outside a very large tent. When he asked the origin of their beers, he was told that it was theirs as they had found it but he was absolutely welcome to help himself as they had far more than they needed or could drink! The beer was indeed from Vaux breweries. When I arrived on the scene, I discovered that the beer was being rapidly consumed by aircrews from the Victor tankers and Vulcan bombers stationed there for the air raids on the Falklands Islands. I explained what the beer was for and they immediately vacated the tent and left the beer, allowing us to arrange for it to be sent to the fleet, where it should have been several days before.

The next day I was called again to HMS *Fearless* for a meeting with the brigade commander. He told me he wanted me to transfer to *Fearless* in order to join his operational planning team to assist in planning the landings. I immediately went to the ship's commander to request accommodation. He replied that that they were completely full and there was no room. I offered to sleep in a bath in a washroom but was told that they were already full of extras and there was no room for more. I returned to the brigade chief of staff who suggested I go to *Canberra* and be prepared to transfer by helicopter every day to *Fearless* to participate in the meetings and discussions.

Aboard *Canberra*, I was put in a cabin with Albert Hempenstall, the padre of 42 Commando RM. I took with me a small pack containing a clean shirt and underwear, washing and shaving kit, swimming trunks and PT kit. I had no idea how long I would be there but assumed it would be a couple of days before I could return to *Sir Tristram* in preparation for the landings.

In previous discussions with the brigade commander we had agreed that the Cadre should not be used as advance forces, but that we should land with the brigade on D-Day and then fly forward. Our task was to provide the initial forward screen about halfway between the brigade around

San Carlos and the Argentines on the outskirts of Port Stanley. I was aware that my teams would be posted about 50km east of San Carlos to provide early warning of any enemy movement towards San Carlos Water. At that time we did not anticipate much trouble from the Argentine Air Force – we got that bit wrong!

Padre Albert was a genial host. I had known him for several years and we made sure my arrival did not affect his work by quickly establishing a reasonable routine, so that I would make myself scarce when he had a visitor, giving them complete privacy. My attempts to get to *Fearless* occupied my first couple of days on board. I was defeated by the fact that all the helicopters had to be thoroughly serviced after the incredible workload demanded of them at Ascension Island. I realised very quickly that I should not be on *Canberra* and began trying to get back to *Sir Tristram* and my job. The day after I joined *Canberra* the order was given for the fleet to sail south. There had already been a couple of false alarms, including the one that caused us to deploy ashore, but this time it was serious and the whole fleet moved out and headed south.

For the first few days I went up to the ship's bridge to ask about incoming helicopters and was told none was expected that day but I would be called if one arrived. As we progressed south two things happened fairly swiftly. Firstly, the weather steadily deteriorated, with white water driven by strong winds becoming the order of the day, and secondly, Albert's visitors began to increase in number. This seemed fine because I did not interfere. After about six days, however, I answered the doorbell to find a senior colour sergeant outside. He asked for the vicar. In Albert's absence, I offered to help if I could, but he responded that it was a private matter and he needed to see the vicar. I asked him to give me an idea so that I could let Albert know and he could arrange to talk to him. He said again that it was confidential, so I went to shut the door and he blurted out 'I need to see him because I'm scared.' I responded 'So am I', and told him he shouldn't worry about it as it was absolutely normal to be scared in that situation. He then said, 'You don't understand. I've been in the Corps for eighteen years and this is the first time I will have been on active service and I need to talk to him.' At this stage it became apparent why I was not a vicar as I responded, 'Get a grip on yourself. You took the Queen's shilling and after eighteen years you are going to have to pay some of it back.' At that moment a quiet voice from behind me said, 'Thanks, Rod, I'll take over from here.' I had not realised that Albert was in the other room in the cabin. After his meeting with the colour sergeant, Albert commented that he was expecting to get a few more visitors like that and maybe I should look for a cabin elsewhere. He was absolutely right. I was moved to share with the young cavalry officer in command of the Scorpion tanks. He was a delightful chap but found my need to launder my clothes daily and hang them to dry in the shower very strange! Not keeping my kit clean would have been very strange for me.

After sixteen days away from my command I managed at last to get hold of a helicopter and returned to *Sir Tristram* on 12 May. My guys had been continuing their training and preparation quite happily and knew that I would return eventually. I was rather tense but need not have worried. They had dealt with my departure as they did everything else – with complete equanimity – and were all ready to go.

Two days later (13 May, I think) I was called to the brigade commander's orders group (O Gp) on HMS *Fearless*. It was the first brigade O Gp I had attended and I found it fascinating. Apart from the thrill of being given our tasks, it brought the first realisation that it really was all about to happen. I found myself looking around the room (from the very back row of attendees) and thinking that I was glad I was on this team and not the opposing one.* It was a tremendous experience for me and I went back to *Sir Tristram* determined to impart that same thrill of commitment to my own guys. The feeling of unity and the sense of purpose I felt after the O Gp was unique and I can honestly say it filled me with considerable resolve to see matters through. I hope I passed my conviction to the rest of the Cadre with my orders.

Corporal Steve Nicoll reminded me of the fact that:

> The brigade commander, Julian Thompson, sent a videotaped message to all embarked forces in the days before the landings on 21 May. Using video technology, it was an impressive way of getting the commander's intentions across to all ranks. Mobile phones and their ability to record anything quickly and then pass it on is now a commonplace activity. Back in 1982 using a VHS videotape for an operational briefing felt as if 'space age' technology was being used to good effect all that way from home. Although it now seems very dated and low tech, I remember how impressive it was at the time.

The period from 13 to 20 May passed in a flash. I spent the first couple of days sorting out my plans from the O Gp and then preparing and writing

---

*I do believe that was the feeling I got from attending the O Gp and I still feel that the comradeship at that meeting was the strongest of any I have ever experienced before or since.

my own orders. We held our own O Gp on 18 May, which gave plenty of time for my orders to be passed on and proper battle preparations to take place. Subsequently I realised that I had based our initial deployment on my experiences in South Armagh in 1976 and maintained a set of teams as back-up to those deployed first, just in case of emergencies. It soon dawned on me that in a real war those sorts of considerations needed to be put to one side. We only had one chance to get results and thus it should be all-out operations. In retrospect, I think we provided all that the brigade commander needed from us but perhaps we could have offered more in the first ten days ashore.

After the main brigade orders group, I had to make my plans and pass my orders to the Cadre in preparation for the landings. For the first time (the Ascension Island operation excluded) the guys had to prepare for proper wartime action. Sergeant Chris Stone wrote a very interesting explanation of this part of the operation as follows:

I can't remember if we started getting 'tooled up' for our tasks on D Day minus one or on D Day itself. What I do remember is going down to the tank deck to draw everything we needed for the forthcoming operations. It was a joy not to be under exercise constraints and limitations on resources. Essentially, if we wanted it, we could have it. It was like being in a military supermarket without having to pay. The danger of this situation, however, is getting carried away and having eyes too big for our bellies. 5.56mm ammunition (ammo) was a given. We filled our magazines plus a bandolier of fifty each. We took an M79 with ammo for it, fragmentation and white phosphorous grenades, and each of us carried 9mm pistols plus ammo in the improvised shoulder holsters we had made on the way south. [Shoulder holsters turned out to be a bad idea as far as I was concerned as the rotten thing dug into my ribs something awful on the march into the OP. I have to admit that by the time we attacked Top Malo it had migrated to my pack.] Having got our weaponry sorted out, we turned our attention to what we were really all about – observing and reporting. We packed our PRC 320 radio, spare batteries, charger, antennae, swift scope and IWS (Individual Weapon Sight). Based on the fact that we would always have two men on watch we took only two sleeping bags and two sets of warm clothing between the four of us. This left us with little space for rations, cooking equipment and fuel so we duly decided that we would live on half-rations for the duration of the patrol. Tony [Boyle] buddied up with me for this purpose and Jan [Rowe] with Matt [Barnacle]. Each of us carried morphine on our dog tags. Other preparations included removing all badges of rank, regimental badges and all personal documentation against the possibility of capture by the enemy. Tony carried the signals instruction in his right thigh pocket. All this sounds very meticulous, and indeed it is, but we were going to be way out on a limb with no one to help us but ourselves, and thorough preparation is the key to a successful operation.

With our preparations complete, we had little to do but take it easy as the landing force sailed round into Falkland Sound overnight. The evening was spent in our various messes having a few beers – nothing else to do. I remember feeling it rather surreal that we were all so relaxed in the mess. There was all the usual banter and piss-taking and anyone seeing us from the outside would have thought we were on a pleasure cruise to a European football match as opposed to embarking on what we all assumed would be full-out war. I think this comes from having total confidence in one's comrades and our commanders, a privilege that I doubted our Argentine friends shared.

The feelings expressed in Chris Stone's last paragraph reflect what I believe were the feelings of all in the Commando Brigade, which now included the two parachute regiments (2 and 3 Para). None of us was foolish enough to think it was going to be a walk in the park but we were all absolutely confident of the result.

A couple of days before the landings began, Jeff Niblett and I shared an experience that was hilarious to us at the time but showed us both how tense many of the other participants were. Every morning at 0700 we were woken by a steward bringing us cups of tea (probably the last remaining perquisite of being an officer serving on one of Her Majesty's ships). As the ship moved further south, and we received less and less favourable news mixed with less and less favourable weather, this task became more onerous and less and less special. The poor steward had started with silver service with a tray per cabin, but by about three days before the landing he was reduced to walking round with a string of cups/mugs and a large jug to dispense ready milked tea. I have never really enjoyed tea and regarded this rather less than potable concoction as being as close to disgusting as it could possibly be. However, in order to support this young man, who was endeavouring to maintain a service, Jeff and I had been very careful always to thank him profusely and then to drink his kind offerings. For reasons that I do not fully remember, one morning both Jeff and I were woken by a particularly grumpy steward who was in a hurry and did not appreciate us taking so long to come to. As a consequence, he demanded that we get up quickly and drink our tea. We reacted accordingly. I remember asking for tea with sugar but no milk, and Jeff said that he wanted tea with neither milk nor sugar. At this our poor Chinese steward just lost it! I don't remember his exact words, but it was something along the lines of 'I get up at 5 o'clock and make tea for all the officers. The ship is rolling around and it is very difficult to get it right and sometimes it is very hard to deliver tea to all the officers that is tasty and hot. Today you say you want special tea and not normal tea and all I can say is that this is the last time I get up early for you two officers so from now on there will be no more f——g tea for you!' With that he stormed out of the cabin and disappeared, leaving Jeff and me giggling helplessly. To this day whenever we see each other our first words are always 'and no more f——g tea for you!', followed by hearty laughter. It was a great morale boost for us and I hope the poor steward suffered no lasting ill-effects.

On the night before the landings none of us could sleep. I remember watching a couple of films that night, awaiting H Hour. One was Monty Python's *Life of Brian* ('Always look on the bright side of life' subsequently became our theme song for the operation) and the other was *Cross of Iron*, a film about the German Army's retreat from Stalingrad in the Second World War. This was not a great morale booster as everyone dies by the end, and rather reduced any desire to watch more films! Standing on the bridge as the first ships approached Fanning Head, I remember seeing great arcs of tracer rounds flying through the air and thinking 'This is it; from now on we're on our own.' Corporal Steve Nicoll remembers:

> I think we were all spectators for Fanning Head. The travel speeds of noise and light made it look and sound disjointed and somehow slower than it really was. After weeks of isolation from the rest of the Task Force all of a sudden we were surrounded by a whirlwind of activity; it was a scene of perpetual motion – and no small threat from attacking aircraft. No one seemed to consider that the threat even remotely applied to *Tristram*. We watched with a cup of tea in hand while the GPMGs blazed away. Some of the Hong Kong* Chinese crew were scared shitless and looked absolutely bewildered and petrified.

* The majority of RFA ships were manned by Chinese crew from Hong Kong. All of them volunteered to stay with their ships for the conflict but they were poorly mentally prepared for what lay ahead of them. Nevertheless, they carried out their duties with great efficiency and no small amount of valour throughout.

At first light we were anchored in San Carlos Water surrounded by the whole fleet. I was then warned that our troops must be ready to fly as soon as a helicopter appeared. In the event this did not happen as Argentine aircraft arrived instead and the day's events had to be altered to take them into account, so that the first three sections were eventually inserted about an hour after sunset. Shortly after noon an enemy aircraft was seen flying over the north ridge of hills and not long after that the first air raids began. We had arrived in San Carlos Water.

Chapter 4

San Carlos – 'Bomb Alley'
(21–28 May)

Around noon on 21 May I was called to *Fearless* to talk to the brigade commander about deployment. We had set up a section location on the flying bridge of *Sir Tristram* which offered the best radio coverage from the ship in order to communicate with and manage our OPs in the field. I left *Sir Tristram* by rigid raider just as the serious air raids started. It was a slow and steady trip, which became quite scary as I felt helpless on the boat. Arriving at *Fearless* I quickly realised how lucky I was. All the people on board were wearing anti-flash kit and they were not happy. I arrived in the operations room just as the 40mm Bofors above it opened up. It made an almighty row and was not at all pleasant. I must admit I was delighted to leave the ship with authority to get ashore by any means possible as quickly as I could and before darkness. I felt very chastened as I left *Fearless*. It was my first experience of being trapped in a metal box with no control over my own destiny. As soon as I returned to *Sir Tristram* I got hold of Bill Wright and told him we were to get ashore as quickly as possible, and visited the captain to give him the same message. As I stood on the bridge watching attacking aircraft flying in very low despite all the ships firing at them I realised that retaking the islands would not be easy if all the Argentine military were as courageous as the aircrew attacking us.

During one of the early air-raids a bomb dropped close to *Fearless*. The explosion caused an enormous waterspout to rise about 20m into the air. As I watched it, a Scout helicopter flew through the waterspout towards *Sir Tristram*. I left the bridge and moved aft towards the helipad on the stern, arriving just as the Scout landed. The pilot was Jeff Niblett and under all his gear he looked very pale. I gestured for a headset in order to talk to him and asked why he was flying through a column of water like that. He was not amused and only realised that I was joking when I laughed out loud at his defence that he 'had no choice'. It had suddenly risen immediately ahead of him, giving no time to change direction. I advised him to keep his eyes open or the ground crew would not forgive him for

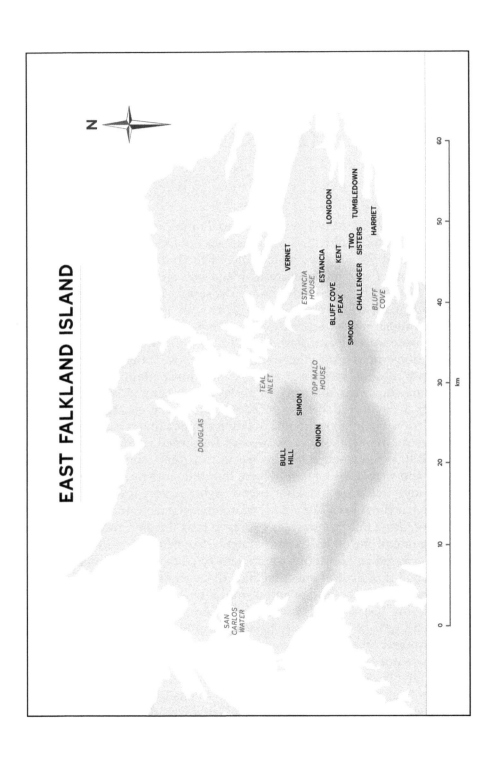

EAST FALKLAND ISLAND

N

DOUGLAS

SAN
CARLOS
WATER

TEAL
INLET

BULL
HILL

ONION

SIMON

TOP MALO
HOUSE

VERNET

ESTANCIA
HOUSE

ESTANCIA

BLUFF COVE
PEAK

SMOKO

CHALLENGER

KENT

TWO
SISTERS

BLUFF
COVE

LONGDON

TUMBLEDOWN

HARRIET

0   10   20   30   40   50   60
km

washing his aircraft in saltwater! We chatted idly for a minute or two as his aircraft was refuelled before he took off for another task.

The scene in San Carlos Water was one of controlled energy. Everywhere you looked there were helicopters of all sizes carrying underslung or onboard loads and apparently ignoring the incoming enemy aircraft.

On my return from *Fearless* I had assembled the guys and asked them to enquire of the next LCU that came alongside whether we could join her to go ashore. It was now mid-afternoon, about three hours before sunset. The crews of the mexefloats (powered barges) had initially scuttled off them as air raids came in but soon decided that they were safer simply getting on with it. It was impressive to see these RCT lads ignoring the noise and danger and just getting their mexefloats ready to begin taking important cargo loads to the shore regardless of all the unpleasant air traffic.

As we made our way ashore a further air raid came in. Bill Wright and I were standing on the cargo in the LCU when two Mirages came towards us from the south. We jumped down into the well of the ship and took cover. As the aircraft flew overhead Bill prodded me and pointed at our 'cover' – it was boxes of ammunition labelled 81mm MOR HE (81mm Mortar High Explosive). Bill's comment was 'Oh hell, Boss, we might just as well enjoy the view as we won't know anything if this lot goes up!' We climbed back up to the top of the boxes and 'enjoyed' the rest of the ride in much more comfort.

Arriving ashore, we offloaded with all our kit and set off up the hill towards the settlement. I was worried about possible mines so told everyone to walk in tyre tracks which I assumed was the safe thing to do. However, none of the tracks seemed to go in the direction we wanted so after a few metres this approach was abandoned and we headed for the top of the hill and the farm settlement. We learned subsequently that San Carlos had seen hardly any Argentine visitors since the invasion of 2 April so there was in fact no risk of mines at the settlement.

Bill Wright spoke to the farmer, Pat Short, to ask if there was somewhere we could use as a base as we needed to be near Brigade HQ. He couldn't have been more helpful and offered us a cow byre, which we then proceeded to clean out in preparation for using it as our base. After about two hours of serious muck removal, fitting blackout covers to the windows, installing our radio station and gaining communications with our sections, I went down to Brigade HQ and announced that we had three sections getting into position. They would be deployed at sunset and we were set up at the farm ready for further operations. By this time Brigade HQ was just coming ashore but its advance party had set up the main HQ and the initial HQ staff were in location. I returned to what I thought was my HQ, and was met by Bill Wright. He later recalled:

> Our occupation [of the byre] was [very] brief as just a short while later, an odd-looking bloke (wearing a red leather flying helmet à la spitfire type) poked his head through our black-out curtain and told us that we'd have to vacate the premises and allow his organisation to take it over. I asked him by whose authority and he quoted Brigadier Thompson. It turns out he was Lieutenant Colonel Michael Rose, who was the CO of 22 SAS which was attached to the brigade. We grudgingly lifted and shifted, and I have to take my hat off to the sig-nallers who were attached as they had to strip down all the antennae that they had spent ages laying out.

I assume that the SAS had seen they byre when they arrived but had been deterred by the presence of so much cow shit. After we had shovelled shit for two and a half hours they obviously felt that it was clean enough for them, so we were ejected.

Bill immediately went back to Pat Short and asked for help. He offered us the use of one of his unused farmhouses, so we moved straight into a three-bedroomed house! I should explain that the only tentage we had were small tents for OP use, and we did not have the facility for a com-mand tent, not even a 9ft by 9ft tent, so we needed to operate from a building of some sort. We thus ended the day sitting in a very comfortable location with a telephone link to Brigade HQ operations and all of us (twenty-four in total) ensconced inside the building. Bill wrote:

> 24 of us moved into the Red Roof House where we all slept in one room of the three-bedroomed cottage and the other room became our ops room. It made for some interesting sorting out of boots one morning as the Boss was an inveterate snorer and during one night he was the target of about eighteen mountain boots, none of which disturbed his slumbers nor stopped the snoring.

After this episode I was allocated my own room in the shape of the cupboard under the stairs, which had a door that could be shut to muffle the inevitable snoring!

Meanwhile the first three sections had remained on board *Sir Tristram* for day one and were deployed well after last light on 21 May, Callum Murray's to Evelyn Hill, Phil ('Monty') Montgomery's to Mount Simon and Chris Stone's to Bull Hill. All were tasked with providing OPs to look out for enemy locations, enemy OPs and to warn Brigade HQ of any enemy aircraft en route from Stanley to San Carlos. They were to be in the field for seven days and it was planned to replace them with the other teams on or about 26/27 May. They left San Carlos in perfect weather, cool and dry with good visibility and no wind. This proved not to be the normal weather window. With increasing altitude the weather would become a real problem as low clouds reduced visibility amid scudding falls of rain, sleet and snow. Eventually the OPs changed locations in order to do their jobs properly.

Details for the three patrols were as follows: '**5 Section (Lieutenant Callum Murray, Corporals Nigel Devenish, Bob Sharp and Steve Nicoll) to set up an OP on Evelyn Hill (GR 9782) to observe arc northwest of Chata Hill (GR 892297) north to Teal Inlet through east to south to Mount Simon.**'

Corporal Steve Nicoll recalled:

Once we deployed forward, we left behind the threats of San Carlos and were immersed into the world of darkness and silence. It seemed very reassuring to be actually under way although we pretty quickly realised some of the realities of war. Operational weights of ammunition, radio equipment and a stack of rations made for extremely heavy rucksacks, the ground was difficult to cover easily and the darkness seemed, well … very dark. We moved slowly as a result.

Corporal Bob Sharp remembered:

when we woke up anchored in San Carlos, we spent the day watching the Argie Air Force firepower display, which luckily wasn't very impressive as they missed their targets, while we waited to get ashore that night on our first task to OP Teal Inlet. I remember someone coming on deck, not from the Cadre, with a hot wet and spilling it on himself when taking cover from a low-flying jet and when he felt the hot liquid he thought he'd been hit. How we laughed.

During one of the lectures on the way south someone asked an ex-NP8901 guy to describe the Falkland Islands. His simple answer was 'take Dartmoor and float it'. The rock bands there weren't Pink Floyd or any other band, just a complete pain in the backside to cross at night. Having been dropped by helo in the middle of one on that first night we got a real close insight as to what to expect from the terrain. It was, however, nothing we couldn't handle.

Once the team of Callum, Steve, Nige and myself had concealed ourselves before first light into the OP overlooking Teal Inlet, we

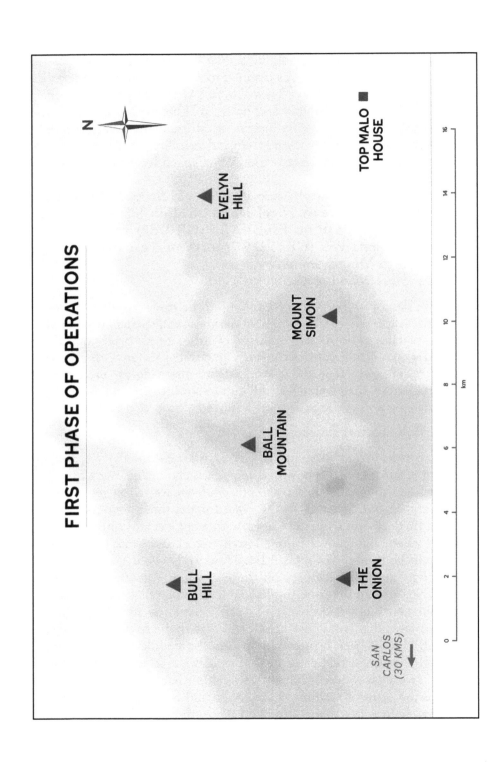

FIRST PHASE OF OPERATIONS

N

EVELYN
HILL

MOUNT
SIMON

BALL
MOUNTAIN

BULL
HILL

THE
ONION

SAN
CARLOS
(30 KMS)

TOP MALO
HOUSE

0   2   4   6   8   10   12   14   16
km

settled into the routine very quickly. Our position was on a forward slope with little cover and was basically a cutting in the peat with a wall of peat behind us and a very small hump of ground a few metres in front from which we could observe the target. The cam net we had brought gave us some cover from above but movement was obviously severely restricted. We only made a wet and cooked at first light and before last light. We weren't moving so only carried half rations anyway. I do remember, as it was peat and very wet, being inside my sleeping bag with waterproofs on trying not to imitate a sponge. It didn't work.

As I remember there were three events during our time in the OP. The first was a daylight flypast by two Harriers flying tactically very fast and low between us and Teal Inlet heading east. The second, once again during daylight, was four enemy Hueys flying around Teal, two gunships, a casevac and one utility all recognised as far as could be observed. They landed for a short while then flew back towards Stanley. Luckily, they did not come our way. The third was a night flight by what we could only guess was a C130, certainly not fast jets, possibly with escort due to the noise, flying towards Stanley. It had no lights on and there was no moon so we could only go by engine noise. These were all reported to base by radio.

'6 Section (Colour Sergeant Phil Montgomery, Sergeant Derek ('Tug the Tourist') Wilson, Corporal Keith Blackmore and Corporal Ray Sey) to set up an OP on Mount Simon to observe the inner valley for enemy movement and to give early warning of air raids from Stanley Airport.'

Corporal Ray Sey described the deployment:

We deployed on 21 May by helo from *Sir Tristram* to GR 915794 [about 3km northwest of the summit of Mount Simon] and then patrolled to our OP on Mount Simon. We were in clag for two days but could hear plenty of enemy Huey activity in the valley below. On 23 May 'Monty' decided to move the OP to GR 950785 [about 1.5km just south of east of the summit of Mount Simon] in order to get eyes on whatever activity was taking place. Unfortunately, the clag prevailed for a further five days and no visible intelligence could be gained. We then moved to Bull Hill on 28 May for an extraction and co-located with Chris Stone's section, from where we were picked up on 30 May.

'7 Section (Sergeant Chris Stone, Sergeant Jan Rowe, Corporal 'Ginge' Boyle and Corporal Matt Barnacle) OP on Bull Hill GR 862832 to act in the same manner as 7 Section.'

Chris Stone's section was given what turned out to be the most difficult of the three patrols. They were sited in a direct line between Stanley Airfield and the southern end of San Carlos Water and all the air raids from Stanley passed over their heads. They were busy, from their arrival, sending important air raid warning messages which gave those of us at San Carlos a good 3 to 5 minutes' warning of incoming enemy aircraft.

This worked well for us until about five or six days in when I received a clear message from Chris warning me that this might be his last message. I could barely hear him through the sound of rotor blades as an Argentine Huey helicopter was hover-taxiing around his location looking for somewhere to land. Chris gave a warning fire control order to his team to prepare to sell their lives as expensively as possible and then called me to warn me to prepare me for the worst. I was about to give him a bollocking about radio security when I realised that his situation was very serious, and further that I could do absolutely nothing to help him and his section. Fortunately, whilst I was worrying about what to do and Chris was preparing his final orders, the cloud base began to drop and the helicopter crew took fright and flew away to lower ground!

Shortly after this, orders were given for 3 Para to prepare to move on foot from Port San Carlos to Teal Inlet and then on to Estancia House. 45 Commando RM were to yomp from San Carlos to Teal Inlet via Douglas Settlement and await further orders. When I realised that the approaching men from 3 Para were in danger of coming across our three patrols, I ordered the teams to congregate at Chris Stone's location and prepare for helicopter pick-up. I knew this would not be easy for them to do but leaving them where they were might cause a 'blue on blue' situation. I had been trying to get them back to San Carlos for about two days already and centralising the three teams seemed the least dangerous thing to do. Both Callum's and Monty's sections had been overflown by Argentine Hueys but not as closely or as dangerously as Chris Stone's section. The risks of leaving the sections in situ was higher than that of centralising them where they would have a bit more strength in numbers.

Meanwhile back at San Carlos the remainder of the Cadre had not been idle. We had set up a routine of watchkeepers on the radio with stand-to positions outside the building in case of alarms. We were linked to Brigade HQ via a telephone line to pass immediate messages to the duty officers. This worked really well as we were able to give at least 5 minutes warning of air raids from the south of San Carlos Water, which was the chosen route for all the raids from Stanley.

In the first three days we settled into our routines and I regularly visited Brigade HQ to see if there were any other tasks for us. After 48 hours it was clear that we needed help to manage the signals watchkeeping as we were getting very tired. I knew that if we maintained this work rate for more than a few weeks we would become much less effective. I requested help from Brigade HQ & Signals Squadron and we were allocated a corporal and two signallers to man our radios at Cadre HQ. Corporal Adey RM and two marine signallers joined us and stayed with us all the way to Stanley. They were brilliant and made us much more effective. To my shame, I do not remember the names of the two signallers.

On about day three I was asked by Major Hector Gullan (the brigade operations officer) whether I could arrange for a recce patrol to go to West Falkland to locate and observe an Argentine OP near Mount Rosalie, which overlooked Falkland Sound and was providing control to the air raids we were enduring. I gave the task to Sergeant Terry Doyle (who commanded 8 Section, the fourth section of the half troop already deployed on D Day). I arranged for two rigid raiders to ferry the guys across immediately after last light. The task was further complicated by the commanding officer of 22 SAS who insisted (because he had a patrol in West Falkland) that we only use a certain beach for landing our patrol to avoid the risk of a 'blue on blue' incident. Terry and his team were to locate and observe this OP and then report back. We could then organise a fighting patrol to attack and destroy the OP. The patrol had all day to prepare and rest before setting out just after sunset. The weather that night seemed benign, although it was a little cold.

The weather in Falkland Sound was quite strange. Throughout daylight hours it was typically clear and calm but as soon as the sun set it became a wind funnel and the winds rose to storm force every night with accompanying waves and turbulence. Terry's crew set off in the calm of San Carlos Water but on leaving it found themselves in awful conditions. They pressed on in a very determined way but after about an hour one of the two rigid raiders filled with water and the engine failed. The patrol now faced a fight for survival. By dint of some fine seamanship by the two boat coxswains, they were able to take the damaged boat under tow and returned to San Carlos bedraggled and wet, but alive. The chastened and exhausted team returned to Cadre HQ several hours later, and I sent them to bed. I then reported our failure to cross Falkland Sound to Brigade HQ with the promise that we would achieve it 24 hours later.

The next day I arranged for an LCVP to carry the team across and they duly set out shortly after sunset. They suffered almost the same fate as on the previous night. It was with some surprise that I met the same bedraggled team later that night, having again failed to cross Falkland Sound because of the atrocious weather conditions. My second visit to Brigade HQ caused much hilarity but I swore that we would get across the next night come hell or high water. I went to the landing craft people and requested an LCU to take the whole troop across the next night.

I had decided that we needed to eliminate this enemy OP as soon as possible and that a full fighting patrol was required to achieve this. With the full troop of twenty-four men we could set up a troop base, locate the OP and then observe it, and destroy it once the recces were completed. I was very confident that we could achieve this so at first light warned the whole Cadre to prepare for a major fighting patrol to depart at sunset or shortly thereafter.

After orders and preparations were made, we were ready to go at sunset. I sent the team to Blue Beach and went to Brigade HQ for final confirmation of my orders, accompanied by 'Mac' Mclean and Steve Groves (to act as my bodyguards!). After a meeting with the brigade commander and Hector Gullan, and despite getting some stick from CO 22 SAS (which I felt was a little unnecessary) I joined my guys and set out for what I believed to be Blue Beach (the pier at San Carlos). I was not aware that the pier at San Carlos was Blue Beach One and the landing craft base was at Blue Beach Two. On arrival at the pier we found ourselves alone. I asked 'Mac' where everyone was. He didn't know. I spoke to a sentry on the pier and he explained that the Landing Craft location was at Blue Beach Two and pointed us in the right direction. Mac, Steve and I then set out along the beach towards the landing craft location. It was extremely dark and after about 10 minutes I walked into something very big and very metal. This turned out to be a BARV in its camouflage net. In the darkness we couldn't see a way round it so, despite being very heavily loaded with kit, we climbed over it and down the far side! I was carrying an AR15 rifle and an M79 with a lot of ammunition for both weapons. In addition, I had a further 500 rounds of link ammunition for the GPMG in my rucksack, as well as kit for three days. As I stepped off the BARV I became entangled in the cam net and fell face first into the water. The composition and sheer weight of my load meant that I could not get up, and I began to drown! After what seemed like for ever, I was able to force my face out of the water and take a huge breath before falling back under. I did this several times before I realised that my two companions were watching me, helpless with mirth at my situation. They were laughing so hard that I became convinced that I would soon run out of strength and air, but they finally got their act together and pulled me clear of the water and the net. I was not impressed but as I whispered my rage their hilarity got worse, so we called a truce and set off to find the rest of the troop. We arrived at the landing craft base with me soaking wet and covered in mud accompanied by two helpless assistants who were quick to share with the others the reason for my state!

Colour Sergeant Bill Wright remembered this incident:

It involved and starred the Boss and could so easily have been a disaster but turned out happily in the end. Terry Doyle and his section had been given a mission on the West Island and had been trying to get there for two nights with no joy due to appalling weather conditions. Finally, it was decided to take all those at San Carlos at the time over the water, to do a proper job on the enemy position. The Boss gave a superb brief and even invited ex-Boss Captain David Nicholls along as a GPMG gunner. Everyone was keyed up, blacked out and raring to go at the appointed time to go to the jetty and embarkation. This indeed had all the hallmarks of a wartime commando raid. As they were about to leave, the Boss was called to Brigade HQ. He asked if anyone would act as guide for the remainder of the Cadre to the Blue Beach. Corporal 'Mac' McGregor said he would as he had landed at Blue Beach the previous night. The Boss then left for Brigade HQ with 'Mac' Mclean and Steve Groves and the main body left for Blue Beach.

Having completed the meeting, the Boss went to join the remainder. When he got to Blue Beach ... no Cadre, no LC. Then he discovered that there were two Blue Beaches and 'Mac' had taken the men to the wrong one. Wishing to avoid confusion at this stage as it was pitch black, the Boss decided to go along the waterline until he found the remainder of the Cadre. Unfortunately, things were not destined to assist him in this task. Parked along the beach at various intervals were several landing craft and BARVs forming a difficult obstacle course even in daylight. Each one was cunningly booby-trapped with a cam net and it was one of these that was to be his downfall. Clambering over the BARV his foot became caught in the netting and he pitched headfirst into the oggin.

The sight of the Boss trying to drown tactically and at the same time extricate himself from the net proved too much for Mac, who at first began to chuckle and then laugh. Luckily, the Boss also saw the funny side of the situation as well. To add insult to injury, they now located the beach (wrong beach). In its approach, and on a falling tide, the LCU struck a rock and refused to come off. End of mission. A very disconsolate group of men later came back to Cadre HQ. We later learnt that all the misfortune was the work of the great mountain god, because the target of the Cadre that night turned out to be not a troop as first indicated, but a company of Argentines. Another funny ending.

On arrival at the beach I grabbed the LC officer and asked where the LCU was. He advised that it had been delayed by its last task but was due any moment. We soon heard its engines heading towards us but as it appeared, it immediately rose in the water and ran aground on a submerged rock. Time was now becoming an issue so I waded into the water, telling a few of the guys to join me, and we tried to push the LCU off the rock whilst the crew went full astern. It was not a great idea as the LCU must have weighed several tons and was not for moving. We could not shift it, and as the tide was ebbing it became ever further stuck on the rock. After about 15 fruitless minutes the LC officer admitted defeat and told me that the trip was off. He did not have another LCU available but thought this one should float off in about 6 hours. I realised that this ended any chance of crossing Falkland Sound that night so told the guys to get their gear together and we then set off back to the Cadre location in a long dripping line. As we approached the area of Brigade HQ a sentry called 'Halt! Who goes there?' I responded 'Friend', but then heard the cocking of at least two GPMGs to our front. It was a sobering moment and I immediately advised we were an M&AW Cadre patrol returning to base. A new and very serious voice responded 'Advance one to be recognised.' I did so and then had to identify every one of my guys before the SNCO and his sentry relaxed. It was nice to know that our sentries were fully alert as it could have been quite unpleasant. Once the team had arrived at Cadre HQ, I divested myself of kit and went to Brigade HQ, where, amid much hilarity from the brigade staff and the brigade commander, I proceeded to apologise for our failure to cross Falkland Sound. I was told to get sorted out and come back to HQ first thing in the morning to discuss the way forward.

I returned to Brigade HQ as instructed the next morning and was told that as we would soon be moving from San Carlos, it had been decided that the fighting patrol would be cancelled. I was to stand down from the task. I was then lambasted by CO 22 SAS with comments about the 'so-called M&AW Cadre not being able to cope with some rough weather'. He was taken to one side by the brigade commander and clearly ordered to wind his neck in. I was rather aggrieved by his remarks and felt that we had really done our best but had been defeated by circumstances beyond our control. After three sleepless nights and a severely freezing swim I was less than pleased with him. Much later I learned from a friend in the SAS that the reason for his CO's irritation was that he had 'lost' a patrol on West Falkland and had not heard from them for some time. The beach that he insisted we were to use was the emergency RV for the patrol and he wanted us to collect them without letting us know that they were there. This seemed a poor idea. We also later discovered from the Argentines that the enemy OP was in fact a reinforced armoured company of about 200 men complete with artillery pieces. Had our raid gone ahead, we would have had little chance of achieving our aim and would probably have been severely mauled in the process.

After five days of watching almost continuous air raids by day and little sleep at night, we were all tired. I suggested to Bill Wright that we needed to find a larger building with more space to sort out the three sections from the field when they returned. Bill discussed the problem with the farmer, who suggested that we move to the San Carlos Community Hall. Once there, and set up in our new HQ with plenty of space, plenty of water and the ability to establish some method of drying soaking wet gear, I realised that I should be concentrating on the whole Cadre rather than just those in San Carlos. I talked it over with Bill Wright and sent a detailed signal to the three sections in the field telling them to get together at Sergeant Chris Stone's location as described earlier.

* * *

The next chapter is introduced out of order with the rest of the book. I feel it is necessary to give a detailed explanation of the difficulties imposed on the Cadre sections by a combination of the weight of the loads they were carrying and the terrain that they had to cross with those loads. The detail contained in Chapter Five clearly explains the problems. This has been confirmed by discussions with all the remaining team members so I con-sider it a very good guide to night movement in full marching order by small sections operating during the Falklands campaign.

As a final comment concerning marching across the islands, I should also explain the difference in the speed of travel of 3 Para and 45 Com-mando in their moves from Port San Carlos to Teal Inlet. Firstly, 3 Para travelled in fighting order with their rucksacks/bergens and other heavy loads carried by tractors and trailers provided by the good people of Port San Carlos. 45 Commando RM travelled a day later and went via Douglas Settlement to Teal Inlet (an additional 10–12km added to the journey). 45 Commando RM was also self-sufficient in that the men carried all their own kit and supplies, and thus their loads were very much heavier than those of the soldiers in 3 Para. 45 Commando RM was the only unit during the Falklands War that carried out the full yomp from Port San Carlos to Stanley carrying all its own kit on the backs of the men for the entire distance.

Chapter 5

Falkland Islands 'Stone Runs': A Personal Recollection

This chapter is intended to explain the problems of moving over difficult terrain with very heavy loads. It is derived from the personal experience of one of the team members, Corporal Steve Nicoll, of 5 Section. It is self-explanatory and does not require anything other than this introduction.

> A stone run (stone river, stone stream or stone sea) is a conspicuous rock landform, a result of the erosion of particular rock varieties caused by myriad freezing-thawing cycles taking place in periglacial conditions during the last Ice Age. The actual formation of stone runs involves no fewer than five processes: weathering, solifluction, frost heaving, frost sorting, and washing. The stone runs are essentially different from moraines, rock glaciers, and rock flows or other rock phenomena involving the actual flow of rock blocks under stress that is sufficient to break down the cement or to cause crushing of the angularities and points of the boulders. By contrast, the stone run boulders are quite stable, providing for safer climbing and crossing of the run.
> Stone runs are accumulations of boulders with no finer material between them. In the Falklands they occur on slopes of between 1 and 10 degrees off the horizontal and are the product of mass-movement and stone sorting during past periods of cold climate.

The accepted textbook definition, above, of the geological feature referred to as a 'stone run' reads quite easily, almost benignly. The reassuring comment that the 'boulders are quite stable, providing for safer climbing and crossing of the run' suggests to a casual reader that they do indeed offer a safe and easy way to experience and witness this geological phenomenon. On a dry, clear day, with no time pressures, or other considerations, to create any unwanted difficulties, they may be exactly that. Yet during the events of Operation Corporate in 1982 stone runs represented an altogether different experience. For any troops laden with field equipment and operational levels of ammunition, moving at night under cover of darkness and with heightened awareness of the possibility of encountering a waiting enemy, stone runs were a unique and challenging natural obstacle. Stone runs were confined to the sloping features of the numerous mountains that dotted the 'camp'. Troops moving across country would have encountered them and negotiated them to maintain progress. For some of the troop movements made throughout the campaign there was no requirement to move over the high ground. Thankfully they were spared the need to become acquainted with the angst of a painful introduction to stone runs. This is my personal recollection of my introduction to stone runs as member of a four-man patrol with the M&AW Cadre.

Any tactical movement at night presents a range of challenges that professional soldiers learn to understand, accept and overcome. They also need to ensure that they are prepared to adapt their planned route and timings, and have a well-rehearsed set of drills for encountering and crossing any obstacle they encounter. The obvious lack of visibility when moving at night makes it difficult to gauge the ground on which you move. Trips, stumbles and falls are a natural, if unwelcome, aspect of night movement. Night vision provides some assistance to an individual as they become accustomed to the reduced light levels, even if depth of field and interpretation of the ground still impair the ability to move with anything close to the speed of moving in daylight. Additional natural obstacles such as streams, rivers and boggy, wet ground will also slow down progress, as well as offering the hugely unpopular disadvantage of wet feet. On a seven-day patrol wet boots in the first 24 hours represent a significant consideration to the wearer in maintaining the welfare of his feet. Wire fences, buildings and other man-made features need careful thought as they suggest the presence of humans and in an operational setting that could lead to detection and compromise or walking into something a little more hostile. Wildlife can detect a human presence long before the human can detect them. Dogs bark, geese cackle, and almost all of them move away or generate some form of alarm call that informs an interested listener that another presence has been detected. Those who lead a rural life are extremely adept at listening to the outside world and what it's telling them.

Navigation at night is a skill that follows the same principles as navigating in daylight but it becomes much more difficult when the lights are out. Everything instantly becomes more difficult. It slows progress, there is no long-range visibility and extra care must be taken when using map and compass. Any use of light is to be avoided where possible. Global

Positioning Systems (GPS) were not available in 1982. All navigation was conducted using traditional methods of navigation, map and compass, and marshalling every scrap of hard-gained experience. Maps of the Falkland Islands were a pale imitation of the Ordnance Survey maps that cover the United Kingdom. Ordnance Survey maps are detailed, accurate and can be read, just like a book, to gain an understanding of the ground to be covered. Comparing 'map to ground' studies is a vital element of pre-deployment preparation. Professional soldiers spend hours studying a map to build a mental picture of the ground, creating a muscle memory that will silently speak to them as they move over the darkened terrain. The Falkland Island maps were adequate but they failed in one crucial aspect: they did not plot the position, extent and types of stone run that criss-crossed the 'camp'. This made any planned movement in a straight line distinctly unlikely and challenging.

For the M&AW Cadre most of their movement was carried out at night using lengthy, silent approaches on foot to establish observation posts (OPs). These were deliberately positioned behind enemy lines where they would remain undetected for several days, observing and reporting. For a tasking of this duration it was necessary to carry enough rations, equipment and ammunition to last several days. Although some weight could be distributed in the belt order, referred to as second line kit, the bulk of each man's weight was carried on his back in a rucksack (third line). First line equipment was carried on the person in pockets, which meant that if equipment, rucksack and belt order had to be discarded, or was lost, the individual had some recourse to basic equipment. Weights varied within any four-man patrol. The radio operator had an extra consideration with his Clansman PRC HF 320 radio and ancillaries. It would be misleading to attempt to estimate the average weight of a rucksack but they were without fail 'heavy', and once on a man's back shifted his centre of gravity above the waistline, making the collective mass top heavy and unstable. On an operation like Corporate the temptation to carry extra ammunition at the beginning of the campaign added to the weight burden. Each M&AW Cadre patrol had similar but subtly different approaches to the carriage and distribution of weight. Spare radio batteries would be shared amongst the patrol to avoid the radio operator being disadvantaged. Some patrols carried two sleeping bags as there would always be two men on watch while the other pair rested; such 'hot bunking' reduced the weight and bulk for two men. Rations could be reduced to the absolute minimum. Once in an OP with little or no movement required, it was possible to exist on a much lower intake of food. Such decisions also carried with them an element of risk, which was considered by each patrol before each insertion. One factor was a constant in all of their deliberations: each man carried a heavy load on his back regardless of what he did or did not choose to carry. Finally, the carriage of an individual's personal weapons ensured that both hands were occupied in carrying the weapon in the 'alert' position, ready to be used as quickly as possible. Although not necessarily heavy, it was the first line of defence if the patrol came under contact. It also effectively removed one or both hands when it came to crossing any natural or man-made obstacles.

Every member of the M&AW Cadre was extremely familiar with most of the difficulties involved in night navigation, including moving over unfriendly terrain, weight carriage and crossing obstacles. All Royal Marines started with basic training at the Commando Training Centre at Lympstone in Devon, graduating to exercises within the Commando Brigade around Dartmoor, Sennybridge, Otterburn, Norway and anywhere else. Wherever Royal Marines carried out their training, it incorporated movement at night on foot and that always entailed crossing obstacles. Further exposure to night navigation also featured on every command course for promotion and Royal Marines Mountain Leaders would have been required to conduct and lead night navigation as an integral component of their specialist qualification. It was understood that night navigation was challenging, difficult and tiring work.

Prior to the first Cadre sections' helicopter insertion on the evening of D Day, 21 May 1982, a great deal of time and thought had been put into how best to prepare for this operational and important deployment. The three sections to be deployed from the LSL *Sir Tristram* were led by Callum Murray, Chris ('Rocky') Stone and Phil ('Monty') Montgomery. One subject that they all discussed and knew about before leaving the warmth of the mess decks and the safety of the flight deck was the Falkland Island stone runs, which represented an extra level of difficulty in addition to the usual considerations for night navigation. The geological description claiming that stone run boulders were 'quite stable, providing for safer climbing and crossing of the run' would be junked for ever by anyone encountering their first stone run on the evening of 21 May 1982. Callum Murray provided a comprehensive brief to his team, Nigel ('Ginge') Devenish, Bob Sharp and me.

We were a pretty ad hoc quartet, to be honest. But that was reflected in every other section as well. Moving from RM Condor in a rush swept up the Cadre staff of instructors as well as the newly qualified students from the Mountain Leader (ML) 2 course. This also coincided with the completion of the more senior Mountain Leader (ML) 1 course. Of the thirty-six-strong Cadre that embarked onboard RFA *Resource* at Rosyth, the split between staff and students was roughly 50:50, all of them officers and NCOs. Callum Murray and Bob Sharp were experienced operators who had proved their worth on the demanding ML2 course. Nige Devenish had completed the ML1 course and had a deep understanding of operating in the harsh environment of mountainous terrain. I had qualified as an ML2 in 1980 and remained on the Cadre staff. Crucially I had attended a combat signals course at Hereford run by 22 SAS in 1981. Eight Cadre MLs had benefited from top class instruction on becoming effective signallers in a combat role. This skill was a timely and important element in establishing and maintaining effective communications. If the composition was ad hoc, it still carried the essential mix of experience, ability and mutual understanding. Although the Cadre deployed three sections on 21 May each one would operate independently of the others. The aim of each section was to establish a covert observation post to report on any Argentine activity in their given area. As the sections were deployed well forward of any other friendly forces it was no exaggeration to describe it as operating 'behind the lines'.

It isn't that unusual to have to negotiate your way round or past boulders and loose rocks, especially in mountainous terrain. They are simply another natural obstacle that is part of the environment you are operating in, so the initial approach to a stone run would have been a relatively straightforward one. Can it be bypassed or avoided? How far does it extend up or downhill? How secure is the stonework? Can a safe exit be seen or estimated? There is always a time factor in considering the actions required to overcome any obstacle. At night the clock is rarely your friend. You must think and move quickly whenever you can. In a four-man patrol the point or lead man would be given the responsibility of route selection and initial decision-making. The bigger the obstacle, the bigger the decision. The process of tackling stone runs quickly became as much a psychological challenge as a physical one. They were difficult, unpredictable and a downright nuisance.

Encountering the first stone run gave a crash course introduction to the difficulties they presented to anyone crossing them. There was never an obvious entry point or clear route across the field of boulders. This made gauging both route selection and entry point little more than pot-luck. The stone runs may have been fashioned over centuries but they remained annoyingly unstable. Despite numerous weight tests before committing to the next precarious step, it wasn't unusual for the stone to pivot, slip or move. This called for some delicate balancing acts and some not so delicate falls. There was the ever-present probability of injuring a knee or ankle and the weight of the rucksack merely added to the levels of discomfort. It was never a silent activity. It couldn't be, as there was always noise generated by the stone's movement and whispered messages of guidance and support between team members. Falling unexpectedly was normally accompanied by some muted oath or muffled groan. If you were lucky, the crossing was achieved at a narrow point and would be a relatively short crossing of 30m or so. We rarely felt that we got lucky very often. Each subsequent stone run was met with a slight sinking of the spirit and recognition that it would be time-consuming, difficult and potentially dangerous. Each stone run varied in width and stone sizes, and each was different in composition. Stone sizes varied from small loose rocks to much larger boulders. All of them were determined to obey gravity and move downhill. No one in our patrol had encountered such a challenging form of natural obstacle before and this was in the context of an environment that contained other challenges. Carrying operational weights and moving in unfamiliar territory with sub-standard maps all added to the mix. Knowing that we were operating well forward of any friendly forces heightened awareness.

Little could be done to avoid stone runs, and nothing could be done to detect a narrow and safe crossing point. The only approach was to get on with it, and to ensure that stone runs were regarded with something resembling respect, and allowing additional time when assessing what was realistically achievable on foot in difficult terrain at night. It didn't require an Oxbridge degree to determine that it meant it took a lot longer to cover the ground and that more time needed to be factored into planning. It was also very tiring work. The effort of maintaining balance, rising from falls, removing and replacing rucksacks all took a physical toll on energy levels.

Stone runs made their mark when our patrol was tasked to move from our OP position on Evelyn Hill overlooking Teal Inlet. We'd been in position for several days and had been following events on our high frequency patrol radios. Tuning into the BBC World Service and Voice of America, it was entirely possible to piece together what had been happening since we landed on 21 May. This was confirmed by a long encoded message sent by the OC, Captain Rod Boswell, on 27 May. We had to vacate our OP at last light and move tactically to a harbour position with two other M&AW Cadre patrols on a feature known as Bull Hill. This was to our southsouthwest and over open terrain. We had to be in our new position by daybreak the following day. We were no longer needed to carry on with the task of observing Teal Inlet. As 3 Cdo Bde began to move eastward from the beach head at Port San Carlos it meant that they would be moving slowly towards our location. As they started their epic yomp, it flushed out several Argentine stragglers from the Fanning Head area. They were reported to be moving on foot and much closer to our location. The task was pretty simple and clear, although we had no illusions that it would be anything other than a pretty demanding night move. Several days perched in a damp hollow in the Falklands turf wasn't ideal preparation for a long night march. As we hadn't anticipated remaining in the OP for as long as we eventually did, our food provisions had become stretched and had to be rationed. Operating so far forward of friendly forces prevented any opportunities for resupply. Every mouthful of food was savoured until it eventually ran out.

That night move on 27 May was memorable, as three separate four-man sections came together on top of a grid reference in open terrain and in darkness. Chris Stone's section was already established on Bull Hill and we would move to their location for a helicopter pick-up on 28 May. As the crow flies, the distance we had to move was 16km, about 10 miles. As we would be moving tactically, it meant that we were denied the luxury of travelling in a straight line. The distance actually covered was well in excess of 16km as route selection necessitated contouring mountainsides. This all added to the distance and, of course, the number of obstacles to be crossed. Rivers and streams criss-crossed the route. Soft, wet, boggy ground and ankle-breaking tussock grass mounds were all encountered, so reaching this vital rendezvous (RV) point was taxing. We were fortunate enough to enjoy dry weather and although visibility was poor, it lacked rain and wind. Additionally, there was an element of undeniable fatigue from days of inactivity and a reduced diet. There was also a heightened sense of possible vulnerability to encountering retreating Argentine troops from Fanning Head and Port San Carlos. Our senses and all our training had to be fully concentrated on our approach to the agreed RV. More than one cow or bull was disturbed by our approach. The sight of a large black silhouette unexpectedly appearing in front made the pulse quicken!

Not surprisingly, we encountered several stone runs en route to the RV. Each one represented a difficult and challenging obstacle to making timely progress. Time was a constant consideration, a concern, as we had to complete the move under cover of darkness. Noise discipline was

severely tested, as were our reserves of patience and fitness. In the satis-
faction of successfully meeting up on Bull Hill, it was easy for the slog of
the previous night to become just another memory in a busy, fast-moving
period. The next priority was to await a safe helicopter pick-up, return to
San Carlos and get ready for the next task. The emphasis was always on
what was to happen next and making sure that you were prepared. What
had already happened was put behind you; the past is gone and can't be
altered.

I didn't always find it so easy to do that. I couldn't recall being so
exhausted and how much effort had been required to push through and
carry on. I was very conscious that it appeared to me that I was the only
patrol member to have struggled and I felt that I, in some way, had slowed
down the patrol's progress. No one had expressed this sentiment. It was
firmly a self-generated internal discussion and I discounted any notion of
talking to the others about it. In my own mind I felt I had been the weakest
link in our patrol at a time when there was a general expectation of a
higher performance. I'd let the team down and I'd let myself down. It
stayed that way with me for years. I recalled that night move on every
occasion subsequently when I had to dig deep and work hard. My internal
voice would say, 'If this is hard, it's nothing compared to the night move
from Evelyn Hill in 1982.' For me that memory served as a powerful
incentive to respond positively to hard physical challenges. It helped me to
put everything into some kind of understandable perspective.

In attending reunions, and particularly Falklands reunions, and meeting
up with other Cadre members from 1982, conversations would inevitably
stray into 'Do you remember …?' These related to recollections of a
shared experience with a focus achieving a little clarity, some nostalgia but
a much stronger flavour of camaraderie. At later reunions I found that
I was a little easier in talking about how difficult I had found the terrain,
and especially the stone runs, in the Falklands. What I hadn't expected to
emerge during these later conversations was that others had found the
terrain and movement over it just as challenging as I had. This information was usually volunteered as part of wider recollections, still providing clarity, nostalgia and camaraderie but with the added ingredient of
personal reflections. Maybe getting older allows us all to be more candid
and to place alpha male misplaced pride to one side. The gradual realisation emerged that I had subconsciously internalised how difficult that
night move had been and my mistaken assumption that I was the only one
who had found it difficult. Perhaps one of the strengths of our four-man
patrols was that they suppressed individual situations to ensure that the

collective objectives were more important. That night move still stands out in my memory as a very difficult and exhausting chapter. It was bloody hard work. The passage of time hasn't dimmed the experience.

Stone runs may still sound like nothing more than an interesting geological phenomenon. Something to witness, perhaps, to gain an understanding of how rock formations occur. Perhaps in daylight and in decent weather they are exactly that, yet crossing a stone run at night, humping a heavy rucksack and unsure of every foot placement, lends them a totally different feel. I doubt that much has changed since 1982 that would make it any easier to negotiate a stone run. Whilst technology may provide some assistance with weaponry and communications, the physical burdens imposed on the foot soldier haven't altered one little bit over decades of conflict. A pair of size nine boots on the ground is still required to carry out all the basic elements and the sharp, business end of conflict. Operation Corporate used the available technology of its time, of course it did. Yet it had to sit alongside the age-old requirement of complementing the needs and aims of foot soldiering. These requirements remain simple and unchanged over centuries – the self-sufficient individual who knowingly subjects himself to the physical vagaries of operating in a contested and challenging environment. All the man-made and natural obstacles have to be overcome and in 1982 that included the fearsome feature of stone runs. They certainly made their presence known and, for me, left a lasting impression.

Author's comment

As an HQ warrior for the duration of Operation Corporate, I was very aware of the time taken to move across country and the difficulties imposed by the terrain. After speaking to all the first three team leaders after their return to San Carlos, I realised that our original plan for night movement was wildly optimistic. Our planning targets for night movement started at about 3km an hour but after the first patrols we made serious changes to our planning times, which were considerably reduced. As a result, we opted for much shorter approach marches to insert OPs. There was a risk that helicopter insertions might possibly be detected by the enemy, but we rated the risk as low and acceptable. We also realised after the raid on Top Malo House that the risk of detection by enemy patrols was considerably reduced but it remained a factor throughout the operations.

The biggest risk to our patrols during the final two weeks of land operations was 'blue on blue' situations. This was exacerbated by the fact that

OPERATIONS AREA OF FRIENDLY TROOPS

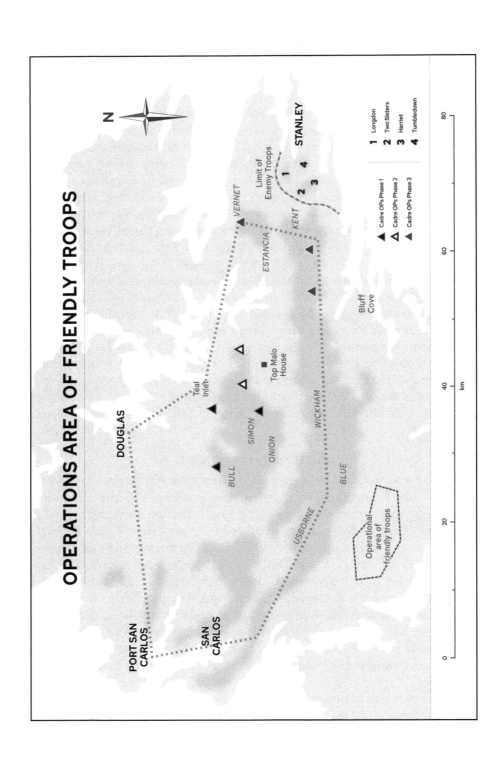

PORT SAN CARLOS

SAN CARLOS

DOUGLAS

Teal Inlet

BULL

SIMON

ONION

Top Malo House

VERNET

ESTANCIA

KENT

WICKHAM

USBORNE

BLUE

Bluff Cove

Limit of Enemy Troops

STANLEY

1 Longdon
2 Two Sisters
3 Harriet
4 Tumbledown

▲ Cadre OPs Phase 1
△ Cadre OPs Phase 2
▲ Cadre OPs Phase 3

Operational area of friendly troops

N

0   20   40   60   80
km

we were never able to find out where the Special Forces were operating, especially the SAS. As the working terrain reduced, so did the safety of all forward operations, and I found it necessary to be very aware of the risk that I was putting my teams more into harm's way than I thought appropriate. Fortunately, we were not involved in any 'blue on blue' situations but they were always a threat. An indication of the reducing size of the operational area as we all moved east is clearly shown on the map opposite.

Like herding cats! A Cadre staff photo at Arbroath, 2 April 1982. *Back row, left to right*: CSgt Bill Wright, Sgt Derek Wilson, Cpl Tim Holleran, Cpl Al Heward, Marine Matthew Blyghton (Storeman), Cpl Nigel Devenish, Marine Ian Forester (Driver), Cpl Graham Foster, Cpl Keith Blackmore, Cpl Tony Boyle, Sgt John Mitchell. *Front row*: Sgt Chris Stone, CSgt Everett Young, Lt John Young, Capt. Rod Boswell, WO2 Brian Snowdon, CSgt Phil Montgomery, Sgt Kevin Mahon.

Climbing on the ML2 course at Sennen Cove in Cornwall.

An ML2 course on their first ski patrol training exercise, led by Sgt Chris Stone.

Introduction of an ML2 course to ice climbing on a glacier in the Lyngen Alps in North Norway.

ML2 course 1/81 on the summit of a mountain in the Alps in northern Italy. At the front is the author, with three Dutch marines, an Australian SNCO and six Royal Marine students.

Ice-breaking drills in Norway in February! One of the few perks of being the 'Boss' is that you do all the really unpleasant demonstrations – watched here by WO2 Snowdon, CSgt Young and Sgt Stone, plus the ML2 Course.

The anchorage at Ascension Island.

Ascension Island. Members of the M&AW Cadre returning to RFA *Sir Tristram* from English Bay after three days on ops guarding the airfield at Wideawake against potential Argentine raiders.

HMS *Ardent* carrying out a morale-improving firepower demonstration a few days before she was sunk by the Argentine Air Force.

RFA *Sir Tristram* deep in the south Atlantic, only a few days before the landings at San Carlos Water.

HMS *Ardent* passing *Canberra* at speed in mid-May.

San Carlos Water. (Top) During an air raid, a Mirage can be seen over the bomb splash (the bomb did not explode) and is strafing with 20mm cannon in front of an LSL (possibly *Sir Galahad*). (Bottom) A Mirage just below the top of the hill strafing the ships, with lines of fire apparent in the water.

Sergeants Mahon and Doyle watching aircraft attacking over the ships but missing the two Skyhawks just above the hill to their rear! The lead aircraft is just about to disappear behind the house and the second aircraft is just to the right of the right hand post.

San Carlos Settlement. (Top) The pier, looking due south towards Sussex Mountain from the farmhouse above Brigade HQ. (Bottom) The grave of Sapper Ghandhi, 28 May. He was killed in the air raid the evening before.

View of the full camouflaged Brigade HQ in San Carlos Water. The dark green line across the promontory is the camouflaged HQ tents and equipment.

Brigadier Thompson with his bodyguard and Air Commodore Pedroza, the Argentine commander of the Goose Green garrison, who formally surrendered his troops to 3 Commando Brigade.

Top Malo House after the raid on 31 May. Mount Simon can be clearly seen in the background.

The Top Malo house area with prisoners under guard by Sergeant Mclean and Corporal Sey, 31 May. In the foreground is the body of Sergeant Sbert of 602 Commando.

Corporal Boyle manning the radio and guarding the Argentine weapons and equipment. The fire group can be seen in the background giving first aid to Corporal Groves, who had been shot in the battle.

Argentine prisoners in Teal Inlet awaiting interrogation by the Brigade HQ intelligence section.

(Top) The Brigade HQ location at Teal Inlet on 1 June, taken from the M&AW Cadre HQ.
(Bottom) The M&AW Cadre HQ building, the closest building to Brigade HQ.

(Top) A Wessex 5 helicopter taking off at dawn from Teal Inlet and heading towards the forward positions, on or about 10 June. (Bottom) A Sea King at the Teal Inlet landing site coming in at dawn to pick up an underslung load.

Moving forward in two BV202 vehicles and crossing the Malo river en route to setting up the brigade patrol control HQ near Mount Kent, 3 June.

The brigade patrol base camouflaged in a rock formation to the southeast of Mount Kent, 3–5 June. There are two BV202 vehicles and a 9 × 9 HQ tent plus bivouacs under the camouflage.

Forward Cadre HQ near Brigade HQ to the north of Mount Kent, 11 June. The lack of camouflage in the snow caused us to move location and improve our camouflage!

The new improved Cadre HQ location, better camouflaged and closer to the Brigade HQ location, 11 June. Sergeant Mac Mclean is on sentry and Corporal Neil West has just been relieved as radio sentry inside the left-hand tent.

Gazelle helicopter flying a white flag on 14 June to signify to the Argentines that hostilities were over, prior to the arrival of Major General Jeremy Moore in Port Stanley to finalise the Argentine surrender.

Government House photographed just before sunset on 14 June after Juliet Company of 42 Commando RM had replaced the Argentine flag with the Union Flag of Great Britain.

Sunset over Port Stanley, looking west towards the mountains, 14 June.

Two dead Argentine soldiers on the coast road on the outskirts of Port Stanley. It appeared that they had been injured and given very basic first aid, then sent back to make their own way to the hospital in Port Stanley. Sadly, they did not make it but died en route and were left by the retreating Argentine troops. The corrugated iron was put over them by members of 2 Para to ensure the bodies were not further damaged by any vehicles. The monument on the left of the road commemorates the Battle of the Falklands in the First World War.

The full length of the runway at Port Stanley Airfield showing no damage from bombs whatsoever, 15 June. The pile of dirt on the middle right of the runway was camouflage put there by the Argentines to simulate a bomb crater. The runway was used by the Argentines to land C130 Hercules aircraft right up to the night of 13/14 June. All of the aircraft in the picture were damaged beyond repair by shrapnel and bullets fired by Sea Harriers during the course of the war.

Ajax Bay on 17 June, showing the 500-plus senior Argentine prisoners held to ensure that the remaining 10,000 Argentines being carried back to their home country would behave properly.

The graveyard at Ajax Bay, photographed from the Gazelle helicopter on 17 June.

The final shot of *Canberra* leaving San Carlos Water on 25 June to head home to an astonishing reception in the UK.

HMS *Hermes* pictured on 26 June with all the Sea Harriers on deck proving how few were actually shot down during the conflict.

RFA *Resource* turning to drop anchor prior to cross-decking her remaining stores to another RFA, Grytviken settlement, South Georgia.

Chapter 6

The Start of the Big Move East
(27–30 May)

Late in the afternoon of 27 May (my 35th birthday) Bill Wright and I were planning to collect the first three sections the next day and return them to San Carlos. We spoke about providing them with dry sleeping bags, a change of clothes and some good food to set them up after what had been a very long eight days in the field. Bill said I should not worry about any of that as he had it in hand and would sort it. He then said, 'I think you should have a night off and enjoy your birthday.' He produced a bottle of very good malt whisky, a mug and a large cigar, saying 'You are now officially stood down until first thing tomorrow morning. Enjoy!' Arguing with Bill was never a good idea, so I just thanked him and took a walk down the hill to the pier at San Carlos. I went to the end of the pier and decided to enjoy my cigar (although I don't smoke!) and my mug of malt (I do enjoy a decent malt whisky) whilst watching the sun set over San Carlos Water.

I had been there about five minutes when four Skyhawks appeared from the southern end of the Water. Two turned left and headed towards Ajax Bay but the other two turned right and headed towards me. This was rather strange as until then the last air raids had all finished about half an hour before sunset and we had got used to a sort of sunset break before overnight sentry duties. I watched in amazement as Ajax Bay was bombed. I then saw the bombs detach from the two Skyhawks above me and the parachute retards activate. Two bombs from each aircraft bracketed me on the end of the pier. The first two exploded in the water and sent up a huge wave that completely engulfed me, and just as I was recovering from that the other two bombs went off at the landward end of the pier and all hell broke loose. I was drenched, my whisky mug was full of saltwater and my cigar had gained a significant droop but worst of all I was soaking wet! I got up, picked up my rifle and set off for home. At the end of the pier there were several guys scrabbling about trying to dig into the first bomb crater. I asked what was happening and was told that the sentry post had been buried under the dirt. Two sappers acting as sentries had been in it. I immediately joined in the dig and about 20 minutes later we were able to extricate the two soldiers. The first man we found had been killed by the blast but the other one underneath him had survived and was physically unharmed, though very shocked. I left them to it and continued up the hill to the Cadre. I must have looked a sight when I arrived as Bill enquired where I had been. I realised I was covered in mud and still soaking wet. I explained and was presented with another large whisky and told to get myself dry. It was a sobering incident. Although a lot had been happening around us during the previous eight days, this was the first time I had come directly into contact with the enemy and it was a significant eye-opener. I also decided that I would not be taking any further time off during the recovery of the Islands.

The following day the brigade commander (as a direct result of being ordered to do so by Commander Task Force (CTF) in London) ordered 2 Para to capture Goose Green. Originally, he had intended them to mount a raid with a battalion fighting patrol to get an idea of the fighting prowess of the enemy but his orders were overruled by CTF. In typical Parachute Regiment fashion this became a major assault which provoked the entire garrison to surrender and 2 Para took control of Goose Green and its surroundings. This battle has been well documented elsewhere and the Cadre did not participate but I was asked to visit their HQ to determine whether we needed to take over any of their OPs. After some discussion with their operations officer it was obvious that this would not be necessary.

One thing did happen that affected me personally. When Lieutenant Colonel H. Jones, the CO of 2 Para, was shot, the battalion requested immediate casevac. Two of the brigade air squadron Scout helicopters that had just carried in some additional ammunition were asked to collect him for treatment. The Scouts were piloted by Jeff Niblett and Lieutenant Richard Nunn. As they lifted off they were immediately bounced by two Argentine Pucara aircraft. A brief and messy air battle resulted in Richard Nunn being killed and his aircraft shot down. Sergeant Belcher, his air gunner, survived the crash in spite of severe injuries, including the loss of a leg.

Richard was an old friend, and his brother Chris and I had gone through training together. Captain Chris Nunn was commanding M Company of 42 Commando RM in South Georgia and had been instrumental in the recapture of the island from the Argentine invaders. The whole enterprise was led by Major Guy Sheridan, who was second in command of

42 Commando RM and was probably the most experienced ML in the Corps, as well as being a world-respected ski tourer who had carried out many particularly arduous and successful ski expeditions around the world. I knew that Chris would want to know what had happened. I made my way across to the hospital at Ajax Bay to talk to Surgeon Commander Rick Jolly, the senior medical officer and commander of the brigade medical squadron at Ajax Bay, to enquire about the incident. Rick was another old friend. He told me about the crash and showed me Richard's body to prove that he would not have survived his injuries, even had he survived the crash of his aircraft. It was a difficult episode but I remain glad that I did it as I was able to write to Chris and his father an honest letter with my condolences. Chris's father Stan had been one of 'the few' in the Battle of Britain and had retired from the RAF as a group captain. He was therefore a veteran pilot and a very experienced officer, but losing a son in an air battle must have been very hard to bear. I felt that I should sit down and write brief letters of explanation to him and to Chris in the hope that it might ease their loss. Stan Nunn had two further personal sources of deep concern with Chris serving in South Georgia and Captain David Constance (Stan's son-in-law) serving with 2 Para as their RM liaison officer.

Because all the brigade helicopters were busy in support of 2 Para, I could not get hold of one to return my three sections from Bull Hill until the morning of 30 May. I was, however, able to send into the field on 28 May the four sections that had been held back at San Carlos since D Day. I was able to get them inserted to the rear of 3 Para in their move to Teal Inlet and they joined the long caterpillar of troops moving across country.

1 Section (Lieutenant Fraser Haddow, Corporal Graham Foster, Corporal Gordon 'Scouse' Heeney and Corporal 'Mac' McGregor) was inserted to set up an OP on Evelyn Hill. This OP was moved on 29 May and re-established on the southwest ridge running downhill from the summit of The Baby feature, observing across the Malo river towards Top Malo House. It was from this OP that the team was able to report the enemy movement towards Top Malo House on 30 May. This provoked the raid on 31 May when the section joined the raiding party and then returned to Teal Inlet to await further tasking.

2 Section (Colour Sergeant Everett Young, Sergeant Jim Martin, Corporal John White and Corporal Jim O'Connor) was inserted to set up an OP to observe the main valley and ended up on a ring contour in heavy snow at GR 985757 (about 3.3km southwest of Top Malo). This became

the OP held by this team until first light on 1 June when they were picked up by helo and moved to Teal Inlet to await further tasking.

3 Section (Sergeant Des Wassall, Corporal Neale Meade, Corporal Steve Last and Corporal Al Heward) was inserted to set up an OP and observe the main valley close to Top Malo House. They held the position until the raid when they joined the raiding party and then returned to Teal Inlet to await further tasking.

4 Section (Sergeant Kev Mahon, Sergeant John Mitchell, Corporal Mick O'Donnell and Corporal George Bickett) was inserted to set up an OP on the southern flank of The Baby feature and to observe towards Lower Malo House and the valley of the Malo river. Ordered to move on 30 May, they were picked up after the raid on 31 May and returned to Teal Inlet to await further tasking. Sergeant Kev Mahon recalled:

> The four sections were dropped by helo at GR 923878 (about 1.8km north-northwest of Bell Mountain) where we were joined by the other three teams and by the mortar troop of 3 Para. The Paras were being transported by tractors, compliments of the Teal Inlet farmers. [Author's note: They were probably farmers from Port San Carlos.] We moved with the mortars until we joined the remainder of 3 Para and stayed with them until about GR 983853 (about 2km south of Teal Inlet) when the Cadre sections split off and headed south. At Petoce Junction (GR 980845) we split up, 1 and 2 Sections going south and 3 and 4 Sections heading southeast. We led with 4 Section a tactical bound to our rear. Our route was to cross the saddle on The Baby feature. On reaching the saddle we decided to clear the feature of enemy as an eight-man section. This was carried out quickly.
>
> At this stage the two sections (3 and 4) split up and we moved into an OP at GR 034803 which was slightly east of our original planned location. All the original arcs could be covered and this OP could offer some additional cover to 3 Section, which had moved further east.

Sergeant John Mitchell was the radio operator of 4 Section:

> We deployed behind a whole stream of Paras heading for battle (they thought) at Estancia House via Teal Inlet. Some locals met us en route and told us that all the Argies had gone from there, but the Paras were determined to attack anyway (typical Paras!). Our task took us over a ridge in the direction of Top Malo House. We over-nighted on top of the ridge in pissing rain. Rod Boswell sent us a very long message changing our orders. They did not make much sense

but we got close to Top Malo House (about 300–400m I think, but it could have been closer). Kev Mahon felt that we needed to get to cover as he saw footprints in the frost-covered ground. We found a hole in the ground and got in it (despite the water in the bottom). By some miracle we managed to get strength 5 voice communication and told HQ of our predicament. I think we reported our findings of Top Malo, but also I think other patrols had reported similar. After a very uncomfortable 48 hours in that hole the cavalry [Cadre assault teams] came in and took out Top Malo House.

Kev Mahon's team discussed whether to attack Top Malo House on the night of 30/31 May in the dark by crawling up to it and throwing grenades through the windows then machine-gunning any survivors as they left the building. Fortunately, they decided not to do that and tried to send a report back to Cadre HQ, but couldn't get through. There was no shortage of aggression in the Cadre teams, as will be shown shortly.

Kev Mahon, meanwhile, had other problems:

Having missed my rendezvous with Des Wassail's section due to the heavy snow slowing our progress, I decided not to wade the river as I didn't want to spend the coming days with wet kit. On checking, I noticed a ford near Top Malo which, although we had seen helos flying in that direction and we knew there were enemy OPs on the high ground, seemed a better option for us. On reaching Top Malo there were footprints in the snow so I assumed the enemy OPs had come down to the house for shelter. We moved on and took shelter in the river bank a safe distance from Top Malo in a position where we could not be viewed from the higher ground, plus we could view and cover our own tracks of that night. I was intending to circumnavigate a safe distance around Top Malo the following night. Having sent a schedule, we had switched the radio off to conserve the battery life. The next thing I remember was a chopper flying low over our heads and seeing Brit uniforms through the open door.

On a less serious note, whilst lying low in the river bank I remember going for a dump which had to be done in the river and also in a crouch! I was doing the business and watching my arcs when a duck swam up behind me and pecked my arse! I literally sh** myself, jumped up and then straight back down like a jack in a box. My head could only have been above the bank for a millisecond! The animals are so tame down there!!

When these four sections were put in the field the overall situation was very different following the success of 2 Para at Goose Green and the need for the brigade to break out of San Carlos Water and head east en masse.

3 Para set out to tab to Estancia House via Teal Inlet. 45 Commando RM yomped to Teal Inlet via Douglas Settlement and 42 Commando RM were transported by helo direct to Mount Kent on 31 May. At the same time Brigade HQ also moved directly to Teal Inlet by helo and BV202.

The Cadre HQ was not at its best in the period 27 to 30 May as I was rather ashamed of what had happened with 5 Section trying to get at the enemy OP on Mount Rosalie in West Falkland and did not fully comprehend the implications of the great move east. This hugely reduced the flexibility of the forward forces and the risk of 'blue on blue' situations became much greater. I sent an absurd set of orders in code to the four newly inserted teams (1, 2, 3 and 4) telling them to move enormous distances. I was very concerned about the risk of 'blue on blue' and ordered all four teams to move well forward, which meant they all faced at least 16km of movement, which would have taken a minimum of two nights. This was completely ridiculous. Fortunately, thanks to their maturity and common sense, the four team leaders all understood the problem and resolved it by judiciously rewriting the orders themselves. So we all ended up at Teal Inlet ready for the next phase of the war.

On the morning of 30 May I was asked to brief the incoming staff officers of 5 Infantry Brigade (who had just arrived in San Carlos Water) on the tasking and current locations of the Cadre. I had been told to keep it short but to explain what our role was and where we had been and were planning to operate. I was also told by our brigade COS that the brigade boundary would be the line of hills to the south of the central valley through East Falkland Island. Some six to ten staff officers duly arrived at the community hall and gathered round our map for their briefing. I was about halfway through the briefing when we heard whistles being blown outside. I and my team ignored them and carried on, but I was interrupted by the 5 Brigade COS asking me what was going on and what the whistles meant. I told him it was nothing to worry about as it was just an air raid and the Argentines were only interested in trying to sink our ships, so we were completely safe where we were. He would have none of this and ordered his men to take cover and get out of the hall into trenches. We watched with barely contained amusement as they sprinted out of the hall, never to be seen again. I remember Colour Sergeant Wright saying to me that they all looked so young and I replied that they wouldn't look quite so young after the ten days that we had just gone through. Interestingly, our main thought was that they were completely unprepared in every way for what lay ahead for them. I put that down to the fact that we had probably looked the same just after we came ashore ten days earlier. I never finished the briefing nor did I see any of the 5 Brigade staff officers at any stage of the rest of the war.

By early afternoon on 30 May the three sections (5, 6 and 7) plus Sergeant Doyle's 8 Section were all together in the town hall at San Carlos recovering from their various ordeals between 21 and 30 May. The three sections that had been on OP tasks had mostly run out of food by 27/28 May and then had to move to a central RV for two further nights before the pick-up at around midday on 30 May. The nights at Sergeant Stone's location were particularly hard. The joining-up of the three teams reduced the overall need for multiple sentries but the teams were all short of dry clothing and sleeping bags as well as rations. I have received several detailed reports of that period and they all emphasise how difficult the conditions were, especially with the amount of snow that fell on the last two nights. Needless to say, they all arrived back in San Carlos pleased with how well they had done in the first ten days and, more importantly, how well the landings were going. They were looking forward to the move east and all that implied for their future tasking. Bill Wright had organised additional sleeping bags and clothing (although only very limited quantities of the latter). The first priority was to warm them up, filling them with food and hot drinks, and then to ensure that they all got a good night's sleep in preparation for their next tasks. A monster stew was made by the HQ team and multiple wets were produced as the guys slowly recovered from what had been a severe test of their professional abilities and personal survival skills.

Their morale and ability to survive in the arduous conditions are best described by Corporal Tony Boyle, who was in 7 Section under Sergeant Chris Stone. He reported:

> The routine within the OP was fine, long days and even longer nights, the hot sleeping bag routine was working well. Day seven (27 May) was a real tester! No food, as we had cut back on so much. We had planned for a five-day deployment mostly on half rations and we were now down to soaking oxo cubes in cold water and eating it with biscuits. Day eight (28 May) we were joined during the night by one of the other patrols. This did cause a sleeping issue as the hot sleeping bag routine was tested to the full. However, we were removed two

days later from the OP and went back to join up with the HQ team ready to deploy again.

There was a view that we were getting things done and doing what we were trained to do. The weather we were used to, a mixture of what we had to deal with in Norway, Dartmoor, North Wales and the Highlands of Scotland. I still walk across Dartmoor with my dog, very thankful that I am not weighed down with a large heavy load.

We had one night in rest and resupply, which was made easier by Shiner and his helping hands who had all the ration packs, etc. to hand. The Boss then said that one of the other sections had reported an enemy unit that had deployed to a farm outcrop called Top Malo House, which was a crofter's house next to the Malo river (a great trout stream). The report was that seventeen enemy had been dropped by helicopter and had established themselves within the house. Our next task, with the information provided from our sections on the ground, [was] to attack the house. We later learned it was [occupied by] 602 Special Commando Unit. They were listed as an elite Argentine Special Forces unit.

The remainder of the troops all felt very much as Tony Boyle did and I was confident that they were up for any task. This was in contrast to the feelings amongst the members of 602 Special Commando Unit, who put out the following report after the war had concluded. I assume it was intended to explain the reason for them taking the appalling decision to take cover in the only building within 8km in any direction when enemy troops were known to be in the area.

Back in Stanley [on 29 May], 2/Ca Cdo 602 had been instructed to occupy Pato OP on Bluff Cove Peak by 1800 and therefore had 12 more hours to prepare, plan and rest. At 1715 the thirteen-man patrol left the racecourse in a B Av C 601 Bell 212 and Augusta 109 escort 'gunship' and 15 minutes later, in the gathering gloom, arrived at the landing site. The Augusta managed to disembark its five-man stick but the Bell 212 and its eight-man stick failed to make the RV. The five, including the patrol commander, decided to carry on with the mission and set off for Bluff Cove Peak but quickly came under mortar and machine-gun fire from the east (the direction of Stanley) near the emergency RV. Fearing the worst, the group sought immediate high ground and lay up for the night. More mortaring and machine-gun fire was heard throughout the night and the group surmised it was the missing patrol engaged in some action.

In the hills, 1/Ca Cdo 602, frustrated with their inability to transmit, nevertheless listened with anguish to the desperate efforts of the eight men of 2/Ca Cdo 602 to breach the perimeter and sympathising as casualties were taken. These events seriously worried them, for the most recent intelligence reports, updated shortly before they had left Stanley, assessed that there were definitely no enemy between Stanley and Mount Simon. The situation looked gloomy and worse was to follow. In Stanley the helicopter carrying a Ca NG 601 patrol crashed, killing most of the National Guard and causing a postponement of the entire operation. No one slept well that night, a chilling, penetrating Antarctic wind sweeping across the ridge and the uncertainty lowering spirits further. There was also the worry of being cut off, although they did not believe they were being overlooked by British patrols.

The following morning (30 May), the events of the night causing considerable anxiety, resulted in some discussion as to what to do. Eventually it was decided to abandon the OP and move south to Fitzroy, evading the enemy, and link up with an engineer detachment known to be working on the bridge. A suggestion to insert the two cavalry warrant officers and their Blowpipes into the British helicopter corridor was vetoed in favour of avoiding all contact.

> Shortly before midday on 30 May the tired, wet and demoralised thirteen men of 1/Ca Cdo 602 abandoned the bleak and inhospitable summit and headed south. After the bad night most had experienced, the combination of freezing drizzle, low clouds, heavy loads and fatigue soon began to take its toll amongst the unacclimatised Commandoes [sic] and the column struggled on without any tactical formation. Navigation was difficult and before long most were exhausted, intent only upon their own survival. By 1800 the patrol had covered 5km and had reached the Arroyo Malo stream, now swollen with freezing winter rain.
>
> Another snow-storm swept across the bleak moorland and, there being no other way, the Commandoes [sic] plunged into the icy water, waded waist high and emerged the other side very wet and even more demoralised. Captain Verseci, seeing the poor state of his patrol, took the advice of two Antarctic veterans and decided not to go to the shelter of the LS, as he had planned to do, but determined to navigate to a group of buildings marked on his map as Top Malo House, not far from where they had crossed the river. This news boosted the patrol and as they neared the buildings they divided into two groups

and made a tactical approach. Finding some evidence of recent occupation, the immediate surrounding area was also cleared and finding no signs of the British, they moved into the welcome shelter of the main house.

When I received the sighting report from 1 Section on the afternoon of 30 May it clearly stated there were seventeen men in the patrol. Lieutenant Haddow had watched the Argentine patrol moving towards and into Top Malo House. This information was immediately signalled to me at San Carlos.

All the post-action reports given by the Argentines talked of thirteen men in the patrol. The additional four men we now know to have been two warrant officers with Blowpipe missiles and a two-man medical team consisting of a doctor and a medical assistant. As far as 602 were concerned the additional personnel were not part of their unit and thus were irrelevant to their thinking and planning. This discrepancy becomes very clear when the casualties taken on both sides are discussed following the raid on Top Malo House.

On receipt of the sighting report I went to Brigade HQ to request an air raid on Top Malo House. The request was put in straight away but we soon received the bad news that it could not be done until the following day. There were only two Harriers configured for the ground attack role and they had just completed a raid on Stanley Airport. During the raid one of the Harriers (from 1 Sqn RAF) flown by Squadron Leader Pook had been hit by small arms fire and he had been forced to eject. He was in the water for a short period and then picked up unharmed, but his aircraft was lost and it would take all night to re-role another as they had to fly in pairs.

I was seriously concerned that we needed to react to this information as quickly as possible as the chances were that the enemy would only stay in the building for the shortest possible time. We needed to take advantage of their tactical idiocy as quickly as we could. At that time the three main units of 42 and 45 Commandos and 3 Para were all on the move and could not be given a change in orders that quickly. 2 Para were still recovering from the Goose Green battle and Brigade HQ was set to move to Teal Inlet at first light the next day. All our artillery was out of range as Top Malo was about 48km from San Carlos and the move of the first artillery pieces to Teal Inlet was not due to happen until late the next day. Teal Inlet was 10km north of Top Malo House anyway.

I gave it a few moments' thought and said to the brigade commander that it looked like a job for the Cadre. We had four full sections as well as the HQ team of four. I could put together a raid of nineteen or twenty men and attack the house at first light. I initially felt that we would be a little short of fire-power but argued we could resolve that problem by borrowing from other units and using M79 40mm grenades and 66mm anti-tank rockets. He asked me if I was sure and I replied that it was exactly the sort of target for which we had prepared. A small and well-armed party would cope without too many problems. I also told him that I had three of the other sections within walking distance of Top Malo. I was sure I could get them to move and secure our landing site so we would not be landing in an unprepared site in the morning. This latter comment was what sold it to the brigade commander (I think) but he also knew how keen I and my guys were to get stuck in after the difficult first ten days of operations. He responded by saying 'OK, you get on with it and let me know if there is anything you need and I will get it for you.'

I returned to Cadre HQ in the community hall and called for attention. I do not remember my actual words but it was something like get your-selves sorted out as we have a job first thing in the morning and I will be giving orders very soon. I was met with some dismay until I remember saying 'Don't worry. It's not another OP task but an offensive raid and we are about to give them a taste of their own medicine!' This was greeted with big smiles and morale rose exponentially.

I quickly got my two colour sergeants together (Wright and Mont-gomery) and told Shiner to see if he could get a few 66mm for us, as well as any GPMGs that could be spared. I told Monty to get a small team together and produce a model of Top Malo House and the immediate area using the aerial photos we had and the maps of the area. I asked Callum Murray to help with setting up an area for orders and I then took myself away on my own and set about writing my orders for the forth-coming raid. Suddenly it was all hustle and bustle. I allowed myself 3 hours for my appreciation of the situation and for my writing of orders, and set the O Gp for 2000. I intended that it would take about an hour to give the orders and then we would all get a reasonable night's sleep and be pre-pared for take-off at about 0600 the next morning.

My first job was to organise the insertion so I wrote a helicopter request for a Priority One operational task for 0600 with the drop-off in darkness at the designated site at about 0630. First light was about 0700 so I wanted to be in position just before that, giving us the element of surprise.

Time flew by and I was largely left alone to get on with the orders. Callum, Bill and Monty, aided by anyone they brought in, sorted every-thing needed for the O Gp. It was a fascinating experience for me as I sat down and thought through how it would go the next day, but it wasn't something I hadn't practised many times. I had had relevant operational experience in Northern Ireland but this was the most important set of orders I had ever prepared or given. I remember telling myself to keep it simple. We had never practised for an operation like this but I knew that making it as simple as possible would work because of the quality of the guys involved. I knew motivation was not an issue. I also knew that as long as the orders were brief, to the point and simple, the plan would work. I decided on a simple full-frontal assault with a fully powered-up fire group on one flank to provide heavy weapons and shock force to the attack.

I needed to be careful where we landed to avoid the pilot overflying the landing site and spoiling any chance of secrecy about our arrival. I got hold of my signals corporal and told him to contact all the teams in the field and get them to secure our selected landing site and to be prepared to join us on the raid once we had landed. This was the only part of the raid that did not work at all. We had a night of failed communications. It was the only time in the whole campaign that we did not have safe and secure communications. I attributed this to the Aurora Australis. Whatever the cause it was certainly no help to us and we did not get the extra (up to) sixteen men that I had anticipated to aid with the raid.

I remember the orders going down well. There is nothing like the opportunity to give something back to a bunch of people who had been bombing and strafing us for ten days. I remember very few questions at the end but those that were asked were all very relevant and undoubtedly helped to form the best plan possible. I told everyone to take their bergens and five days' rations in case it all went wrong and we had to make a fighting withdrawal, though I did not for one moment think that was likely. I must admit to an abundance of confidence and I thought the plan would work really well. Corporal Tony Boyle felt the same:

> I recall the Boss giving orders which was like something from the Junior Command Course and an example to all that our NCO and officer training was some of the best. I recall talking to Sergeant Terry Doyle who is also a qualified PW2 [Platoon Weapons Instructor] telling him I needed a revision on the structure of the sight pattern of the 66mm LAW [Light Anti-tank Weapon]. It was a weapon that we didn't regularly get our hands on too often and a refresher lesson was well received.

On completion of the orders we set about sorting out our kit and making it ready for the morning. I remember talking at some length to Shiner

Wright. He would be running the base location and I had to ensure that he was happy and ready to do anything to assist us if things got difficult. Shiner was his usual confident and supportive self and assured me that he thought it would be a walk in the park and was completely confident that it would go like clockwork. By now I was not so sure and admit to sleeping very little that night for fear of forgetting something and screwing up everything. I was glad to be called at 0400 to start the next morning. I awoke to find myself surrounded by a lot of banter and cheerful piss-taking but underneath it all, more importantly, there was a serious intent to get the job done.

We set out in single file from the community hall, walking up the slope to the landing site at the top of the hill to await our aircraft's arrival.

Chapter 7

The Raid on Top Malo House
(31 May)

We arrived at the landing site at about 0430, an hour and a half before first light. We felt very alone. At about 0600 the first helicopter flew in. Several more helicopters came in to land and load and then take off again. I was trying to find out when ours would arrive but had little luck. Eventually, after at least 20 minutes of failing to get a helicopter to take us, I was becoming angry and stormed on board one to demand that the pilot hand over the trip to me whether he had been tasked for it or not. Fortunately, the pilot was Lieutenant Commander Simon Thornewill, CO of 846 Naval Air Commando Squadron (846 NACS), and he was not going to be bullied by a raging RM captain. He calmed me down and asked me what the problem was. I explained that, unlike the brigade move, my 'stick' was an Operational Priority One task to assault an enemy location about 45km east of the landing site. I further explained that we were supposed to be making a first-light attack on an enemy patrol base and any chance of surprise was diminishing as the daylight grew. Once I had calmed down sufficiently to explain the mission, he got straight on the radio telling the pilot of the second aircraft (currently waiting to land) to cancel his planned flight and take orders from me as soon as I boarded. Satisfied, I left the helo and returned to my 'stick' and warned the guys that the next aircraft was ours and to prepare to embark, but not until I had fully briefed the pilot.

As soon as the first aircraft took off, the second landed in its place. I went on board straightaway to speak to the pilot. He was fully prepared. When I showed him the map and pointed out where we wanted to land, he asked only one question: 'How close are the Argentines?' I told him at least 3km and impressed upon him that we needed all the secrecy we could manage as we were running very late and should have attacked about 20 minutes before! He said, 'No problem!' and I then left the helo to tell the guys to load as quickly as possible.

We had to load nineteen men plus nineteen bergens, and a few extras such as a dozen 66mm LAWs for the assault. This did not take long and

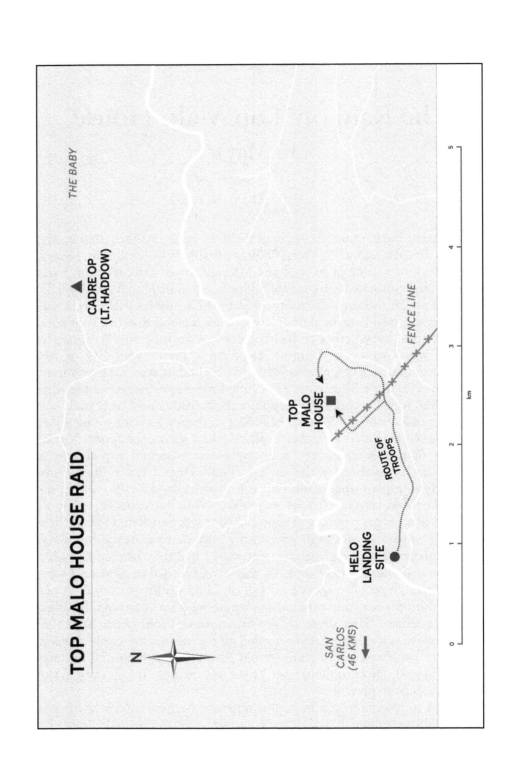

I was the last to board the helo. I had to load on the last five or six bergens to fill the bird, leaving me to climb the pile of bergens and sit on the top with my feet against the top of the aircraft door – an interesting position, but I wanted us to get going. The pilot, who many years later I learned was Lieutenant John Miller RN of 846 NACS*, then took us on the most exciting and impressive flight I have ever taken in any aircraft! It was more than 48km, but at no time did I see anything other than grass or stream beds out of the door which remained open throughout the flight. The door could not be closed because of the bergens and I swear that Miller was grass cutting for most of the route! It was truly impressive and a perfect example of the NACS' capabilities. We arrived after about 20 minutes and landed at a stream junction. I slid down the pile of bergens, grabbing a couple as I went and pulling them off the helo with me. Safely on the ground, I then ran about 15m and stood guard as the other guys fought their way off. We formed a protective screen around the helo as we had always been taught.

Soon there was a great mound of bergens and a full team of men ready to go. I quickly checked with each team leader then looked towards the aircrewman standing in the aircraft doorway, giving him a thumbs up to say we were all off. He returned the thumbs up so I gave the wave off order and the helo lifted off and disappeared towards the west.

As silence re-established itself, the teams started building a pile of the bergens against the rising bank of the stream junction while I consulted my map. I soon appreciated Miller's outstanding flying skills. Apart from the initial delay, the Jungly† pilot had made a perfect flight and had deposited us exactly where we wanted to be. This was doubly remarkable as he had had no time to prepare a flight plan. He had simply taken my finger mark on a map and then, at zero feet and about 150 knots, navigated his way over 48km and landed on the eye of a pin. It was beyond superb.

I quickly called the section commanders together and explained that this would be our emergency RV. All but one of the bergens would remain here for us to get to should we have to fight our way out. As the nominated signaller for the operation, Corporal Tony Boyle had to carry his bergen to carry the radio. He was not best pleased as it was in the pile somewhere, but he very quickly found it as we piled the rest into cover.

* 846 Naval Air Commando Squadron was one of three squadrons allocated to 3 Co Bde for operations, the other two being 847 and 848.
† Derived from jungle operations in Borneo, 'Jungly' is the term used by the Royal Navy to describe personnel-carrying helicopters and helicopter pilots. 'Pingers' are anti-submarine helicopters and pilots of the Royal Navy.

Once I had ensured that all was in order, I set off towards the location where we would split into fire section and assault section. We were about 1,800m as the crow flies from Top Malo House at the selected landing site of GR 992772 (a stream junction 2km southwest of Top Malo House). The route in was to follow the east-bound stream bed for about 1.5km, cross a small saddle and join another stream that we would follow for a further 600m to a fence line. There the patrol would split, Callum Murray and his six-man fire team heading northwest along the fence line until they came in sight of Top Malo House. They would then select the best location to offer us full covering fire.

The rest of us (the twelve-strong assault group) would continue to follow the stream for a further 800m, ensuring we constantly had high ground between us and Top Malo House for security. I would then locate a position from which we would launch our assault. The going underfoot was good and firm and we set off at a fast rate, arriving at the fence line fairly quickly. After a swift word with Callum and a shared good luck to each other we continued on our way.

A few minutes later I looked to my left to see Sergeant 'Mac' Mclean moving swiftly towards my party. I stopped and waited for his arrival. He had been sent by Callum, who had spotted a large peat cutting at almost exactly the right position for us to use to start our assault. This was valuable information and once 'Mac' had shared it, he skedaddled back to the fire group. We continued on our way around a reasonably large hill that gave us cover. When I thought we must be due east of Top Malo House I stopped the patrol and, taking Monty Montgomery, Chris Stone and Taff Doyle with me, carefully moved up the hill until we had sight of the building. It was just like the air photographs we had studied the day before. It stood out in the bright sunshine with the ground covered in a

---

Top Malo Raiding Party

Fire Group: Lt Callum Murray (*OC*); Sgt Mac Mclean; Cpl Steve Groves (*Sniper*); Cpl Bob Sharp; Cpl Steve Nicoll; Cpl Nigel Devenish; Cpl Matt Barnacle

Assault Group: Capt Rod Boswell (*OC and overall commander*); Sgt Chris Stone (*second-in-command of assault*); Sgt J. Rowe; Cpl Ginge Boyle (*Radio operator*); CSgt Monty Montgomery (*Left flank team commander*); Sgt Derek 'Tug' Wilson; Cpl Keith Blackmore; Cpl Ray Sey; Sgt Terry Doyle (*Right flank team commander*); Cpl Mac Macgregor; Cpl Tim Holleran; Cpl Sam Healey

dusting of snow. This was not good news as we were all wearing DPM camouflage clothing which offered us no camouflage at all against the snow. We withdrew and a brief whispered conversation took place. Changing the initial plan, I told the guys to line up for the assault and then we would all crawl forward until I felt we were getting too close and would then initiate the attack.

After a crawl of about 15m or so, I halted our movement and raised my bayonet to tell the assault party to fix their bayonets. As we were doing so, Chris Stone said to me, 'There's nobody there, it's a bloody bite!' I responded, 'I don't care. We've come all this way and the building's going to get it whether it's occupied or not!'

At that point I looked across towards the fire group. There they were in exactly the right position, lying in the snow and waiting for the attack order. I raised my mini-flare and fired a green flare in their direction. It seemed to be hours before anything happened but suddenly four of them got up on one knee and fired the 66mm LAWs at Top Malo House. I watched the first salvo heading towards the house. It was extremely disappointing. One seemed to go over the roof of the house and disappeared northwards at a great speed, and another exploded short of the house; I didn't see where the other two went. A few seconds later the second salvo went off but only three this time. It was, however, spectacular. All three hit the main house and the roof lifted off in its entirety. There were three very big bangs and the house started to flame.

At the same time Corporal Steve Groves, who was a qualified sniper in the fire group, had caused the first casualty of the action. Steve had not had a chance to check fire his weapon and was worried that his sights were off, so as the four men rose to fire the salvo of 66mm LAWs he set his sights on the cross in the centre of the upstairs window, intending to fire at the cross to see where his bullet landed and then adjust his further shots for maximum advantage and accuracy. As luck would have it, as he was looking at the cross in the window an Argentine face appeared, so Steve fired and the man fell immediately from view. The Argentines always claimed that he was their sentry, but in view of their other totally unprofessional activities, I am convinced that he was just a curious soldier looking out to admire the view. It cost him his life.

Ironically, our first casualty was Corporal Steve Groves, who remained in the kneeling position as the salvoes were fired at Top Malo House. When the enemy ran out of the building, he continued to fire at them from that position. Shortly into the firefight he received a round that took him out of the fight. As the Argentines escaped from the exploding, flaming building, they fired their weapons from the hip in all directions and by a piece of random bad luck Steve was hit by one of those rounds. (This incident will be expanded in the next chapter.)

I stood up and shouted 'Let's go!', or something similar, and we all stood up and charged forwards about 50m, after which I stopped. We then sent in a smaller salvo of two 66mm designed to cause further confusion amongst the enemy and I set off with my four-man fire team expecting the others to put down covering fire as ordered. This did not happen. All twelve men got up and we charged towards the house screaming at the top of our voices and firing automatic bursts of fire as we went in. It was the most exciting and spectacular thing I have ever done. It was an extra-ordinary feeling to know that every man was up and running towards an enemy whom we had not seen until that moment.

At this point I should confess to a moment of madness on my part. As we set off for the second charge of about 150m, I realised that I would not be able to keep up the aggressive AAAAAAHHHH scream we had been taught in training for that length of time. I therefore started screaming 'Yahoo' and 'Sky Dive' at the top of my voice. This cheered me up and made the distance seem much shorter. The follow-up to this came about two years later at a reunion. Chris Stone took me to one side and asked me what I was screaming on the charge into Top Malo House. When I told him, he laughed and said, 'That's what I thought I'd heard but I could not believe that anyone would shout something so strange when doing a bayonet charge!' I seem to remember with some embarrassment saying something to the effect that 'You are supposed to scream aggressively to scare the enemy and boost your own confidence. That seemed much better at the time than just exhaling violently for the run in!' It certainly made me feel better!

The adrenaline rush did not last long, however. About 40m short of the house Taff Doyle shouted 'Enemy front, enemy front.' I looked across at him and saw that he was on the ground. I shouted across to him not to take cover but to get up and get closer to the enemy, whom I had not yet seen. Corporal Tim Holleran, who was next to Taff Doyle, shouted back that he hadn't taken cover, he'd been shot. I then watched in horror as Tim Holleran proceeded to give Taff Doyle first aid in full view of the enemy and under obvious and direct tracer round* fire from the enemy positions.

---

*We found out after the firefight that all the Argentines had filled their rifle magazines with a mixture of ball, tracer and armour-piercing rounds, hence the apparent preponderance of tracer fire around Tim Holleran.

I took stock of our situation. Chris Stone, Tony Boyle and I were standing beside one of the outhouses about 20m from the raging fire that was Top Malo House. None of us could see any enemy but we knew they were there because Taff Doyle had been shot. We could hear very heavy fire being poured in by the fire group, as well as explosions from rounds 'cooking off' in the fire. None of us could hear enemy fire, although the tracer rounds going past Tim Holleran told us that they were firing at him and obviously returning fire towards us. I turned to Chris Stone, standing a metre or so away from me, and asked if he could see any of the enemy. He responded that he couldn't and then said, 'I'll run down the slope and that should make them see me and you can take them out.' I shouted 'No way' but he said 'Too late, I'm off!' He covered a couple of metres and then fell to the ground like a sack of potatoes and lay still. I ran over to help him and saw that he had been shot. Odd lines were appearing in the snow and grass around us both and it didn't take me long to work out that we were being shot at by the enemy and so I withdrew a few metres until the firing stopped.

Events were now rather strange, to say the least. Tony Boyle and I were in a position that was completely safe, but around the other side of our outbuilding and to the rear of Top Malo House I could hear Monty shouting 'Lay it on, Sam' and 'Keep firing, Sam – you're doing really well.' Corporal Sam Healy was in his section so I knew who he was talking to, but then I heard a strange Spanish voice shouting '*Manos aribas*' ('Hands up'). I thought that was a bit of a cheek considering that we had just assaulted them and they must certainly be taking severe casualties. I then heard, again in strangled Spanish, '*Manos detrás de tu cabeza*' ('Hands behind your heads') and recognised Corporal 'Mac' MacGregor's voice. He had learnt these phrases from a Spanish language book on the way down 'to the great amusement of the rest of the Cadre' but suddenly it seemed to have been a very good idea.

I still had no real idea where the Argentines were. I knew that they had to be close to Top Malo House, having run into our very heavy fire as they rushed to escape the burning building. It soon became apparent that once they had got outside Top Malo House, they had immediately taken cover in a small stream bed about 15m away. That is where they stayed until they had had enough. Subsequent stories from the Argentines that they launched a counter-attack from the river Malo and stopped us in our tracks bear no relation to the truth of what happened.

I decided to throw a couple of grenades towards the enemy in the hope it would make them show themselves, but when I went to get a grenade

I realised I had lost them all in the run in. I asked Tony Boyle for an HE grenade and he looked strangely at me but took one out of his pouch. I pulled the pin and threw it as far forward as I could. It may not have worried the enemy but it made me feel good! A professional soldier might ask what happened to my grenades. The answer is simple. As we were lying waiting for the 66mm salvoes it occurred to me that if I needed a grenade it would be in a hurry. My pouches were full of HE and WP grenades but I reasoned that it would take a bit of time to get them out, and more time would be wasted re-closing my pouch. I therefore decided to hang all my grenades about my webbing so that they were immediately to hand and would be ready for action. Obviously (hindsight having 20/20 vision) the energy expended on the charge caused every one of them to bounce off and fall to the ground, rendering me grenade-less.

After telling Tony Boyle to stay where he was and to prepare to send a contact report, I moved forward to see if I could help but as I stepped forward I suddenly realised I wasn't alone. There was an enormous Argentine soldier about 15m in front of me and looking directly at me. I think we both reacted at the same time. I fired at him straight away and could see my rounds hitting him; after he had been hit about three times, he very calmly put his rifle down and raised both his hands. Moving towards him, I noticed that the firing seemed to be reducing and that more of the enemy were raising their hands in surrender. I turned to Tony Boyle and threw him my mini-flare gun and told him to fire off some red flares to stop the fire group and to send the contact report.

As I moved towards the remaining enemy, I shouted 'Cease firing.' The sudden silence was startling. We began to disarm the enemy and tried to get them together in order to control them and prevent any risk of them attacking us. Whilst we were doing this several of them put crucifixes in their mouths and a number of them began to scream. I realised the Argentines were convinced that we were gathering them together so that we could finish them off. This was so obscene a prospect that I did not believe it at first. Subsequently, I wondered if that was what they were expected to do with us had the boot been on the other foot. Fortunately, I can never prove or disprove this thought. The screaming did not last long as by then people like 'Mac' Mclean and Sam Healy were already giving the Argentine wounded first aid and binding their injuries.

We were now in a small group with our own casualties and a bunch of enemy soldiers. There were five uninjured Argentines, seven casualties and one dead enemy soldier. This made thirteen enemy. We were unable to get close to Top Malo House as it was still burning fiercely, but at least the rounds were no longer cooking off. I was concerned that there were still four enemy unaccounted for. I also noted that the fire group had gathered around someone on the ground. Having disarmed one Argentine, and moved him to a central location, I was not needed at the house as it was all under control. Both Doyle and Stone were being treated, so I went over to the fire group to say thanks and to see what was going on. I discovered that Corporal Steve Groves was badly hurt, having been shot very early on in the contact. He was getting very good treatment from the others and I told Callum to bring his guys down to Top Malo House so that we could set up a protected area.

I checked in with Tony Boyle, who assured me he had sent a contact report with a casevac request and was awaiting an update. No surprise there, I thought, as all the radio operators were first class and completely reliable. In spite of Tony Boyle thinking he was hard done by when I made him the radio operator for the raid, it had already paid off.

One of the Argentines asked me in good English what we planned to do with the dead Argentine soldier lying on the ground about 20m from Top Malo House. I had not given it much thought but suspected that we would leave him there. The Argentine asked if they could take him with them to give him a proper burial. This made complete sense to me, so I turned to 'Mac' Mclean and asked him to go and get the body and bring it to the house so we could put it in the plane with the prisoners. His surprising response was 'F—k off, Boss, I'm not an undertaker. They can do that themselves.' I was taken aback but it made sense, so I replied 'Okay, in which case give me a hand and we'll bring him here together.' I picked up the dead man in a fireman's carry and dropped him next to the Argentine POWs. It seemed a small thing but it calmed the Argentines a lot and made life easier for all.

At that stage I looked down towards the river Malo to see a four-man patrol crossing the river and heading in our direction. They were waving a very large Union Flag. It turned out to be Fraser Haddow's section, who had had a grandstand view of the raid and had decided to join us.

I now realised that we had not fully cleared all the buildings. Top Malo House was demolished, while the small shed where Tony Boyle was established contained only the carcase of a sheep that the Argentines had obviously butchered, and the peat shed next to Top Malo House was full of peat. The outhouse, about 40m downhill in front of the house, was still shut. 'Mac' McGregor was nearest to it so I shouted down to him, 'Corporal McGregor, clear the shithouse.' He looked up at me, then turned on the small building and fired a full magazine of ammunition into it. He then opened the door, looked in and shouted back 'Shithouse cleared, Boss!' It seemed appropriate that one crazy action completed another crazy action, but I have to make it clear that there was no explosion and the 'shithouse' did not disappear in a puff of smoke as legend would have it. It is still there and I saw it in 2012 when I returned to Top Malo House with my wife.

There followed a very long wait before we managed to get our casualties evacuated, as well as getting ourselves and the Argentines away from the area. This was largely caused by the large distance from Brigade HQ and the fact that the wrong officer was on duty at the flight desk that day. We had already started our attack about two hours later than planned because someone who did not know who we were had filed our helicopter request as an administrative move and put it to the back of all the other requests for that day. It was only because the CO of 846 NACS understood the urgency of our task that we were moved forward as a priority. Now, after the action, when we were loitering 40km or more into Argentine territory, we were again dismissed by an ignorant staff officer who could not be bothered to help us out. Unfortunately, he was an RAF officer. Rather than ask 'What is the M&AW Cadre?', he decided to use his limited initiative and ignored our requests. After about the third attempt to get confirmation of our casevac requirement, I spoke to Bill Wright at San Carlos and told him to sort it out. Bill descended on the air desk at Brigade HQ and demanded that an aircraft or two be sent immediately to Top Malo House as men were dying because of a failure of support. He was heard remonstrating with the desk officer by the chief of staff, who immediately ordered the recalcitrant staff officer to do as he was asked and resolve the Cadre's transport problem. This he apparently did willy nilly. Even so, the first helicopter to arrive at Top Malo House to collect the casualties did not arrive until almost 2 hours after we had requested the casevac.

Once the first helo arrived, things went smoothly and our three casualties and seven injured Argentines, along with three of our uninjured men as escorts, were all taken to the 'Red and Green Life Machine'* at Ajax Bay. The five Argentine prisoners and the remaining Cadre members were moved with all the bergens to Teal Inlet, the POWs for interrogation and the rest of us to find somewhere to establish our new headquarters.

*The name given to the Royal Marines Field Hospital manned by Royal Navy medics supported by Army medics from 5 Brigade. Their great claim to fame was that every man who entered the hospital alive during the course of the war left it alive.

The lengthy delay did not cause any real problems for the casualties but it certainly ruined my day and I was very disappointed with the poor efforts of the staff officer on the air desk. Having arrived at Teal Inlet, I went straight to the new Brigade HQ to report in. I saw the brigadier and gave him a shortened version of the action and handed over all the kit, weapons and equipment we had removed from the Argentine prisoners.

I then needed to be alone and to sort my head out – I was still full of adrenaline and had to walk it off. I strolled around Teal Inlet until I came across 45 Commando RM HQ and paid them a visit. The operations officer was an old friend, Captain Mike Hitchcock, who told me subsequently that I was virtually incoherent with excitement but that I slowly calmed down as I cooled off.

All in all, the raid had gone well, although I still feel bad that we took three casualties. It had all gone as planned and we had managed to prevent the Argentines from gaining intelligence from forward patrols. It is of note that two further Argentine 602 Commando patrols saw the action at Top Malo House. Both patrols made their way towards the British forces and surrendered, one to 3 Para and the other to 45 Commando RM. After the raid 602 Commando of the Argentine Army ceased to exist.

So ends my memory of the raid on Top Malo House. I have told my story first but at this point I shall include some of the reflections of other members of the Cadre who participated that day. The following chapter consists of their memories of the raid on Top Malo House.

Chapter 8

The Top Malo House Raid by Cadre Participants

Sergeant Chris Stone's recollections started with the orders:

> The plan for our raid was very simple, as the best plans are, but as the old maxim goes, 'battle plans rarely survive the first shot being fired'. In essence, we were to fly before first light to a drop-off point out of ear-shot of the enemy (As it turned out, we underestimated this distance, as captured Argies under interrogation revealed that they had heard the chopper coming in and were expecting visitors), patrol to the area of the house and after a final recce split up into a fire group and assault group. From there it was to be a straightforward right flanking attack. Rod Boswell was obviously to be in command of the entire operation and the assault group, and not so obviously I was to be second in command of the raid and the assault group. There were other officers present who outranked me but once again the normal military hierarchy didn't always apply within the Cadre. Still, who was I to argue?

Having moved from the community hall in San Carlos to the landing site at the top of the slope above Brigade HQ we set up and waited for a helicopter to take us east to Top Malo House.

Corporal Steve Nicoll remembered:

> At the landing site we were part of a fairly crowded gathering. Groups were coming and going like a busy taxi rank. All the time it was getting lighter [but there was] no sign of any helicopter for us. I met up with some friends in Air Defence Troop. We greeted each other with 'man hugs' at a time when tactility wasn't commonplace; senses were heightened. After a lengthy wait and still no sign of any helo we realised that it was now complete daylight. We'd all had the 'hurry up and wait' experience too many times and this just seemed like yet another. With nothing else to do but wait, it began to feel like a busted flush and [we thought] the whole job would be called off.

At this stage I was getting very agitated and climbed aboard the next helicopter with every intention of hijacking it (described in Chapter 7). Steve continued:

> Another helicopter approached the landing site. The Boss went on board and the crewman looked out, pointed at us, gave a thumbs up and we were off. Attacking a house in daylight with no comms and no update was something new and different. Regardless, we were on our way.

Sergeant 'Mac' Mclean stated:

> The thing was supposed to be a dawn attack, but it didn't materialise because of the heavy commitments of the choppers and what have you. Although we had priority to a degree, [our chopper] didn't arrive until midday. It didn't matter, we were going to do it anyway. We were so keyed up to do it that we didn't give a monkey's what time it turned up.

Corporal Steve Groves again:

> We landed about a kilometre to a kilometre and a half away and moved in patrol formation from this location eastwards down the valley. Once we got to the fence, we divided the patrol, with the fire group, of which I was part, following the fence towards Top Malo House. The assault group moved further down the valley in order to get to the east of Top Malo House and in a position to assault. I was part of the fire group and we got into position about 150m uphill of the house and directly south of it. We had good reason to overlook the objective but we could only see the top half of the building and the roofs of the other buildings which were single storey. We were obscured by the shape of the slope and the dead ground it created. We then had to wait there until Captain Boswell sent up a green flare which was the go-ahead for the attack.

Corporal Bob Sharp remembered:

> Once we located the house we could see there was no cover; we were on a forward slope and we stuck out like a leper in a brothel due to the light covering of snow and our dark clothing; it was down on hands and knees and crawl. I had my mittens, outer, arctic on for the crawl. I had two 66s close to my chest with my left arm, and my rifle in my right hand. Steve Nicoll was near me as I got into a firing position,

away from the others, taking into account the backblast area, and waited for the flare to say the assault group was in position. I readied the rockets and calculated the distance to be about 150m to the house. It seemed like ages but when the green mini-flare was seen the first rocket headed towards the house. As it was a wooden structure I aligned and aimed for the stone-built chimney stack so at least it would hit something solid. The second one I aimed at the corrugated metal roof to fan the flames that were already doing their work and to take out the top floor.

Just after this Steve Groves came over to me and said he was moving left, looking for a target, and wanted me to do fire and movement with him. This worked well for a couple of minutes until a sniper somewhere in the house had him in his sights. Almost immediately after Steve was hit his feet and legs went up into the air. I found out later that he was checking to see if his spine had been hit as well. I started putting rounds into the house, which was still partially standing, and into the outhouses at possible sniper positions. Fortunately, no other rounds came our way. Once the fighting was over, I started to give Steve first aid. What I first thought was the entry wound was the exact shape of a round but was in fact the exit wound. The entry point was near his armpit. We later found out that the Argentines had loaded their magazines with ball, armour-piercing and tracer throughout.

When the casevac helo arrived I checked out the outbuildings and found a sheep carcase in one of them. I thought this would be good for fresh rations in Teal Inlet so took it to the helo when we withdrew. The aircrewman nearly fainted when I put it on board, he must have thought it was human!

Whilst the fire group was getting into position, the assault group was also finishing its approach. Having arrived at the best position for our attack, I checked up and down the line to see that all was okay. I then put up the green mini-flare and watched as the fire group got up on one knee and sent off the 66mm LAWs. 'Mac' Mclean commented 'I think the first 66mm fell short, so did the first M79 grenade and I can remember being screamed at by someone!'

Steve Groves continued:

I was employed as a sniper and I had an L42, which is a sniper's rifle. Previously I had been unable to zero the weapon in, that is, to correct the sights so that the bullet hit what I was aiming at. So when I got on the ground I had to somehow adjust the weapon to the distance [required] and the only way I could do it from that position was to fire at one of the top gable-end windows, [aiming] at the middle cross of the window, [then watching to see] which window it hit. Well, after I had fired my 66mm I took aim at the window and one of the guys in the house must have thought 'What the hell is going on here?', ran to the window and just as I was about to fire his head came into the window and I fired. I don't know what it hit, it must have hit the frame, but it took out the frame, the window and the guy as well. Anyway, the battle then ensued.

Lieutenant Fraser Haddow and his section, who had sent the sighting report the previous night, were about to get a grandstand view of the entire operation. He wrote afterwards:

> At that time we were amazed that such a small force was carrying out the attack. It didn't seem to be the normal three to one forces in our favour. But, since it was such an isolated location, there was possibly no other way to carry out the attack. We were amazed and surprised at how quickly the Argentines reacted to the attack. Although they had shown no sign of movement in the house, within the first five seconds of the house being hit there were men with their equipment and rifles running from the house, taking up fire positions and returning fire.

While this was going on, I continued to watch the fire group as the second salvo went in. It was perfect. All three rockets hit the building and one must have hit the chimney, causing the roof to lift about 15m. I have a vivid memory of the roof just flying high through the air. I counted each of the rockets because I did not wish to charge in and run straight into further rockets being fired at us. One had failed to be fired and I thought it must have been a misfire. I learned later that 'Mac' Mclean had not actually set it up as he had injured his hand in the process and so just failed to fire. He said afterwards that it must have been shot out of his hand but realised later that it was an error of drill that caused him to hurt himself. This particular incident has led to 'Mac' being taken by various authors, without recourse to proper research, as being the fourth British casualty of the battle but it was not so. Notwithstanding that, the initial fire group action was a success as it caused all the Argentines (who were not already dead or seriously injured) to get out of the house and take cover straight away.

Steve Groves continued:

People were coming out of the house. They weren't people to me. They were targets that came into the sight of my sniper's rifle. I then began to open fire on them, fire the shot, kill them, move on to the next target. There were no two ways about it, you can't afford to think of the human factor and you can't afford to think, 'Well, am I doing the right thing?' in moments like this. As a fire group you've got to be able to give good covering fire. You've got to be able to keep the enemy's heads down ... so that the assault group can move through and, obviously, kill the enemy. If you can't do that then you must move position, which I did at that time. I moved forward with my number two (Corporal Bob Sharp). We moved forwards into a better position and, as I fired another couple of shots, I heard two rounds come very close to me and thought 'Time to move out of here.' I ducked down to crawl away to another position and as I ducked, I was hit. I thought immediately to myself 'Well, that's your own stupid fault for being out here in the first place, you know.' OK I'm out here trying to protect my guys doing the assault but I'm too far away, I'm too exposed. I shouldn't really be here, but I tried, and I didn't get away with it, which is a fair one.

On the left flank of the assault group Corporal Jim McGregor was very busy:

When you're being shot at you don't think about anyone else but yourself. It's a cruel thing to say but it's very true. When you're being shot at you think 'Right, this is what it's all about. This is what I've been trained for.' You do everything that you are trained to do and if anyone gets shot around you well that's hard luck, that's by the by, you are still moving, you are on your own, you are all right. It is a very cruel thing, and you might not understand it afterwards, but at the time you are the one and you are alone in the moment. You are the one that counts, and you've got to keep going. You never consider that you are likely to be shot. Having gone through Borneo and Aden it's exactly the same; there is no way that you are ever going to be shot until you are actually shot. Then it's too late but there is no way mentally that you are going to be shot.

On the right flank of the assault group Sergeant Terry Doyle's section was the first to sight the enemy and Doyle shouted out 'Enemy front, enemy front.' I looked across at him and he appeared to have taken cover. I immediately screamed back 'Get up, don't take cover, get up and get down into the valley, into the stream bed.' Corporal Holleran screamed back 'He can't, he's hit', and then knelt and started giving him first aid. This was a very brave act. It was at that moment I realised that we were under quite heavy automatic fire. It hadn't occurred to me until that moment that we were under fire. I saw what resembled fireflies (a lot of them) going past the two men. They were tracer rounds. Corporal Holleran was kneeling in full view of the enemy giving Sergeant Doyle first aid, fully conscious of the danger he was in, I am sure.

Corporal Holleran remembered:

> Initially I was going to leave [Doyle] as we had been ordered to do, but there was a lot of fire going down and I was able to get across to him. His arm was shot up pretty badly. From what I heard later it was a bad arterial wound, the whole of his arm had been shattered and his artery had been punctured. There was blood pumping out everywhere. I think that, had he been left, he would have been very seriously injured. I am not sure he would have died but he probably would have been in a worse state than he is now.

Sergeant Terry Doyle's memories are a little different:

> I had a grenade in my hand and was about to throw it and the first thing I felt was a bit of a thump, being thrown backwards and a very strong smell of burning. I was later to find out that the spare magazine in my chest harness had been hit and exploded all the rounds. I ended up with three rounds in my arm, one of which was a 7.62mm tracer round which was Argentine and two 5.56mm rounds which were ours. The burning smell was from my arm and my initial thought was that the grenade had gone off. I remember looking back along my arm and thinking 'The bastards have shot my arm off, you know, the grenade had gone off and the arm's gone.' I was looking along my arm and I saw a little blue glove with the fingers waggling when there was a sudden sharp pain and all the nerves detached. From about three inches above my elbow downwards there was no feeling whatsoever. At that time all I could think of was that there were no problems, we had taken them out. I needed to get casevacced and get myself stitched up. I had no real negative thoughts, it was just a matter of 'we've done the job and it's time to get stitched up and working from here'.

Steve Groves was in a world of pain and discomfort after being shot:

> The first thing that came to my mind was, has it gone through my
> spine? I tried to move my legs and I remember afterwards, a long
> time afterwards, the guys looking at me as I got hit. I hit the ground
> and the first things that came up were my legs flipping up and back
> down again. What it was, I was checking to see if I could still move
> my legs. I kind of knew they were all right, so I was quite happy with
> that, that it hadn't shattered my spine. But it did a lot of damage,
> which I found out later, broken ribs, a punctured lung. It's not [the
> bullet] that does most of the damage. It's the vacuum behind it and
> the shockwave in front of it that does the most damage. The shock-
> wave caused damage to my kidneys, liver and spleen and blew up my
> intestines so that I looked like a pregnant woman. The most difficult
> part of the experience is the feeling of vulnerability. One of the things
> that went through my mind whilst lying there was that I couldn't fire
> back. I would have to rely on my friends to cover me. Someone's
> going to have to look after me in a minute because I'm losing a lot of
> blood. The firefight is still going on; what if we lose the firefight, if
> the enemy move forward or counterattack? Because I was left entirely
> alone, the guys can't afford to pick me up and run with me because
> were so short numbered. I was really worried that I would be left and
> that was one of the first things that came to my mind.

At this stage our momentum in the attack was slowing down. The right
flank section had been halved and the remaining two (Corporals 'Mac'
McGregor and Sam Healey) had moved to their left and joined Colour
Sergeant Montgomery's section on the left flank. In the middle with me
were Sergeant Chris Stone and Corporal 'Ginge' Boyle (the nominated
signaller for the assault). Soon after this, Chris Stone charged out to draw
the Argentines' fire. He only moved a few paces before he was hit. He
remembered:

> The momentum of the attack had to be kept going and so I advanced
> towards the enemy's location. By this stage ... some of them were
> starting to surrender and others were still returning fire. I remember
> getting hit and went down like a ton of cold sausages and I got hurt
> quite bad. Now there are mates of mine who have been shot and said
> that they didn't feel much in the way of pain. 'Scouse' Cox who was
> shot in Ireland said he thought he had been kicked in the arse and it
> was only ten minutes later when his leg began to get hot and wet that

he realised the truth. In my case there was intense and immediate pain, mostly in my arm and back. I knew I'd been hit by something as the pain was chiefly in my back. I knew it was serious as I was now aware of breathing through a hole in my back. It was making a hoover-like noise every time I exhaled. Also, a noise like a milk bottle being emptied came from somewhere deep inside me which I knew must be internal bleeding. Finally, I started to cough up bits of tissue which I assume were bits of lung. It transpired later that a 7.62 round had entered my shoulder and shattered my collar bone. The round then appears to have fragmented and taken a downward trajectory, blowing off the top of my lung and nicking my subclavian artery and nerve, giving me pain for months to come. To this day it still visits me occasionally to remind me of my foolhardiness. All in all, I had plenty of reasons to feel sorry for myself, which I most certainly did! I remember being under heavy fire while I was trying to move … to get my morphine from around my neck. Every time I moved, I seemed to come under heavier fire and I remember seeing the ground being churned up as if there were wires under the ground. It was very heavy fire and I'll never know how I didn't get hit again but I didn't.

I tried to run over to Chris to drag him back to safety but the Argentines then decided to take it out on me. I noted the lines appearing in the ground around us and realised that we were under serious fire. I withdrew out of range which meant that they stopped firing at Chris. It was better for me to keep out of the way and he would be all right.

By now the assault group was reduced to nine and I was hoping that the fire group was still intact. I was unaware that they had one casualty already (Corporal Steve Groves), so we were now outnumbered by the enemy. The Argentines had managed to get thirteen men out of the house in various states of disrepair, and it appeared to me that they were all firing back at us. Their shooting, however, was pretty ragged and the amount of fire they were putting down was not giving them the results they needed to stop our attack.

Chris Stone again:

As I was lying there, I heard shouting of '*Manos ariba*'. We had learnt this from a sheet of Spanish we had been given on the way south. I thought it was the Argentines shouting at us, telling us to put our hands up. I remember thinking 'You cheeky bastards, we've just

zapped the shit out of you and you're telling us to put our hands up.'
I then realised it was 'Mac' McGregor.

Corporal 'Mac' McGregor's reading of the situation is worth noting:

> I kept on firing in my advance and Sam Healey and I shouted at the
> enemy '*Manos ariba*', which means 'put your hands up'. Now the
> enemy in the valley had just come out of a house that had been blown
> away, so they were a little disconcerted to say the least. They must
> have thought that there were at least two to three hundred of us
> when in fact there were only nineteen of us. They did in fact put their
> hands up which was quite amazing to me. Then I shouted '*Manos
> detrás de tu cabeza*', which means 'put your hands behind your heads',
> which they did.

While I had been involved on the right flank, Colour Sergeant Montgomery and his team, supported by Corporals McGregor and Healey, had
done their job as briefed. They had gone around the left side of the
building and were the final straw for the Argentines. They came around
the building (or what was left of it) very aggressively, very fast, straight out
into the open. As they were upwind and in clear smokeless air, they put
down some very effective fire and started to get very close to the Argentines. Monty and his men had closed to about 10m and were getting ready
to move to hand-to-hand fighting. I think the Argentines realised this
and their resistance crumbled. They all surrendered. At that stage they
were all screaming to surrender so I threw the marker pistol to Corporal
Boyle, saying, 'Put up a couple of red flares to stop the fire group.' There
was no other way of communicating with them. He put about three red
flares up and they stopped firing.

Corporal Tony Boyle remembered:

> Towards the end when there was slight confusion there were people
> with their hands in the air, some of them screaming with sheer terror,
> and if the guy has his hands in the air you can't shoot them; I can't,
> in any case. However, there were still some Argentines firing back, so
> you've got to draw the line somehow, you know. You're the guy in
> the face of the battle let's say, the fight, and you fire at a guy who is
> firing at you. In the course of that you might not notice the guy with
> his hands in the air. At the end there were about three or four of them
> and they were really screaming. It was quite eerie really, [to] hear men
> screaming in terror.

At this stage I had my encounter with the very tall Argentine with whom I swapped shots, as described in the previous chapter; fortunately my rounds hit him and his rounds missed me. The building had by this time completely collapsed. There was one final task for Corporal McGregor:

> Captain Boswell shouted at me to 'clear that shithouse', and I think that what he expected me to do was to go over and knock on the door and say 'Excuse me, would you like to come out and join us? We've had a little fight here.' As it was, I turned around and thought there's no way I'm going over there to see if one of them happened to be in there. So I let off the whole magazine at the toilet, and that was the end of the raid on Top Malo when the toilet was cleared by me.

As it went quiet, we started moving towards the centre to gather the prisoners together in order to guard them and prevent them attempting to escape. A few meetings were going on and our own wounded were being tended. Chris Stone was initially looked after by Sergeant Derek ('Tug the Tourist') Wilson, who finally got to him and gave him morphine. Chris recalled:

> The man who finally gave me morphine was Tug Wilson, obviously that was a great relief to get the morphine. They then sat me up against my fighting order. I said I would be happier [sitting up] because I could hear the wound sucking at the back like a vacuum cleaner. I knew I had a sucking chest wound and they readjusted the dressing to make it airtight and it stopped sucking so badly as a result. It was at this point when I said I was leaking at the front that Nigel ('Ginge') Devenish, said 'Yes, Sherlock, you've been shot, mate!' and then put a dressing on the front wound as well.

After Chris had been given first aid and left propped up against his fighting order for comfort, 'Mac' Mclean arrived and said to Chris, 'Get on with it you daft bastard. Didn't anyone tell you that bayonet charges went out in 1918?' Chris then replied with some indignation 'I've been shot and would appreciate a little more empathy! 'Mac' then ran off, leaving Chris there; Chris thought 'Mac' wasn't aware that he had been 'punctured'.

Corporal Nigel Devenish remembered sitting with Chris Stone and praying that he would not bleed out from his chest wound:

> As we sat there, Chris was getting noticeably colder; he said 'I feel extremely wet – can we check the in-out holes?' I opened the front of his windproof, lifted his thermal top, and it took some time, a long

time, to locate the entry point – about the size of a 1 pence piece! There was little or no blood secreting from the entry point. I then examined the area at the exit point just below his clavicle on his back, and the wound was as big as your fist. I said to Chris 'I found the leak, mate, I just need to add some padding', and with that I stripped off and used my smelly and sweaty T-shirt to pad the exit wound. We had run out of first field dressings (FFDs). Chris now had my T-shirt, my Gucci duvet gloves (which I had just nicked from one of the Argentines) and my best warm hat. He then appeared more com-fortable. The wind and excessive blood loss were making him very cold. We just sat chewing the fat, praying (I was) that the helo would get in very soon. I think it took three hours. [It actually took almost two hours but seemed very much longer.]

Corporal Steve Groves had been having a difficult time since being shot:

As I lay there, my number two [Corporal Bob Sharp] carried on firing, which was a funny thing because as I lay there, I didn't know what was hurting me most – the hole in me or the fact that my number two was firing directly over me. The blast from his weapon was really, really hurting my ears. I thought to myself 'I must lie on my bad side, so I don't flood my good lung, try and put pressure on it and lie on my arm.' I had blood coming out of my nose, my mouth, all that sort of thing but the pain in my ears was much worse. What I tried to do was put my finger in my ear to stop the pain. The shock of the bullet strike had gone through my whole body and I was trying to move my arms and poking myself, up my nose and in my mouth, until I eventually found my ear and stayed that way to the end of the battle. When the boys came over to give me first aid, I still had my finger stuck in my ear. They questioned what was wrong with me!

Chris Stone's recollections of the aftermath are worth including:

There followed what seemed an eternity (was it an hour or more?) of waiting while our extraction and a casevac was being organised. There had been an almost total blackout of HF communications over the entire island and nobody was talking to each other. But good old 'Ginge' Boyle somehow managed to raise San Carlos on the radio, gave a perfect contact report and requested the necessary helo mission. At long last the chopper arrived and a doc came hot-footing round the casualties to assess our damage. I think he put a saline drip in me and all the wounded, dead and prisoners were bundled into the chopper. And I do mean bundled. I remember looking around and seeing bloodied bodies everywhere in various attitudes and wondering who was alive and who was dead. Matt Barnacle, under orders from the doc, sat behind me with his knee jammed against my back to keep the wound as closed as possible. Poor Steve Groves in particular looked quite dead and definitely in a worse state than me. Seeing him like that, I really didn't think he was going to pull through.

On arrival at Ajax Bay we were immediately stretchered into the old sheep shearing station which served as our field hospital. The building was dark and dingy and full of casualties brought about by the bombing and the Paras' action at Goose Green. One of the Paras was obviously having an adverse reaction to his morphine and was giving a rendition of 'When the red, red robin comes bob, bob bobbing along' at the top of his voice. We were triaged and then literally placed in a queue for the operating tables. I took some comfort in realising I was not at the front of the queue and that there must be others that were in more need of urgent treatment than me. Then one of the bootneck medical assistants, no doubt by way of an apology for me being back in the queue, explained that they were waiting for the effects of the morphine to wear off so they could give me a general anaesthetic and that otherwise I would be near the front. You've got to love them! The queue gradually shuffled forward and eventually it was my turn to get tidied up. The doc attending to me was a major attached to the Paras and I once again sought assurance from him that I was going to 'pull through' and once again I was reassured that I was going to be absolutely fine. However, he did add that was provided that the hospital didn't get bombed again, in which case it was unlikely that any of us would pull through. I had a little morphine-fuelled chuckle at that. Then it was blackness and I have only fleeting images of the next several hours. Apparently, this is one of the times I made an appearance on UK TV, lying in recovery with Matt Barnacle (who had been commandeered as an untrained MA) holding an oxygen mask over my face. My parents actually saw the footage, but owing to the fact that my face was covered in cam cream and a newly grown moustache, they didn't recognise me. One of the things I do remember is being visited by Shiner Wright, who had bummed a lift on a chopper to visit the Cadre wounded. When he got to me he was told there was no chance of waking me up out of the anaesthetic. His response reportedly was 'Oh no? Watch this!' Shiner, knowing that I could be a bit of a poseur, shouted in my ear 'Wake up Chris!

You're on national TV!', at which point I opened my eyes. I still remember the laughter of those present!

When the battle at Top Malo was over, our next task was to gather the prisoners to disarm them and to give them first aid. The Argentines were convinced that we were going to kill them. They were all very subdued with the shock of capture and their injuries. Two or three of them actually put their crucifixes and rosary beads in their mouths. It was unpleasant and was, of course, the last thing on our minds. I am not at all convinced that they would have treated us well had our roles been reversed.

'Mac' Mclean explained it as follows:

> There was a very compassionate feeling for the Argentine prisoners. I don't know, they just looked such a sorry sight and all I could do, once everything else had been sorted out, was to make sure they were taken care of. Which is what I think any normal human being would do. I had a word with an Argentine officer (I think their second in command) and he said something like 'Perfecto' or something like that. I replied, 'Yes it was' because it was, it was a good job.

Corporal Steve Nicoll remembered the closing moments of the raid:

> Although the prisoners were all disarmed and searched, we didn't segregate them. There was a nil chance of any attempt by them to counterattack or resist capture. The shock of their capture meant they resigned themselves to their fate and looked after number one. I was shocked that they showed little or no concern for each other's welfare. We treated most of their wounds and probably saved one or two of them from bleeding out. The body of Sergeant Sbert was buried as an unknown Argentine soldier until his identity was established by DNA many years later. The Argentines appeared totally callous and displayed a deplorable absence of dignity for their fallen comrade. Something like that would plague my conscience had I been in 602 (the Argentine unit). [*Author's note: In addition, there was absolutely no consideration given to the remains of Lieutenant Esposito or the other dead Argentines left in Top Malo House, which we think totalled another four men. With the seven injured and five unharmed prisoners, this fully accounts for the seventeen men seen entering the building.*] Eventually their leader, Captain Verseci, must have performed a head count and realised that several of his men were missing. He must have concluded that they could not have run away and therefore assumed they

had been killed in the building. Another terrible example of their appalling leadership.

In order to give the Argentines a chance to report on their part in the battle at Top Malo House it is worth quoting further from the article referred to in Chapter 6:

> 1/Ca Cdo 602 had spent an uneventful night, although the apprehension that no sentries had been put in place had simmered amongst the patrol. Stand-to was not called and a leisurely time was spent preparing for the march to Fitzroy. The helicopter had been heard and generated some discussions if it was Argentine or British.

An Argentine officer inside Top Malo House recalled:

> It was snowing, visibility was bad, but we heard the turbines of the helicopter ... This generated considerable discussion as to whether it was ours or theirs. We were unaware that Darwin had fallen, and the enemy were now advancing on two fronts. Suddenly one of the lookouts [*Author's note: What lookouts? They had earlier admitted that they hadn't posted any.*] reported that the helicopter did not have the yellow stripe* on its tail. [*Author's note: I believe this is the wisdom of hindsight designed to obscure their inadequacy and professional ineptitude and written well after the war ended. In addition, this goes against their assertion above that the visibility was poor due to snow falling.*] That was our alarm and a few seconds later Lieutenant Espinosa, who was upstairs, shouted 'Here they come!'
>
> There was a frantic rush for weapons and equipment, ready to defend the house or withdraw. Outside an intermittent snowstorm swept across the moorland, blotting the watery sun that had risen a short time earlier. [*Author's note: This is also fiction. From the moment we had taken off from San Carlos until sunset that night the sky was completely clear with a bright sun and clear visibility. See the photographs of Top Malo House taken after the skirmish for confirmation.*]
>
> Above Top Malo House, the M&AW Cadre believed that because there had been no movement outside the main building, they had achieved total surprise. A green mini-flare, fired from the commander, with the assault group, soared into the air and looped gently earthwards, signalling the start of the attack. [*Author's note: Again, some literary licence is used by the Argentines. It should be noted that from the*

*All Argentine helicopters had a yellow stripe painted around the tail.

arrival at the landing site the Cadre had taken about 40 minutes to get into position for the assault on the house. This paragraph gives the impression that it was a very swift transit, which is not accurate.] A 66mm LAW barrage ripped into the building, smashing through timber walls. [*Author's note: The building was made of corrugated iron and not wood.*] A second volley took the roof off.

The explosions initially had a paralysing affect [*sic*] on the defenders, shocked by the shattering noise and destruction and yet stimulated into action. The MAG* on the first floor stammered into action. [*Author's note: Fired blindly – if at all – through the corrugated iron of the walls as there were no windows apart from the one at the gable end, which was at waist height.*]

The report continued:

> The British opened fire with anti-tank and automatic weapons in a violent attack that immediately achieved two things. First the house became semi-derelict in an instant, as bullets came at us from all directions. Lieutenants Martinex and Helguero were both wounded by shrapnel, Sergeant Medina was pinned underneath a falling wall and Sergeant Castillo leapt down the blazing staircase. The second affect [*sic*] was to produce amongst us a paralysing psychological affect caused by the explosions and shock of noise and action. Nevertheless, the men reacted well although they may not have been able to fire back. Meanwhile the house was beginning to burn. We decided to evacuate the place, and all assembled at the front door, before bursting out of the door and ground floor windows, firing in all directions, not entirely sure from where the attack was coming. It seemed the right thing to do. Upstairs Lieutenant Espinosa manning the MAG gave us covering fire but was killed when a grenade hit him in the chest. [*Author's note: Not true. Espinosa was killed by Corporal Groves with a single shot from his sniper rifle at the moment of the first salvo of 66mm rockets being fired.*] Lieutenant Brun was badly wounded in the head. This all happened in the first few seconds of the fight.

> Coming out of the house, another grenade exploded close to me and I was wounded in the head, stunned by the noise of the blast, more than anything else. Nevertheless, I quickly recovered and joined in the fighting.

*An Argentine belt-fed machine gun.

On the ridge, the fire team lifted its covering fire and orders were given for the assault force to advance, in skirmish order as planned, four men leapfrogging the remaining eight. In total disobedience to the plan and to the utter astonishment of the OC M&AW Cadre, the entire assault force rose and yelling and screaming, charged down the slope, momentarily leaving their commander behind. One section of four detached itself and angled towards the burning house, wounding Lieutenant Brun in a fierce engagement. [*Author's note: This statement is, I believe, taken directly from a BBC television programme made in 1983 and sold to Argentina. It could not have come from the Argentines who at this stage had managed to get 15–20m from the front door of the building and then taken cover in a small stream bed.*]

The Argentine officer continued:

The enemy were now visible, about 15m away. They were still without any protection, as they thought they were not going to have any resistance, believing us to be dead and wounded. The great volume of fire that fell on the now abandoned house from us justified their mistaken belief. In the midst of the confusion of shots and explosions I made automatically for the stream [*Author's note: The Malo river?*] away from the maximum volume of fire, as did almost everyone who was still standing. [*Author's note: This is fiction. The only one who attempted to move was Sergeant Sbert, who was seen and bracketed by two M79 grenades from which he died instantly.*]

It was about 200m from the house to the river, totally clear ground, devoid of cover. Our only protection was covering fire, so we ran a few metres, threw ourselves on the ground and fired at the enemy. Some even fired while running. Sergeant Sbert who had joined Captain Verseci and Lieutenant Gait giving covering fire from the fence was killed, going to the rescue of the wounded Lieutenant Helguero, wounded again by a grenade splinter. Meanwhile the British continued to advance. [*Author's note: The only part of the previous paragraph that bears any resemblance to truth is the last sentence.*]

The fighting became chaotic and close as both sides exchanged shots at close range, although the momentum of the M&AW charge was checked when it became apparent that no-one knew exactly where the enemy were. There was a short pause and then the Argentines giving covering fire from the corral fence broke cover and headed towards the stream. Another heavy fusillade fell on the Argentines and the Cadre advanced on the stream. [*Author's note: The stream that was running about 15m in front of the burning building. This is fiction as the short pause was caused by the Cadre losing sight of the enemy in the thick smoke coming from the burning house. At no time did the Argentines attempt to 'break out', with the sole exception of Sergeant Sbert who paid with his life. By now many of the Argentines were screaming to surrender with their hands held high. Very few continued to resist.]*

The officer recalled:

> The British passed the house and came towards us in a classic assault, straight out of the school-books, shouting and firing according to the requirements of their advance, as if they were following a teacher.

The remainder of the Argentine report is largely fiction and does not bear comparison with actual events. They claim to have caused several injuries. The only three injuries received by the Cadre all occurred in the first few moments of the firefight and were mostly caused, I believe, by indiscriminate unsighted fire from the hip when they were rapidly evacuating the house. The injury to Sergeant Stone was almost certainly caused by a well-aimed shot, but the other two were definitely lucky for the Argentines and a result of the indiscriminate spraying of fire in all directions. The final part of the Argentine report is, however, worth quoting:

> We were surrounded with the enemy advancing upon us, but the end was very different from the books I have read and films I have seen.
>
> The end was not easy, and it became very dangerous. In the beginning, it was not easy to decide to give ourselves up, above all one carried the responsibility of the mission and the responsibility that it was being carried out by Commando Troops. I still had my commando beret and that was a great responsibility. Surrender is something unacceptable and I had always thought that the outcome of a commando mission should be either success or death. To succeed is to return alive to continue fighting, that was the idea. We had never thought of the possibility of surrender.
>
> Despite the calls to cease fire, I continued firing. At that moment and to my right, two British came towards me firing. They were very close but as I was fairly drowsy, it took me some time to realise that they were shooting, but such was the weight of enemy fire, it sounded like rain falling on dry sand. When I saw these men, I swung round and fired, hitting, I believe, one of them in the stomach. I tried to shoot the second but I no longer had any strength and I slowly, it seemed, fell into the ditch, semi-conscious. I looked to see one of the

men pointing his weapon at me and thinking he was going to shoot me, without fear, I entrusted myself to God. However, following the rules of war and seeing that I was wounded, he lowered his weapon, dragged me out of the ditch and relieved me of my weapon and said, 'No problem, its war.' He took off his parachutist's scarf [*Author's note: His camouflage neckerchief.*] and made a tourniquet for my leg. He asked me if I had any medicine, but my kit was in my back-pack, left in the burning house. He then took out some morphine capsules that he carried in an inside pocket, so that they did not freeze, and gave me an injection in my leg. He then made some signals and British began to appear from all sides. Some of my companions also came, some prisoners, one wounded by a bullet in the heel, without knowing it. It was cold but the morphine was working and gave me some strength. One or two of the Argentines were continuing to resist, further down the stream, and we were in danger of being caught in pulverising crossfire. The calls for surrender became less frequent but more urgent and so it was that the survivors of 1/Ca Cdo 602 realised the hopelessness of the situation, threw their weapons on the ground and surrendered.

The fighting was over, all the wounded were collected together and first aid given. The five unwounded prisoners were centralised, searched and in the camaraderie of respect between two enemies, who have been through identical violent experiences, the OC M&AW Cadre remarked to Captain Verseci 'Never in a house', referring to the unwise and yet understandable [*Author's note: Understandable to Argentine forces.*] move of seeking shelter in the only building for many kilometres around.

The Argentines' story as told above should not be condemned because of its inherent inaccuracy. They had made so many basic errors of soldiering that it was incumbent upon the survivors to tell a story that gave some credibility to those who lost their lives in the skirmish. Of the seventeen men who entered Top Malo House on 30 May five were now dead, five were uninjured prisoners and seven were casualties. All of them recovered from their wounds, as did the three Royal Marines who were injured, largely thanks to the high-quality first aid treatment given by the Cadre after the battle.

Chris Stone mentioned that 'according to the medics at Ajax Bay (where all the injured of both sides were taken), the first aid administered to both

Brits and Argies was first rate and commented on by the doctors at the field hospital. So, take a chuck up boys!'

It is worth pointing out at this stage that after the war the Argentines awarded several gallantry awards to the troops who fought at Top Malo House. Two posthumous VC (equivalents) and a further six MC (equivalents) were awarded; all the injured soldiers were awarded an injured in war medal, plus all were awarded a battle medal. The Cadre earned one mention in dispatches, awarded to Sergeant Chris Stone, and one commander in chief's commendation, awarded to Corporal Tim Holleran. It would appear that there are many differences in the various national methods of commending soldiers in war but it remains my belief that we were correct as we had all carried out the job we were paid to do and with these two noted exceptions, all had done their job to the best of their ability and no more.

It was the only planned daylight battle that took place on land during the Falklands campaign. Even though it was planned to begin in darkness, it actually started at about midday in bright sunshine and clear visibility. I remain delighted by the effort, courage and professionalism shown by my men that day. It will never be forgotten.

Chapter 9

Teal Inlet
(31 May–10 June)

We arrived at Teal Inlet after the raid on Top Malo House with three injured at the Ajax Bay hospital and one injured from 1 Section. We had HQ Section and 1, 3, 5,6, 7 and 8 Sections with 2 and 4 Sections still in the field.

My first task was to reorganise the Cadre because of the casualties. I had lost two section leaders and a sniper from HQ Section. The reorganisation turned out to be quite straightforward. 8 Section was disbanded after the loss of Sergeant Terry Doyle and the three remaining team members were moved thus: Corporal Sam Healey joined 7 Section, where Sergeant Jan Rowe replaced Sergeant Chris Stone as section commander. Corporal 'Mac' McGregor replaced Corporal Neil West (who had injured his knee on the night of 30 May and was moved to the HQ Section) in 1 Section. Corporal Tim Holleran, who was the 8 Section signaller, was also moved to the HQ Section to reinforce our signals capability. The Cadre was thus reduced to seven sections with an increased HQ Section of five men.

Teal Inlet was becoming increasingly crowded. 3 Para had already moved forward towards Estancia House, where they would establish their headquarters, with the remaining troops deployed on Mount Estancia and around Estancia House. 42 Commando RM had flown one company to Mount Kent and the remainder to Mount Challenger on 31 May. 45 Commando RM was beginning to arrive at Teal Inlet, where they would rest up for a couple of days after their very testing yomp from Port San Carlos via Douglas Settlement. 29 Commando RA had put one or two batteries of 105mm artillery in place southwest of Mount Kent, so for the first time since 21 May it was able to provide supporting fire against all the westerly Argentine positions. This situation would slowly improve over the following week. The priority for helicopter use was ammunition for the forward artillery guns, followed by full ammunition support for all the remaining 29 Commando RA batteries. This was to ensure that all the guns would have sufficient ammunition to cope with the battles to come.

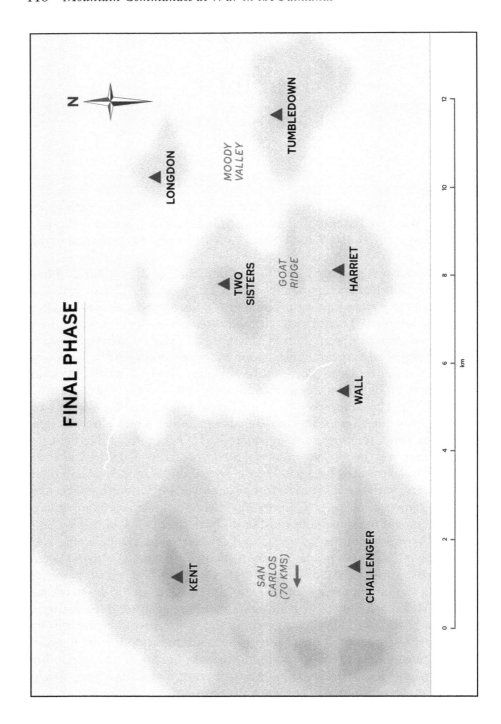

I realised that we were running out of viable terrain for us to continue our task of protecting the flanks and the forward line of our troops. The main units were now very close to the enemy. I was therefore tasked to provide immediate flank protection to the south and to the northeast of the brigade's forward positions. I recalled 2 and 4 Sections and they were collected by helicopter on the morning of 1 June.

Three sections were also inserted on 1 June. 5 Section was to overlook Fitzroy and Bluff Cove from an OP on Smoko Mountain, while 6 Section deployed to the west end of the ridge from Mount Challenger to provide rear protection to 42 Commando and to observe to the south and east, ensuring that there was no enemy movement from Stanley towards Bluff Cove. The two sections were about 10km apart, with Stanley about 20km to the east of 6 Section on Mount Challenger.

7 Section was deployed by rigid raider with a team from the SBS to provide an observation post covering the north and east of the forward brigade locations. The SBS task was unspecified but the decision to share transport made sense as the Cadre team had to move north and east from the drop-off point and the SBS team to move south and east from the same location. Conditions were difficult, with thick fog, and navigation on the way in was provided by a portable GPS held by the SBS. The journey by boat was approximately 25km and not a great experience for all involved. Arriving at the drop-off beach, the two section commanders took some time to confirm that they were, in fact, at the correct location. Sergeant Rowe was convinced that they had been dropped off a little too far east of where they were supposed to be. As a result, he suggested two things. First, that he be given the opportunity to get above the fog and confirm the actual location, and second, that when the SBS moved off, his section would stay in place for at least 30 minutes to guarantee that they would not accidentally bump into one other. This was agreed and 7 Section set off uphill to get above the fog and confirm their location. Rowe established that he was correct, though they were a little further east than he thought. Returning to the drop-off point, he found that the SBS team had already left, having failed to wait for him. 7 Section stayed in place for the agreed 30 minutes and then set off on their planned patrol. Their task was to set up an OP at the eastern end of Green Hill, providing observation to the south and east and covering any potential enemy movement towards Mount Longdon, Two Sisters and Mount Kent (*see* map on p. 68). The rest of the patrol went without incident but sadly the SBS patrol bumped into an SAS patrol whilst on the move and in the ensuing firefight an SBS

member was killed. Sergeant Rowe and his team were unaware of this incident until they were picked up and returned to Teal Inlet seven days later.

I was appalled by the incident because I had no idea that there were any SAS patrols in that area. It seriously concerned me that there might be other SAS patrols wandering around close to my teams. I contacted the brigade intelligence officer (Captain Viv Rowe, another ML officer) to see if he could provide me with information concerning the SAS patrols but was informed that their operations were 'need to know', and I was not on the list of those who needed to know!

I ensured that all my future patrols were very carefully briefed about their routes and locations. I also made sure that the SAS were made aware of my patrol routes and locations so that there should be no further unnecessary 'blue on blue' situations. This very sobering incident was caused by the fact that the SAS had become accustomed to operating in full secrecy during operations in previous years. This had made them very insular and non-communicative. Since the Second World War the SAS had largely operated independently. They were not used to fitting in with the main force, and tended to adopt a 'prima donna' approach, including demanding absolute priority for assets. They assumed an arrogant attitude over what they did, and failed to divulge their operations. This obsession with secrecy and special status had been encouraged by the highly successful SAS operation to rescue hostages held by dissidents in the Iranian Embassy in London two years previously. In essence, there were too many forward operating troops in an area that did not justify that many. The SBS was always deployed with 3 Cdo Bde and was much better at communicating with Brigade HQ using liaison staff but the independence of the SAS had become a problem, resulting in the death of one of the SBS.

It is worth at this stage introducing a personal report from one of the members of 7 Section, Corporal Matt Barnacle:

> Several things make this patrol stand out, particularly as it started only a couple of days after we had done the raid on Top Malo House and we had to reorganise the section when Chris Stone, the team commander, was shot. It was also my birthday, the first day of the patrol, and for me it was to be the first joint patrol that I had ever been involved in with the SBS. I really don't remember the briefing phase of the process at all, which would suggest that it was either only attended by Jan Rowe or was very brief and uninspiring. However, I do vividly remember the boat trip, which was, to say the least,

bloody freezing! The journey was long and uncomfortable and I remember thinking how professional the two LC marines were. Geoff Nordass and Barry Gilbert were, in their whole approach to the task, utterly professional throughout. They were unflinching in the freezing spray and wind and fully focused on the need for accurate navigation. When we arrived at the disembarkation RV, bearing in mind the trip was 26km in the pitch black, we established that we were not exactly where we should be and I think this was because of the depth of the water. It was not as deep as it should have been and we couldn't go as far as had been planned. However, it really wasn't that significant, only a few hundred metres.

I was point man of the patrol as we set off towards our first navigation checkpoint. The going was okay, just soft green grass slopes, but relatively quickly it deteriorated into the nightmare of stone runs with interestingly big boulders. I remember stepping into bottomless holes on several occasions, much to the amusement of the other guys in the team. Although the navigation was not directly my role (I had enough on my plate trying to find a route that could be followed without someone breaking a leg), I did have to maintain a bearing with Jan [Rowe] and Tony [Boyle] checking navigation with the 1/50,000 map and monitoring distance the best they could. Something that did strike me though, as a very young and inexperienced 21-year-old, was the total lack of input of the four SBS guys. I don't remember them having anything to do with the navigation until I went to ground in the RV that was the separation point of the two teams and I pointed to a high peak on the skyline which was the bearing to their next RV. Jan Rowe had to make it clear that we were at the separation point and then which direction the two four-man teams were to go. I took this discussion quite simply as an explanation, almost a briefing, as the SBS guys had at this point had so little to do with the navigation. We remained in the separation RV for a while then moved off to complete the remainder of our yomp. This went without incident and we quickly arrived at our final RV and moved into an acceptable location for our OP for the next few days until relieved on the 7th June.

Sergeant Jan Rowe's recollections are also worth including:

When given the patrol I went to the SBS and met up with the SBS team leader and discussed how and where we were going to do this job. He told me I would have to lead the patrol as I was probably better at map reading.* I knew the SBS leader well as we had both attended the same senior command course at CTCRM before being promoted to sergeant. We were inserted by two boats and dropped off. First problem that arose was that we were told that we were at the drop-off point by an SBS officer who had navigated the two boats using a GPS. I was not happy about our drop-off location but we could not hang about arguing where we were and so we moved off with my team leading. I am not sure how long we were moving but I noticed what I thought was a set of tracks moving north–south and where I was going to make my way to my RV position. The SBS disagreed and we got clear and went to ground to check the map. He said that the mountain to our front was where he had been told to go and said that we had been dropped off further down the creek so that the tracks could not have been arrived at so soon. I was having doubts at this stage and I now needed to confirm our position. I asked the SBS team to stay where they were as I wanted to go ahead with one of my guys [Tony Boyle] to check our position. On checking I found I was right and we were in the wrong place. I returned to where I had left the guys who told me that the SBS team had already left. I got my guys together and we made our way to our OP position. At the 0700 radio schedule later that morning I received the message that it was imperative that I checked my position. I checked it and confirmed we were where we should be but they came back again telling me to thoroughly check my position. I thought they were taking the piss but confirmed I was at the right location. I heard no firefight that night and had no idea what was going on to the west of us. When I got back to base on 7 June 'Ginge' Devenish said 'sorry to hear about the loss of the SBS guy' and that was how I found out about the 'blue on blue'. I have problems with this today, going over what I should have done, but I had a job to do as did the SBS team and they needed to get on, as did we. Also, it is worth noting that this business of not being able to communicate between different groups back then was complete crap and totally unacceptable.

I remain seriously upset about the entire incident. As far as I am concerned Sergeant Jan Rowe and his team made every effort to confirm their

* Sergeant Jan Rowe was one of the most reliable and accurate map readers with whom I have ever had the good fortune to work. When he was a marine in my Recce Tp in the mid-1970s he was the man to whom I turned if there was a serious difficulty with locating our position. He had an almost uncanny ability to read map to ground and vice versa.

location and did not progress until they were absolutely sure of where they were. The fact that we were unaware of the location of the SAS patrol was not acceptable at all; the SAS should have informed Major Hector Gullan, as the 'patrol master' of the brigade, of their plans.

Late in the morning of 2 June I received a clear and detailed report from 5 Section that the Argentines were reinforcing Bluff Cove by helicopter. The section had seen a Scout helicopter and heard a Chinook helicopter discharging troops just north of Bluff Cove. They asked for artillery support and prepared themselves to fire on the helicopter when it returned with its next load of troops. I went straight to Brigade HQ and spoke to the duty gunner, arranging a three-battery fire mission on the given location. He assured me that the time of flight of the shells would be 28 seconds so we agreed that we would order 'open fire' as soon as the troops began unloading from the helicopter. This would ensure that we would cause maximum damage to the helicopter and its passengers before they had the chance to organise themselves at the landing site. I relayed the information back to 7 Section and with Corporal Steve Nicoll on his end of the line and me on the other, we waited for the Chinook to return. I had already found out that the RAF Chinook was occupied doing administrative work for 5 Brigade and was absolutely nowhere near Bluff Cove, nor anywhere east of Goose Green. I remember standing next to the radio with two handsets, one to Corporal Nicoll and the other to the gunners. We kept both routes open and got a warning order from Corporal Nicoll when the Chinook came into sight. All seemed to be going well when suddenly Corporal Nicoll started transmitting 'Check, Check, Check, Check.' I waited for a break in transmission and requested clarification. He explained that as the aircraft turned to land, he saw that it did not have a forward right door. As we all knew that the RAF Chinook had been flying without the forward right door this made it our helicopter and not an Argentine one. I immediately told the gunners to cancel the task, explaining the reason, and we all breathed one heck of a sigh of relief. Of such are 'blues on blues' made. The story of 5 Brigade and 2 Para's enormous leap forward could have proved the most expensive mistake of the entire Falklands war as the Chinook had at least eighty passengers on board. They would have been severely mauled by our own guns had 5 Section not been so observant and careful. I reported the incident to my brigade commander, who passed it immediately to the divisional commander, who I assume passed it on to 5 Brigade commander. I was not impressed.

On 3 June Major Hector Gullan was tasked by the brigade to set up a
location in order to ensure that all friendly patrols were to be coordinated
by one person. He would effectively become the brigade 'patrol master'.
Hector was accompanied by the brigade commander's assistant, Lieutenant James Montefiore, and he asked me to join him, so we set off in two
BV 202 vehicles from Teal Inlet. Six hours later we arrived at the western
end of Mount Kent and then moved around the mountain. We set up a
very well camouflaged position beside a large rock formation about a third
of the way between Mount Kent and Mount Challenger.* Radio communications were established with the relevant unit headquarters and we
prepared ourselves for whatever might happen next. After we had been in
position for about 24 hours, Hector and I were planning a night patrol in
order to get to a position that would enable us to provide Brigade HQ
with a set of photographs of the enemy positions on Mount Harriet when
there was a series of six or seven very large, very loud and very close
explosions. The first explosion actually lifted the BV 202 off the ground
and caused us both to take cover in the footwell of the vehicle. This was no
mean feat as the space was very small and we are not small men! With our
faces about 2 inches apart, Hector looked at me and said 'What the f—k
was that?' He had fought with distinction in Oman and Northern Ireland
and had led the assault on the Iranian Embassy in London in 1980, and
had considerable experience of active service. His comment frightened the
life out of me and I replied 'Don't say that! You must know what it was', in
a very tremulous voice. We laughed out loud and said to each other
'Whatever it was we got away with it but what's coming next?' We then
cancelled our planned patrol for the night and spent the next 12 hours
stood to in case it was the prelude to an enemy assault. This fortunately
did not materialise.†

This experience achieved two things. First it made me realise that I was
responsible for thirty-two other guys, most of whom were in danger and
were relying on me and my HQ to be available to help them at any time,

* This was probably Bluff Cove Peak, but I am not at all sure as it was not a peak, just a very
large rock formation.
† At the end of the war we learned that the Argentine Air Force was rolling bombs off the
tail ramps of Hercules aircraft, with directions being given by the radar controllers at Port
Stanley Airfield. On this occasion we assumed they were targeting 42 Commando on
Mount Kent. They were OK for distance but got their line incorrect and the bombs landed
nearer to us. The next day we paced out the distance – the first bomb had landed 175m
away, with the remainder in a straight line towards Stanley. The holes were each big
enough to contain a double decker bus, hence our nervous reactions.

and second that going on a trip such as this was satisfying my need for action but taking me away from my real job. Fortunately for me, before I raised this point with Hector, we received a message from Brigade HQ telling us that the brigade was moving to set up a forward location on the north side of Mount Kent and we were to join it there as soon as possible.

I called back to Teal Inlet and told Bill Wright to send a small team (Sergeant 'Mac' Mclean and Corporal Neil West) to come forward with the Brigade HQ forward staff and be ready to set up a Cadre HQ next to the Brigade HQ forward location.

On 4 June the CO of 42 Commando RM asked the brigade commander for two Cadre patrols to be allocated to his unit to assist with patrolling in preparation for the attack planned against Mount Harriet. I was asked to allocate two patrols and selected 1 (Haddow) and 3 (Wassall) Sections. However, I also insisted that they remain under command of the Cadre so would not be tasked directly by 42 Commando. The tasking should be requested through Brigade HQ and agreed by OC Cadre before being given to the two patrols.

The first task given to them was to carry out a reconnaissance patrol to Wall Mountain to confirm that it was not occupied by the enemy. Wall Mountain, immediately to the east of Mount Challenger, is the last high ground before Mount Harriet. I nominated 3 Section (Sergeant Des Wassall and his team) for this task. The patrol was carried out during the night of 4 June and was difficult but necessary. It proved conclusively that Wall Mountain was devoid of any Argentine personnel and that there had been no previous occupation by them. This latter point was easy to confirm as there was no litter or detritus left on the mountain, and there would have been had the Argentines been there before us. Des Wassall and his team returned to Brigade HQ on the morning of 5 June, at which point they were stood down for a full rest day after a very serious night's work.

On 8 June I was called to Brigade HQ to meet Captain Viv Rowe, the brigade intelligence officer. An ML officer, Viv had taken over 40 Commando Recce Tp when I finished my tour there in 1977. Viv was concerned that there was a shortage of information about the area to the north of Mount Harriet and south of Mount Two Sisters and the area west of Mount Tumbledown. He wanted to get hold of detailed and reliable information about this area in preparation for the forthcoming brigade attack on these three mountains. He passed his request through the brigade commander, who agreed with him that this was an important task and also that it should be carried out by the Cadre. Viv Rowe had been trying to obtain aerial photographs of the area but had been unable to get any. The

PRIC photos acquired by the Cadre in Arbroath only covered the area from San Carlos Water to just east of Mount Simon (fortunately including Top Malo House). He therefore needed to send a reconnaissance patrol into no man's land and get up-to-date and accurate information about this triangle of ground that was out of sight of our troops. I appreciated the difficulty of this task, as well as the risk involved, so I detailed the two sections to work together to carry it out, inserting overnight on 8/9 June and staying in position for the whole of 9 June. They were to withdraw after sunset on 9 June and return to Brigade HQ with the information required. I called forward Lieutenant Fraser Haddow and Sergeant Des Wassall and their sections (1 and 3) to carry out this task. I made it very clear to them both that this was a joint patrol.

I told them that Brigade HQ required good field sketches of the area between Harriet and Two Sisters and as much as possible of the area between Harriet and Tumbledown. I told them to ensure that they were secure and as safe as possible but to get this information for the two COs of 42 and 45 Commandos as they would need it to formulate their plans before attacking the relevant mountains in the very near future. Whilst they were organising their guys, I contacted 42 Commando RM and asked for assistance in inserting the two patrols by letting them tag along with a fighting patrol of 42 Commando that night. K Company of 42 Commando was tasked with providing a troop-strength fighting patrol. Led by Lieutenant Mark Townsend RM, it was tasked to confirm that there were no enemy soldiers on Goat Ridge and then to drop off the Cadre patrol before heading south towards Mount Harriet. It was to engage the enemy there and cause as much disruption as possible to assist the infiltration of the Cadre patrol.

The joint patrol left from the eastern end of Mount Challenger at last light on 8 June. About 250m from the west end of Goat Ridge the Cadre patrol halted and waited for K Company to head towards the northern slopes of Mount Harriet. As the commandos approached the enemy positions, they engaged an Argentine heavy machine-gun position with an 84mm Carl Gustav anti-tank round before withdrawing to better cover. The Argentine response was the usual heavy fire as the patrol carried out its fighting withdrawal. Most of the fire went over the heads of the 42 Commando patrol but landed amongst the hiding Cadre patrol, who had to take cover to avoid risk of injury. The two section leaders made notes of the firing positions of the Argentines for their later patrol report.

Once the fire had died down, the Cadre patrol split into two. Haddow's section moved up the north side of Goat Ridge and Wassall's up the south side. Each patrol spent the entire night checking out the full length of Goat Ridge until they met at the eastern end in the early hours of 9 June. Their patrols had confirmed that the enemy strength on both Harriet and Two Sisters was much greater than had been assumed by the brigade intelligence staff.

The two section commanders then set about finding a location at which to establish an OP to observe the two mountains during the daylight hours of 9 June. The narrowness of the rock formations on Goat Ridge made this task extremely difficult. They eventually found a spot about halfway back along the ridge towards the eastern end. They set themselves up with the two section commanders in position, sitting back to back under a rock and looking north and south. The remaining six men set up 5 to 6m away, providing rear and flank protection for their commanders. Deep within the two main Argentine positions, the two men were about 40m away from the track that provided the administrative link between the enemy units on Mount Harriet and Two Sisters. The patrol remained in position all day watching the two Argentine positions and each producing a field sketch of any sighted enemy locations and trenches. This included a large command wire bomb consisting of barrels buried in the ground on the south side of Two Sisters with the command wire leading away to a fire trench well clear of the intended explosion. This discovery was a major coup as any assaulting troops would be severely injured if this bomb exploded during the fight for the mountain. The two field sketch maps provided much important and detailed information about the siting of the Argentine positions on the two mountains and would prove very valuable in the planning of the forthcoming attacks.

A couple of hours after sunset, when the night was as dark as possible, the two sections rejoined forces and made their way off Goat Ridge heading west to 42 Commando's HQ location. There they briefed 42 Commando's second in command Major Guy Sheridan (another ML officer and previous OC of the M&AW Cadre) before going on to HQ 3 Cdo Bde to brief the patrol master Major Hector Gullan and Captain Viv Rowe. The two commanders then went to the relevant COs (Haddow to Lieutenant Colonel Andrew Whitehead of 45 Commando and Wassall to Lieutenant Colonel Nick Vaux of 42 Commando) to brief them with their findings and to hand over their field sketch maps. The brigade staff sent the details of what had been seen on Mount Tumbledown and Mount William to 5 Infantry Brigade for them to be used by 5 Infantry Brigade in their follow-on attacks after the capture of Two Sisters, Harriet and Longdon.

This was an outstanding patrol carried out very close to and probably in full sight of the enemy. It was so well done that they were able to provide a lot of information to the four relevant COs, who were able to adjust their battle plans accordingly. This almost certainly saved a significant number of British lives in the ensuing attacks.

Before moving on from this patrol, it is worth including a joint report made by Corporals Steve Last and Neale Meade of 3 Section. It very clearly describes the personal and private experiences they shared during this extraordinary feat of military professionalism and personal courage:

> Our OP patrol consisted of two teams brought together for the job. Des Wassall was in command of one team with Neale Meade, Al Heward and me (Steve Last), with Fraser Haddow, Graham Foster, 'Mac' McGregor and Gordon 'Scouse' Heeney in the other.
>
> We started the patrol from 42 Commando's location from K Company whose task was to recce the area and terrain in the Mount Harriet area and to probe the defences where possible.
>
> We left their location via a 29 Commando battery and I recall going to the gun control, I assume with Des Wassall. There I registered about six or eight X-Ray fire missions around Goat Ridge should the shit hit the fan on infiltration or exfiltration and to get Zulu targets from them. (Senility may have dulled my memory here and I could be totally wrong but I seem to recall fire missions were Zulu targets if they had been fired in and registered and X-Ray targets if they were prospective cover/targets). At every chance I got I ran through my target numbers to try to memorise them so they could be called in quickly if need be.
>
> We both recall that the going was tough on the route in, varying from firm to very boggy, to tussock grass and those bloody stone runs. They were a pain in the arse with anything from small rocks up to large boulders, all quite unstable and loose with loads of ankle-breaking voids between them.
>
> We approached from the west below Wall Mountain and moved to low ground between Goat Ridge and Mount Harriet. Neale, who had the patrol IWS, could see light from many positions on Mount Harriet as we approached. We then broke away from 42's patrol and took a rising traverse to get onto Goat Ridge, which ran roughly east–west, whilst they moved towards Harriet. We were about half-way up the ridge when 42 made contact and a fierce firefight developed between them and the enemy on Mount Harriet. We just

carried on in the hope that with every eye on the fight it would cover for us moving into the OP position. It all went fairly well until near the top of the ridge when we started getting a lot of incoming rounds, presumably because 42 were breaking contact at this time and seemed almost in a direct line between us and Harriet and it was probably overshoot or ricochets.

Here we both have some amusing recollections from that time. I recall looking up-slope at Neale and Fozzy Foster, I think, taking a breather against a steep slab of rock before having to sprint for cover whilst the slab was being peppered with incoming rounds. Neale recalls me trying to take cover in a crack in the rock. I thought I would back into the crack to keep the radio out of the line of fire (knob!) but this didn't work as I soon found that the fissure was too shallow. The radio was okay but it left me stuck out in the line of fire! I remember looking about 10m down the slope at Meade and Foster laughing their tits off at my antics in the crack. I think they were trying to tell me to come down to them in cover but they couldn't get the words out for laughter! I saw Gordon 'Scouse' Heeney, closer and off to one side behind a rock, so I scuttled down to take cover with him but tripped and fell onto him breaking his whip antenna (which I never heard the last of), to find the rock barely big enough for us both, leading 'Scouse' to tell me to bugger off as he was here first. More nervous laughter!

Eventually things died down and we moved along the ridge to the east trying to find a suitable position. This proved quite hard as the ridge was not that wide until we dropped off the crest and went further east. We eventually found a horseshoe-shaped depression about 5m across with shallow rock walls on either side and to the front offering some cover from view and fire and with a good view to the east to Mount Tumbledown. I stayed at the rear of the position with Gordon 'Scouse' Heeney, who was also a section signaller, as this was a bit higher than everyone else and hopefully better for comms. Neale Meade and Al Heward were down to my right with Des and Fraser in the front and 'Mac' McGregor and Fozzy Foster on the left.

On the way in I had set up a trailing wire antenna to try to get comms as it soon became apparent that any other form of antenna would be seen as soon as daylight came. In the event the comms were non-existent on voice or morse. I spent most of the night with 'Scouse' trying to inform Shiner Wright back at brigade by codeword that we were in location. I'm sure Tony Boyle is right with the codes;

we had one time pads [OTP] should we have to work via the SF Hereford rebroadcast system, Slidex for working back to brigade and Nuco and Pele for calling in naval gun support fire. I think all the signallers carried a white phosphorous grenade in their code bag to destroy them all if need be.*

Come daybreak it was clear how bare-arsed the ridge was and how exposed we were from the east. Luckily, Mount Tumbledown was some distance off and we had some cover from the sides. I recall that 'Scouse' and I, being higher and more in view than the rest, pulled up tufts of grass to put on ourselves, we were that exposed. I began to get bad cramps too from being still for so long and couldn't wait for the cover of night to come.

At one stage during the day I remember hearing noises off the side of the ridge on the Harriet side. Al, I think it was, looked over the rim and turned around with eyes on stalks giving the thumbs down enemy sign. We all stood to for some time expecting poo to hit the spinny thing [Author: shit hit the fan!] but luckily nothing transpired. At one point during the day a pair of Chinooks landed and unloaded something. Des had binoculars; he thought it might be mines and made detailed sketches accordingly. This all helped later when Des's report and our knowledge of the route and area enabled us to lead the Guards and Gurkhas to their start lines. 'Scouse' and I thought about bringing some fire down on them as they were down for some time unloading but we still had no comms.

There was frequent artillery fire from both directions during the day and night, theirs and ours, sounding quite different and clearly coming from opposite directions. At one point I remember a lump of shrapnel bouncing off the rock rim between Al and Neale and landing in the middle of our position. I was a little peeved to say the least as many of the rounds from our guns seemed to be landing dangerously close, especially as I had deconflicted with gun control on the way out. On return we had a chat with guns but nobody owned up and they swore it was not them. I don't think it was naval gun support fire as the angles were wrong and you could easily tell the difference

---

* The variety of signalling methods and codes was particular for the Cadre teams in order to guarantee communications at all times. The various systems gave each of the sections a variety of options to ensure their messages got through. At one stage HQ was receiving messages that were rebroadcast from the UK because the OPs could not get through directly to HQ, 45km distant. They could, however, send signals 13,000km to the UK, who then sent the messages back to us at HQ!

between the quick-fire 4.5inch naval guns and our 105mms. The mystery remains! We both remember the way the fire missions hit Harriet causing a big 'firework-like' display from the shrapnel on rock. Also, the sound of the para-illum [parachute illumination] shells at night popping open overhead with the empty shell carrying on and sounding like someone blowing across the top of a bottle as they tumbled on.

Darkness was very welcome when it came because it meant we could move to ease cramped limbs prior to moving out. We were all ready to move when Al called a halt, saying that he needed a dump first. All waited patiently until the deed was done, whereupon Al declared that he had just laid the biggest turd the Falklands had ever seen. Unsurprisingly, no one was keen to verify his alleged achievement.

Whilst we were making our way down the ridge, I knocked my knee against the magazine release of my rifle, dropping the magazine onto the slab where it skittered down for about 3m making one hell of a racket. It sounded to me as if I had emptied a bucket of spanners down the rock and I waited for the flares to go up and the rounds to come in but nothing happened and it seems most of the others never even heard it happen. Just goes to show how your perception of sound changes with heightened senses. Neale also remembers that on our first rest stop having got off the ridge, but still very close to Harriet and in clear view of anyone with a night sight, one of the patrol wanted a fag break. Neale remembers being gobsmacked at this so close to the enemy positions and words were exchanged, leading to no fag break. It transpired later that they had a much better night vision capability than our measly IWS, having bought new up-to-date stuff from the Yanks.

The next point to note, after the bloody stone runs again, was approaching 42's location. The night was black as a witch's tit, with Neale in front with the IWS, then Al. As we got close Neale picked out their dugouts and sod bunkers with the IWS and we moved forward very slowly. We carried on into the position and walked right into unit HQ.

We then carried on back to Brigade HQ and whilst Des went to a debrief we were putting up bivvies well away from the 'brigade target' in the cover of some peat cuttings. We remember Max Hastings (one of the attached journalists) came and bivvied with us and did his best to grill us on our tasks, obviously to no avail.

The two sections rested up all day on 10 June and were next deployed on the night of 11 June.

During the Goat Ridge patrol, on the morning of 9 June I was called to the brigade commander. I was tasked to visit 42 Commando to confirm their fitness and whether they were able to carry out the next phase of operations. This would be the brigade's assaults on the first set of mountains: Harriet, Two Sisters and Longdon. I wasn't too happy with this task as I had many friends in 42 and did not want to jeopardise their friendship but I fully understood the brigadier's dilemma. K Company of 42 had been on Mount Kent since 31 May without bivouacs and sleeping bags and with poor supplies of rations. All this whilst under sporadic Argentine artillery fire and in weather conditions that could readily be described as horrific. Although not seriously cold, the combination of close to zero temperatures with snow, sleet and rain and a constant southerly Antarctic wind produced a serious windchill effect well below the actual air temperature. After ten days of this it was no surprise that the brigadier wanted assurances that they would be able to carry out his plans and not become casualties with cold weather injuries hindering their ability to soldier.

I set off from Brigade HQ quite early on 9 June and travelled to the main 42 Commando position on Mount Challenger. I did not go to Mount Kent because I thought that if the rest of the unit was in fine fettle then K Company would fight through with them and I was not going to be a cause of distress to K Company. I first visited Lieutenant Colonel Nick Vaux and Major Guy Sheridan (the CO and his second-in-command) in their two-man tent as Guy was producing a very good wet for himself and his CO. We had a quick chat, and I explained that I was visiting to see how my patrol on Goat Ridge was getting on (although I am absolutely sure they saw through this wafer-thin story), and they confirmed to me that the HQ was fine and ready to go. I then went to visit support company, whose boss was Captain Phil Wilson, recently posted from Brigade HQ. Phil was in a sordid bivouac with his recce troop commander, Lieutenant Chris Mawhood, who had recently passed his ML course and was a square peg in a square hole doing a very good job for 42 Commando. After the usual piss-taking, I found that they were all in fine fettle and raring to go. After that I visited those members of the recce troop whom I knew and chatted to a few other NCOs and Marines I knew from support company. It was clear that this was a fine unit and very ready for what was ahead. I moved around the area talking to a few people and generally checking out their physical status. It was clear that they were all okay but definitely starting to feel the effects of the weather and the hardships of the situation, but they were determined to see the thing through to the end.

I made my way back to Brigade HQ and reported to the brigade commander. I told him that in my opinion 42 Commando was ready to go, with fine morale, and although suffering from the conditions the men were certainly up for any task he could throw at them. I did point out that if we were to stay in the same locations for more than another few days, he might have to consider withdrawing 42 Commando to the rear for a short period in order for them to get some proper rest out of the weather as much as possible. I felt that if the next battles were not started soon, 42 would not be in a position to give their very best. He responded by saying that my opinion fitted in with those of Hector Gullan and Viv Rowe, who had also visited the unit the day before, and I should not worry because they would be fighting their battle within the next 48 hours. This was the first time I had known when the next battles were to begin and I returned to the Cadre HQ to get prepared for the workload that was about to get a bit heavier.

During the period after 8 June the 2 Section OP on Mount Challenger, led by Colour Sergeant Young with Sergeant Jim Martin and Corporals John White and Jim O'Connor, had been carefully observing the Argentine positions on and around Mount Harriet. They had been sending numerous sighting reports and requesting several artillery fire missions which had all been successfully managed by the section. The priority of the gunners was to build up artillery ammunition stocks to cope with the oncoming brigade assaults on the Argentine positions. As a result they became more and more possessive over their ammunition, and less prepared to use their guns to harass enemy locations. One of the tasks requested by Colour Sergeant Young was to shell an Argentine queue that had formed up to collect their breakfast early one morning. I passed the request to the gunners but it was refused on the grounds that it would be 'a waste of their ammunition'. I took exception to this decision and visited Brigade HQ and asked the particular gunner why he did not wish to cause some very heavy casualties to an easy and necessary target. He told me he thought it would be a waste of valuable ammunition. I therefore went over his head and spoke to the brigade chief of staff, Major John Chester, explaining that my section was established in Argentine territory and taking more than a few risks. The least we could do was support them, especially as it would certainly cause serious harm to the enemy. John Chester agreed with me and ordered the gunner to carry out the mission. With some grumpiness he agreed but insisted that he wanted a full report on the effect of the fire on the enemy once the mission was completed. I passed this on to Ev Young, who was surprised but got on with it. After the mission had been completed, I received a clear and honest report back from 2 Section. The report stated that the mission was successful and the queue had disbanded; no Argentines got their breakfast and casualties were caused to the enemy. This was not considered enough by the now very grumpy gunner who asked for more. I asked Ev Young to elaborate and he responded that they had caused many casualties and he had seen many bodies and bits of bodies flying through the air, so many that he couldn't actually count the numbers. I relayed this to the gunner who was rather upset by the level of detail, but I was even less impressed by his complaint and spoke again to John Chester, asking him to provide my guys with the support they deserved when I forwarded requests for artillery support in the future. This he did.

This OP stayed in position providing constant and very useful information about the Argentine locations on Mount Harriet until the day after the enemy capitulation on 12 June, when they were withdrawn and returned to Teal Inlet.

Chapter 10

The Final Battles and the Move into Port Stanley
(10–14 June)

After the completion of the Goat Ridge patrol two things became apparent. First, that the war for the little units was effectively over on East Falkland. Second, that there was a reasonably large Argentine garrison on West Falkland, which we would have to take under control. I therefore started to rest up my sections at Teal Inlet in order to prepare for the new tasks.

On 10 June the Cadre was deployed as follows. HQ Section was divided in two, with Bill Wright remaining at Teal Inlet and a 'Cadre forward HQ' with the Brigade HQ at Mount Kent. 4 Section was positioned in an OP on Mount Vernet, prepared to cover any Argentine movement towards the brigade from the north and east. 2 Section had moved to an OP on Mount Challenger, to cover any possibility of an Argentine counter-attack from Stanley, and to provide artillery control for any enemy positions seen on Mount Harriet or its immediate area. 1 and 3 Sections were withdrawn to Teal Inlet to prepare for assisting 5 Brigade with its approach to the start lines for their upcoming battles. 5, 6 and 7 Sections were to remain in Teal Inlet and prepare for operations on West Falkland.

None of us had much idea of what was to come but we were all sure that the battle for Stanley was about to begin and that the outcome would be a British victory. The first battles for Harriet (42 Commando), Two Sisters (45 Commando) and Mount Longdon (3 Para) were to take place over the night of 11 June. The orders were that once the battles had been won the three units were to exploit forward towards Stanley, with 3 Para taking Wireless Ridge, 45 Commando taking Tumbledown and 42 Commando taking Mount William. The first three battles took longer than initially planned, and so the decision was taken not to exploit beyond the initial targets. This was because it was thought that daylight battles should not take place in such open country. The consequence of this was that the second phase of the divisional assault was to be by 5 Brigade, with the Scots Guards taking Mount Tumbledown, 2 Para (back under command of 3 Cdo Bde) taking Wireless Ridge, the Gurkhas taking Mount William and then the Welsh Guards (reinforced by support company and two rifle companies of 40 Commando) taking Sapper Hill and the immediate approach to Stanley. This could not happen on the night of 12 June for a number of reasons and so was set to take place on the night of 13 June.

The Cadre had no involvement in the 11 June battles. We were, however, asked to provide 42 Commando with a protection team for two Blowpipe sections that were to be tasked with providing anti-aircraft cover for their battle on Mount Harriet. When asked to provide two sections for this task I asked the brigade commander to reconsider. I was not at all sure that it was a job for the Cadre and felt that the risk of 'overs' from both Mount Harriet and Two Sisters would make it a suicidal operation. I remember telling the brigadier that if he ordered me to do it then I would, but that I would rather not. I felt that the risk of nocturnal air attacks was very low and the risk of unnecessary casualties very high. He agreed with me and that patrol did not take place, much to my relief.

I remember watching the battles from the safety of Mount Kent and being astonished at the amount of firepower used by both sides. All three battles must have been very bloody affairs. When the final casualty reports were sent to Brigade HQ on the morning of 12 June I was surprised and delighted at the unexpectedly low number of casualties suffered by our three units. I was particularly pleased to hear that K Company of 42 Commando (who led the battle for Mount Harriet) had taken few casualties, even though the Company HQ had taken a direct hit from Argentine shellfire. I remembered my conversation with Kay Babbington in Arbroath about keeping an eye out for her husband Peter, the commander of K Company, and was anxious to find out who had been injured.

That morning (12 June) started with the news that 3 Cdo Bde was settled on the tops of Harriet, Two Sisters and Longdon. A break had been ordered in the battles to give 5 Brigade the opportunity to get organised and to prepare for the next phase. This was to be the 2 Para attack (as part of 3 Cdo Bde) on Wireless Ridge, with 5 Brigade, led by the Scots Guards, attacking Mount Tumbledown. I was tasked with sending 1 and 3 Sections to lead the Scots Guards to their start line to the west of Mount Tumbledown. They were the obvious choice because of their participation in the Goat Ridge patrol and their intimate knowledge of the ground between Mount Harriet and Mount Tumbledown. The intention was that 1 Section would lead the Scots Guards to their start line and then 3 Section would join the Gurkhas and lead them to their start line for the follow-on attack on Mount William.

In the meantime, a Cadre patrol was tasked on the morning of 12 June to clear four grid squares of a possible Argentine OP in the area to the south and west of Mount Kent. I found this rather strange at the time as the Argentines had sent so few patrols west of the main mountains during the campaign and after the attack at Top Malo House any attempts to patrol west of their main positions had stopped altogether. I was very surprised therefore to learn that an Argentine OP was suspected 3km into what was now clearly British territory. Nonetheless, 1 Section (Lieutenant Haddow), 3 Section (Sergeant Wassall), 6 Section (Colour Sergeant Montgomery) and 7 Section (Sergeant Rowe) were each tasked to clear one of the four grid squares during daylight on 12 June. This they did very successfully, finding nothing untoward, and then returning to Teal Inlet to await further orders. Colour Sergeant Young and his section (2) were withdrawn from their OP just after first light on 12 June and also returned to Teal Inlet to await further orders.

By the evening of 12 June therefore the majority of the Cadre was at Teal Inlet, with 4 Section still in an OP at Mount Vernet and Cadre HQ at Mount Kent with Brigade HQ. 1 and 3 Sections were waiting to move to assist the 5 Brigade attack and were also close to Brigade HQ.

The next day, 13 June, was a quiet day for us all and by late afternoon 1 and 3 Sections were with their respective units preparing for the move up to their attacks that night. The Scots Guards, led by 1 Section, moved to the fence line just to the west of Mount Tumbledown, which was their start line. 3 Section meanwhile had joined the Gurkhas ready to take them to their start line for the attack on Mount William as soon as Tumbledown was secured.

Once the two section commanders had been briefed and set off for their tasks, I realised that we were very short of rations. I took advantage of the quiet time to get on a Gazelle helicopter and return to Teal Inlet to acquire more rations for the HQ. I also had the opportunity to talk to Bill Wright, which I had not been able to do for over a week. As always, he was full of beans and ready for anything. We kept our discussion brief. I told him that as soon as it was over, he was to get everyone and all the kit to Stanley as quickly as possible. I would let him know where to rendezvous with us at the HQ. Returning to Mount Kent with my box of rations, I was told in no uncertain terms by the brigadier to hurry up and get out of the helo as he needed it right away. This was very unlike him but I did as I was told. As he took off, I was left to enquire of my HQ team what I had missed. They told me that the Brigade HQ had just been bombed by some Skyhawks. Although nobody was hurt, it could have been a major disaster as all the COs had been there only moments earlier for a final Orders Group. It could have been a major coup for the Argentines and a disaster for all of us. I then understood the brigadier's impatience.

Sergeant John Rowe described his experience of the bombing:

> I remember being with Brigade HQ & Signals Squadron the night before the surrender and an air raid warning red came in and some-one in HQ & Sigs said 'don't worry, we're too far back to be affected'. I was just packing my bivvi gear away and could hear what sounded like gunfire and as I looked up the first wave of three Argentine A4 jets were coming straight for us. I managed to fire off a full magazine of ammunition at them; the aircraft to my right was so low and close, I could see that the pilot had a moustache. He then released a bomb from which a small parachute deployed and then I hit the deck. Luckily it landed in soft ground and did not cause any injuries. Right near my bivouac I picked up some pieces of shrapnel as souvenirs, which some thieving bastard nicked from me later. At this time a guy called Junior Young, who was with air defence troop, was stood up aiming a Blowpipe missile; realising the planes were in too close, he ditched it and dived into his trench. When he popped back out, I shouted 'Junior you're supposed to fire the f—ing thing, not throw it', to which his reply was a two-finger salute! The brigadier was nearby and I did not realise how fast he could move. His chopper had a hole in the windscreen. However, no one was injured in the attack because we were in a dip and as the aircraft came over the hill, they could not dip their guns to put fire down on us. Being killed at any time is not good but the day before they surrendered would have been shite!

This explained why the brigadier was a little tense when I arrived with my rations, not realising what I had missed!

When I had given 1 and 3 Sections their orders for the night ahead, I took care to brief both Lieutenant Haddow and Sergeant Wassall that they were not to get involved in either battle but to take the battalions to their start lines and then withdraw as soon as possible back to our lines. This was for two reasons. First, neither had worked or trained with their respective battalions and thus did not know what they would get up to once the proverbial hit the fan and second, they had already done enough and I did not want any of them to risk casualties unnecessarily. For

Sergeant Wassall this was academic, as ultimately the Gurkhas were not required to carry out their battle. For Lieutenant Haddow it was a little different. Once he got the Guards to their start line, he reported to their CO, who then told him to lead off up the hill. Haddow politely refused, explaining that it was not his battle and anyway he had been ordered by his boss not to cross the start line but to leave it to the Guards. This was accepted, so he and his section withdrew back to Brigade HQ.

The morning of 14 June was a beautifully clear day. I was on standby at Brigade HQ for any orders, should the Cadre be required. Shortly after first light we were told that the Argentines were leaving their locations and streaming back to Stanley. It appeared that they had had enough and had decided there was little point in resisting further. Brigadier Thompson called me in and told me to get into Stanley and find a location for him to set up the Brigade HQ there.

I got hold of a Gazelle helicopter and pilot and asked him to take me to Stanley. The pilot was Lieutenant Bill Scott, an old friend who had been in 40 Commando when I commanded the Recce Tp six years before. I had the heaviest rucksack I have ever carried, having put an entire PRC 320 radio and ancillaries into it along with all my usual stuff. As I picked it up to put it into the helicopter, the entire right shoulder strap separated from the rest of it. It had completely given up the ghost! It was a struggle to load it into the aircraft in this state and as I climbed into the Gazelle I caught my rifle on something. I pulled it clear with some irritation and the muzzle jerked up and pierced the roof of the aircraft. Bill was not best pleased and I remember him telling me that that was the only undamaged part of his aircraft until I turned up! None the less, we took off for Stanley – and what a sight it was.

By then the Argentine retreat was just about over but everywhere we looked there were troops making their way towards Stanley. We were a bit behind the curve, thank goodness. We hover-taxied along the coast road towards Government House. When we reached the last of the British troops I asked Bill to drop me off on the road. He moved down and towards the road (breaking some telephone wires as he did so!) and put his skids down. I jumped out, keeping my headset on until I was completely clear. As I was about to take my headset off, Bill told me to look up. I saw Max Hastings, one of the journalists, waving his hands and gesturing for a ride in the helicopter. Bill asked me what he should do. I told him to let me get clear, and then take off and return to Brigade HQ for the brigade commander, who had higher priority than a press man. Bill chuckled and said 'Wilco!' I removed my headset, returned it to the cabin and lay down over my gear as he took off. Once he had gone I picked up my rucksack and watched Max Hastings throw a complete tantrum, smashing his walking stick on the road. After four or five hits it broke into two or three pieces, rather to his surprise. He shouted at me that he had wanted that helicopter and I should have held it for him. I was not impressed, and told him so.*

I made my way along the coast road towards the entrance to the race-course, where I had seen a large detached building that I thought would be a good spot for Brigade HQ. The whole road was full of paras (2 Para, I would find out later), all wearing their red berets and all cock-a-hoop about being in Stanley. On entering the big building I met some 2 Para officers and explained that I had been sent to find a location for Brigade HQ. They kindly offered me the upper floor of the building, as they had already claimed the downstairs for themselves and their HQ. I went upstairs and set up my radio and sent a short message to Brigade HQ advising them of my location and saying that I would remain here until they arrived. I also told my HQ team to get to Stanley as fast as they could and establish our HQ with the Brigade HQ. Having received confirmation to both messages, I relaxed and looked at my surroundings.

I was surrounded on all sides by soldiers, mostly Paras but also many Argentines, all fully armed and walking amongst one another with little or no sign of aggression. The Argentines had obviously had enough, as had the British, but the Argentine reaction was surreal. They were neither surly nor aggressive, but entirely passive in their comprehension that it was all over. It appeared that it was not at all dangerous and I saw no examples of aggression from either side. The opposing forces were studiously ignoring one another. The Argentines were all trying to head east towards the piers at the eastern end of the coast road and the British appeared to be milling around the racecourse, having been told not to go beyond Government House (about 200m beyond the racecourse). I waited for the arrival of Sergeant Mclean and Corporal West, along with the rest of the Brigade HQ. Time seemed to stand still and I have no idea how long I waited. Eventually I met some of the brigade staff, as well as my team, and we set up our HQ in one of the upstairs rooms.

* Many years later Bill Scott, by then a very experienced pilot for Virgin Airlines, told me that when he got back to Brigade HQ he was ordered to return to Stanley to pick up Max Hastings and take him to HMS *Fearless* so that he could send a report of the surrender back to the papers in the UK!

During this wait I was asked by Major Hector Gullan to assist him with getting hold of the various COs in order for the brigadier to hold an Orders Group. Our first port of call was downstairs, where we walked into one of the rooms looking for the CO. In the room were seven or eight Paras all sitting around a pot stew with their spoons in their hands sharing a meal. I asked for the CO and was greeted with a rather sarcastic comment from one of them to the effect of 'What are you doing here? Why aren't in the rear with the rest of the Marines?' At this point Hector appeared and told the cheeky Para to 'Bottle it – he's done his fair share of the work.' Hector recognised Lieutenant Colonel Chandler, the CO, and asked him to make himself available for an O Group upstairs as soon as he had eaten. The CO said he would and Hector and I left. Hector apologised for the Para's comment but I brushed it aside. Inter-service rivalries were bound to return sooner or later, and it would appear it was to be sooner! Hector offered to get the rest of the COs himself and thanked me for my help.

After that I went for a walk to see what was happening and headed towards Government House. Just before I arrived there I saw the telephone and telegraph office, so I thought I might see if I could phone home. I met the operator inside and asked him if it was possible to make a phone call to my family in England. He requested the number, dialled it and handed me a phone. I called my eldest sister June, whom I knew would be at home with her family, and she could tell the rest of our family that I was fine and it was all over. After three or four rings my brother-in-law answered. He was delighted to hear from me and called June to the phone. I told her that I was phoning from Stanley, that the war was over and I was fine and unharmed. She was very down to earth and said immediately that she would call the rest of the family and pass on the news. After that I really had nothing to say and I think she realised that I had run out of steam so she wished me well, promised again to tell everyone and we rang off. I asked the operator how much I owed him and would he take a credit card, and he simply replied that it was he who owed me, that my money was no use to him, and to have a nice day! It was my first experience of the kindness of just about everyone I met after it was all over, both in the islands and the UK when we returned.

It was then that I decided to find out what had happened to K Company in general and Peter Babbington in particular. I thought that if I was to find him, I shouldn't go empty-handed so I took a walk towards Government House, to where I had seen a whole load of Argentine stores containers, to see what I could find. As luck would have it, the first container

I looked into was full of Argentine rations and cases of 2-litre plastic bottles of Argentine wine. I filled up my combat jacket with six or eight bottles of the wine and headed west, searching for K Company. About 450m on I came across fellow green beret wearers and asked who they were. They were from 45 Commando so I asked the whereabouts of 42 Commando. They pointed west and directed me to the edge of town where they said they had seen 42 starting to bivouac.

Shortly after speaking to the 45 guys, I noticed a couple of Argentine bodies on the side of the road. Someone (probably from 2 Para) had put some corrugated iron over them to give a little protection from vehicles. It looked as if they had been injured and told to make their own way back to the hospital. Both died of their injuries en route. It struck me as a further example of the appalling way in which the Argentines treated their own men. Sadly, we were to see more of the same as the days progressed.

I walked on down the road and the next bunch I spoke to were 42 Commando. They pointed me towards an enormous hangar-sized building, which I was advised was K Company's location. I asked to see the company commander and was shown to a small room which held the HQ team. They all had metal mugs in their hands and were drinking a communal wet of something or other. Following the usual greetings, I proudly asked if that was the best they could do and produced a few of my bottles of wine. The hot wets were immediately ditched and we had a toast or two with Argentine Malbec. Peter was unhurt but his second in command, Lieutenant Chris Whitely, had been injured in the shelling, as had Sergeant Shepherd, one of his SNCOs. I was sorry to hear this news because I knew Shepherd well, as he had been one of my snipers in 40 Commando Recce Tp, but I was very pleased to see that Peter was alive and well.

I noticed that all the guys were holding their hands over their mugs whilst drinking tea and had continued to do so after it had been replaced with wine. I asked why, and was told that the upper floor and the roof must be leaking as drips were continuously falling from above and they didn't want them to fall in their drinks. It was discovered the next morning that the Argentines had used the upper floor as a temporary mortuary, where they threw all the bodies of soldiers who had succumbed to their wounds, along with any amputated parts of soldiers who had had surgery. With no heating it was particularly cold, and it worked very well as a mortuary until a hundred or so hot Royal Marines increased the temperature to above freezing and everything began to thaw – hence the drips!

Whilst we were enjoying our illicit wine Peter's forward observation officer, Captain Chris Romberg RA, appeared at the door and asked us what we were drinking. Peter replied 'Good Argentine wine', but Chris responded 'Well, throw that away and try some really good Scottish malt whisky!' Chris had done the same as me but had actually visited Government House and raided the cellar, where he found the whisky supply. We all emptied our metal mugs and replenished them with some very fine malt.

The next few minutes were spent enjoying the company of old friends and the success of the mission. A few silly stories were shared and a few lies were told but after about half an hour I started to feel guilty about what I was doing. Just then there was a knock at the door. A messenger had arrived to tell Peter that his presence was required at Brigade HQ as he had a task to complete. I told Peter that as I was based at Brigade HQ and knew exactly where it was, I would walk there with him. Having not drunk any alcohol for over three weeks I was already feeling a little light-headed, as was Peter, so it was a timely call for us both.

We set off for Brigade HQ along the coast road. When we arrived, I slid off to the room where my guys were settled. Having greeted them both, I leaned forward to get a couple of bottles of the wine out of my combat jacket. As I did so, my rifle slid off my shoulder and landed on the top of Sergeant 'Mac' Mclean's head. 'Mac' was not best pleased but soon forgave me when I apologised and offered him some wine. Suddenly we heard the brigadier's voice saying rather loudly, 'I understand that there is some looting going on in Stanley. We need to put an immediate stop to it as I will not allow it to happen.' We instantly hid our remaining couple of bottles of wine and tried to look completely innocent (very unsuccessfully) as we continued to drink the illicit Malbec.

Meanwhile, Peter was being given orders by the brigadier to get his company ready to provide protection for the Argentine officers' mess near the town pier. Apparently, the Argentine soldiers were getting ready to burn it down and the Argentine senior officers had asked for assistance and protection from attack by their own soldiers! Fortunately for K Company and Peter, the riot came to nothing but it was a tense moment for all concerned.

The day was over. The Cadre was mostly in Teal Inlet with one section (4 Section, Sergeant Kev Mahon) on Mount Vernet and three of us in Stanley. I spoke to Bill Wright on the radio and told him to get the rest to Stanley as fast as possible and I would meet him at Government House when he arrived.

For the first time in thirty-six days I had a clear and full night's sleep, on the floor of the room in Brigade HQ.

Chapter 11

Port Stanley
(14–22 June)

Early in the morning of 15 June I was called to see the brigade commander. He told me to get my guys out of the field and into Stanley as soon as possible. I was able to reassure him that the move was already in hand. He wanted to know the condition of the runway at Port Stanley Airport. He told me to get out there and let him know how much damage, if any, had been done to the main runway and to see if it was usable for C130s.

By that stage we knew that the Argentines had formally surrendered on East Falkland and that they were all being moved to the airport for easier management of the very large number of prisoners for whom we were now responsible. I grabbed Sergeant 'Mac' Mclean and Corporal Neil West as bodyguards and set off for the airport. As I was leaving Brigade HQ the SBS liaison officer, Captain Barry Heath, a friend of many years, asked me where I was going and when I told him his immediate response was 'Can I come too?' I asked him what weaponry he had, and learning that he had an automatic weapon I said of course. It turned out that his weapon was a 9mm Ingrams automatic pistol (great for movies but completely useless for anything other than very close work!). We all walked out onto the coast road and when the first vehicle appeared I stood in the middle of the road and stopped it. I commandeered it, telling the Argentines to get out. To my surprise the officer, who spoke very good English and was a brigadier and an engineer, immediately handed over the vehicle. We loaded up and set off for the airport.

At the end of the coast road we had to negotiate our way around J Company of 42 Commando, who were very busy disarming every Argentine en route to the airport. I briefly spoke to Major Mike Norman, the company commander, and asked if there had been any problems but he was busy and a bit short so I simply asked for directions to the airport. He pointed east, telling me to follow my nose! It became a rather surreal experience. There were hundreds of Argentines on the road, not all of them disarmed, heading the same way as us. I soon appreciated that they were not at all interested in making a nuisance of themselves; as far as they were concerned, the war was over and they had had enough. Barry noted that there were a lot of guys dismantling weapons such as 20mm AAA (automatic anti-aircraft weapons) and various artillery pieces. As that made life easier for us, I was happy to ignore them.

When we arrived at the airport I drove straight onto the runway and proceeded to drive its periphery for the entire length taking photos when I could and noting the condition of the surface. It was uncanny, as I was expecting damage both from the Vulcan bombing before D Day and from various RN Harrier attacks throughout the fighting. I found no damage whatsoever. There was no sign of any damage repair. In one area some attempt at camouflage had been made to make it look damaged, with paint and some soil. The airfield runway was in my opinion completely un-damaged and ready for use. The four of us held a little meeting and we agreed that that was the case. We loaded up to get back to Brigade HQ and report to the brigadier.

As we were leaving the airfield, I noticed two long wheelbase Safari Landrovers parked on the side of the road. They were both left hand drive and ideal for use in Norway or on the continent. I stopped our vehicle and walked over to a bunch of Argentines to find out who was in command. A smart major appeared and responded in English that he was in com-mand and that the vehicles were his. I told him I was commandeering one of them. He replied that the keys were in them. I selected the one that looked the cleanest and smartest and requested that he take all the Argen-tine kit out of it as they would be needing their stuff. He agreed but looked rather surprised and turned to some of his men, ordering them to clear the vehicle. I told 'Mac' Mclean to follow close behind and we set off towards Stanley. After about 30m I realised that the clutch did not work and the vehicle was unserviceable. I stopped, told 'Mac' to wait and walked back to the Argentine to tell him that the clutch was not working and the vehicle was useless. He replied that had I asked him, he would have told me that himself as they had had to tow it there in the first place! I told him we would be taking the other vehicle and he shrugged and ordered his men to clear it of their kit and equipment. As we stood waiting for the vehicle to be cleared, I noticed that the other vehicle bore markings indicating that it was an Argentine Marines vehicle. I asked the major where he had been fighting in the battle for Port Stanley. His response was that he would happily give me his name, rank and number but was not prepared at all to talk about anything to do with the fight for the Malvinas. I advised him that I had little interest in any military information from him but was just passing the time of day. I also told him that I had been involved in fighting for the return of the Falklands Islands to the UK and had no interest in *Las Malvinas* or Argentina's involvement there whatsoever. We parted with smiles. I was impressed with this man's stature and obvious professionalism and rather hoped that we would meet again under different circumstances at some time in the future. He was the only Argentine with whom I felt any comradeship during the entire period and I would have liked to know his name. I found out later that he had been the commander of the Argentine Marines defending Mount Tumbledown and had behaved with courage and professionalism throughout the war. I was not at all surprised.

The second vehicle was fine so we returned to Stanley in a convoy of two vehicles. Mine was a left-hand drive UK Landrover and the other an Argentine Mercedes Benz. We had not gone far when a vehicle appeared driving towards us. He was driving on the right of the road and I was driving on the left. As we approached Barry commented 'This could be interesting!' After my previous encounter I was determined to get the upper hand over someone, so I pressed on and the two vehicles stopped about 20m apart. We stared at each other. I was about to get out when the passenger in the Argentine vehicle gestured to his driver to pull over to his left and then drove past us on our right. I'm sure we weren't the only ones to have such an experience but it felt as if we were the first to make the Argentines drive on our side of the road rather than theirs!

At Brigade HQ I went directly to the brigadier and informed him that the airfield was dirty, and there were many damaged aircraft parked around the periphery of the runway, but the runway itself was completely undamaged and usable and a C130 could land on it right now if needed. We all knew that the Argentine Air Force had been landing C130s right up to the night of 10 June, but this was valuable information for the brigadier. He told me to get my guys into Stanley and to find accommodation as close to Government House as possible as he needed his personal bodyguards to be close at all times. This comment gave me a great boost and I went back to my guys feeling a lot taller!

The remainder of 15 June was spent getting into two buildings just opposite the post office: the Malvinas guesthouse and its next-door neighbour. I then managed to acquire a helicopter in order to fetch my sections out of the field and bring those in Teal Inlet into Stanley. I finally ensured that all our kit and equipment had been transferred or was being transferred from Teal Inlet to Stanley.

I met Bill Wright, my CSM, and passed on the immediate plan which was to get settled into Stanley and clean and re-ammo ready for any operations on West Falkland. As usual he took this with aplomb and told me he had organised a helo for the pick-ups and was also sorting out the other tasks and making preparations. I was introduced to the owners of the Malvinas guesthouse who apologised for the name and told me that they would be renaming it very soon! They invited us for a meal for all the guys on the house that night. I asked if they could postpone it for a night as we would have the whole team in Stanley by then and they agreed. However, they needed to dig up their wine cellar first and asked whether we would be prepared to give them a hand. It transpired that when the Argentines had invaded, the owners had dug a pit in the back garden and buried their entire wine cellar and camouflaged it by moving their garden shed over the hole. They were not prepared to let the Argentines have any of their wines so our first job in Stanley was to dig up the contents of their wine cellar!

The next night was a strange but enjoyable one. We had gathered all the Cadre in Stanley and were firmly established in two large houses next to the green leading to Government House. We were stood down and no longer on standby for West Falkland operations. We were scruffy and dirty after four weeks in the field but still invited to a formal dinner of roast mutton by the owners of the guesthouse. I don't remember much of the night but I do remember lots of toasts from all sides, singing the National Anthem at one stage and my unrestrained hilarity and relief that it was over and we had all made it.

My memories of the period from 15 June until we embarked on RFA *Resource* on 21 June are completely confused. I remember a host of incidents and experiences but am unable to put them in any sort of chronological order so what follows are my memories as they come to me.

I do know that after the surrender on 14 June and the negotiations that followed, the Argentines stated that as far as they were concerned all hostilities in the Falkland Islands were over. This was not passed to the rest of us for a couple of days so until early on the 16th we were still preparing for the next phase. After hearing that it was all over, we switched to getting sorted out, cleaned up and back to normal.

On the afternoon of 16 June I was called to Brigade HQ and told to produce my citation recommendations for honours and awards for Cadre personnel. I had to submit them by first thing the next morning! I had been thinking about this already and had planned to sit down on the trip back and make a proper job of it so that I could get the best results for my guys. This short notice order was provoked by instructions from the UK and applied to all the troops in the Falkland Islands. Needless to say, there were many of us who had a sleepless night. I called my section commanders together and asked for recommendations; with their information I sat down and spent the hardest night I can remember of my trip south. In the end I forwarded nine citations and was eventually successful with seven of them: a Military Medal for Sergeant Des Wassall, Mentions in Despatches for Lieutenant Fraser Haddow, Colour Sergeant Chopper Young and Sergeant Chris Stone, and Commander in Chief's Commendations for Colour Sergeant Phil Montgomery, Sergeant Jan Rowe and Corporal Tim Holleran. Sadly, from my point of view, the final two I put forward (Lieutenant Callum Murray and Colour Sergeant Bill Wright) did not receive the awards which they both thoroughly deserved and I hold myself responsible for failing to get them the proper recognition.

One of the jobs being issued to all units in Stanley was to clear their immediate areas of the mess and detritus left by the Argentines. They had left Stanley in a disgusting state. It was a very dangerous area for everybody, and especially for civilians and children. Two incidents come immediately to mind. First, I visited the HQ of 45 Commando to say hello and met their operations officer, Captain Mike Hitchcock, an old friend, sweeping up with a broom a mixture of unfired rifle ammunition and hand grenades that had been left behind by the enemy troops. Second, I was given the post office as the Cadre's cleaning task. I thought it was a good deal until we entered the building. It had been used by the Argentines as a latrine and was disgusting. It was covered in excrement and urine and made a clear statement about the lack of discipline in the Argentine forces. Needless to say, we got stuck in with a will and sorted the mess out as fast as we could.

Once the post office was as clean as we could make it, the postal workers agreed to open up for business. Chopper Young had advised me earlier that as soon as it was open we should get in quickly and buy all the first day covers for sale. I was the very first customer and I bought every single first day cover they had for sale for both the Falkland Islands, South Georgia and the other dependencies. It was not a large quantity, as their stocks were quite limited, but I thought I had scored a tremendous coup thanks to Chopper's knowledge of philately. Unfortunately, he had failed to tell me that I needed to get them all stamped with an Argentine post office stamp for authentication and for it to be dated 14 June 1982. Therefore, I bought a whole load of first day covers that could have been bought anywhere in the world at any time! The post office staff destroyed all the

Argentine stamps and paperwork as their first job after taking back control, so I was unable to follow up on a later date. I still have a few which are, of course, worth very little but remain interesting to me, as do all the other first day covers held by the guys to whom I gave copies.

One of the difficulties we all experienced was personal hygiene. I (and most of my guys) had been lucky and had been able to have a bucket bath in Teal Inlet. We were, however, suffering from a month of wearing the same clothes and by the time we got to Stanley we were less than clean and tidy. One of the LSLs was docked in Port Stanley and became the cleaning/showering/dhobi ship for the force. A rota was established for the major units but not for the minor ones and it was because of this that I realised that now the war was over we were effectively orphans and had to look after ourselves. This was not a big revelation but it did influence our modus operandi so, guided by Bill Wright, I began to make plans for our return to the UK. We all needed a good shower and a full change of clothes before anything else. This we accomplished by marching up to the LSL and explaining to the mate that we were only thirty-three strong and could readily get ourselves sorted with the minimum of fuss and did not need to get any special timings as a result. He reacted by saying 'No problem, get yourselves on board and help yourselves to whatever you need.' This came as no great surprise at all to me, since this was exactly how the RFA had been operating throughout the whole campaign. We tramped on board with towels and dhobi kit and shared the remarkable experience of scrubbing off four weeks' worth of grime. To say we were ecstatic would not be an overstatement, and the feeling of cleanliness was definitely life-enhancing.

We now needed to get all our kit together. We had left two Chacons on RFA *Sir Tristram*, having only taken one ashore. The two remaining on board contained all our Arctic kit, along with our personal stuff. The one ashore had all our operational kit. I thus became a past master at getting hold of helicopters in order to consolidate our kit. Bill, meanwhile, had decided that we needed to repay the hospitality shown to us at Teal Inlet. The places where we had stayed had fed us, baked bread for us and generally used all their stored winter supplies to make life easier for us. Bill's first bit of foraging took him to an Argentine quartermaster's store from where he appropriated a few beef carcasses and several hundred-weight bags of flour, along with lots of other goodies like salt, spices and tins of vegetables. This made an almost full load for the Chinook helicopter so he arranged for it all to be taken to Teal Inlet in one go. It was very well received by all concerned!

After our kit had arrived in Stanley, we needed to get to Bluff Cove to see if our two Chacons on board RFA *Sir Tristram* could be removed to Port Stanley. We arrived in Bluff Cove to find *Sir Tristram* aground on the beach and her entire rear part destroyed by fire. Gaining access was easy but disappointing as the two Chacons had been completely wrecked. The damage was not caused by Argentine bombs but by British soldiers on a looting spree when they were on board without proper supervision. I found this particularly upsetting and swore to get justice. None of our personal kit was salvageable and was either missing or destroyed, so we were all left with what we had carried for the previous four weeks. Bill Wright and I flew back to Stanley seriously angry that our own side had poorer discipline than the enemy. Arriving back in Stanley I went straight to Divisional HQ and spoke to the chief of staff, who had taken me through training some thirteen years before. He was horrified at what we had found but the policy decision (as this had happened to other units of the brigade) was that all claims for loss would be treated as caused by enemy action and thus be fully replaced in a like-for-like manner. I found this unfathomable and was absolutely furious. I did not agree but I was told in no uncertain terms that the war was over and no further action would be taken to spoil the reputation of any army unit. I moved on.

Once the decision was made to return the Argentine prisoners to their homeland on board the SS *Canberra*, the writing was on the wall for the return of 3 Cdo Bde to the UK. I visited the brigade commander and was given permission to organise my own unit's return journey. RFA *Resource* had arrived in Stanley on 17 June and on about 20 June Bill Wright and I went on board to see if we could scrounge a lift back with them. It seemed right as we had sailed from the UK on her and this would complete the circle. I went to visit the captain and over a cup of coffee I asked him if he could help me out. He said he would love to but was now under full peacetime rules and could only carry passengers up to the amount of lifesaving equipment he had on board. He had already agreed to return the SBS to the UK, so the ship was effectively full. I asked him what was needed for thirty-three men. He said if I could find life rafts for thirty that would be sufficient. I knew where there was one 10-man life raft, and I was sure that with our resources we could obtain a further two from somewhere on East Falkland. He told me that he would be sailing in a couple of days so I would need to get them quickly as he would not allow me to join the ship until all three life rafts were on board. I set off back to the gangway, calling for Bill Wright on the way. We re-embarked aboard the LSU that we were using and I told him the story. His immediate reaction was 'Bugger, I'll have to use the one I've got for my yacht!' We therefore already had one and I knew of another on a damaged Argentine patrol vessel in Goose Green. Bill said he would talk to the RN clearance diving team to see if they knew where one was. By the time we got to shore we had created a plan to source the two required life rafts.

I sent off a small team to Goose Green to find the damaged patrol boat and to bring back the best of its life rafts. Meanwhile Bill and I went to visit the clearance diving team to see if they could help. They, like us, had begun to feel like orphans as they were also a small unit, though, unlike us, they were still deeply involved in making safe the large quantity of Argentine ordnance that had been left behind. They would not be leaving in a hurry so were willing to help us. Shortly thereafter I received a message that they had found a 10-man life raft on a semi-sunken Argentine ship alongside in Port Stanley. We arranged to meet and set off to collect this one. The pick-up team consisted of Bill Wright and me, accompanied by Everett Young (my TQ), David Nicholls (my predecessor at the Cadre, now working in Divisional HQ) and the CO and his WO1 from the clearance diving team. We successfully collected the raft and were making our way to the coast road before taking it to our HQ when an Argentine Mercedes stopped in front of us and out stepped a Royal Military Police corporal, complete with red cap! In conventional style he asked 'What's going on here?' To which Bill Wright replied 'Sir!', and then explained 'There are two Royal Marines captains, a Royal Naval lieutenant commander and a Royal Naval WO1 with two Royal Marines colour sergeants, so you should complete your question with "Sir".' This flustered the corporal who started to bluster about stealing equipment and was instantly stopped by Bill, who explained that the life raft was required by RFA *Resource* and we were on the way there to deliver it, so he should get out of our way because it was very heavy and we had a long way to go. Confronted with such bare-faced cheek, the RMP corporal tried to save face by saying okay but looting was a crime. Bill replied cockily, 'In that case get out of our way and make sure none of it is taking place elsewhere so that we can finish carrying out our duty to RFA *Resource*!' It was clear that I was in the company of a master acquirer, which came as no surprise as I had known Bill for ten years, and we prepared to carry the raft the 300m or so to our lodgings.

On the morning of 21 June I cleared it with the brigade commander that we intended to embark on the *Resource* that day and he agreed that we could, and so we arranged to get ourselves and our kit on board that afternoon.

My first job was to get the long wheelbase Safari Landrover that I had acquired from the Argentine Marines delivered to the *Resource* for transport back to the UK, where our fleet consisted of three vehicles and one driver and we were always short of transport. This extra vehicle would come in very useful, especially as it was left hand drive. I briefed the guys that if asked they were to say it was a diesel vehicle and thus acceptable for carriage on an ammunition ship such as *Resource*. I was not aware that Colour Sergeant Montgomery was also attempting to get an Argentine army vehicle on board, a Mercedes Benz jeep. When the first vehicle (the Landrover) was about to be landed on the deck of the *Resource*, the chief officer appeared and asked Corporal West whether it was petrol or diesel powered. Disastrously he replied 'petrol', and the chief officer refused to allow it on board. I had planned to completely drain it of all fuel, etc., as soon as we got it on board but had no chance as he was adamant and the order stood. The jeep was also disallowed! Corporal West made himself scarce for a couple of days whilst all calmed down!

My next job was to arrange for our Chacon and all our kit to be put into nets and transferred by helo to the *Resource*. This was going really well until the very last underslung load, by which time it was getting dark and we had no communications with the helo. The last sling was lifted but instead of heading out over the water the pilot set off in the direction of Bluff Cove. There was absolutely nothing we could do about it until the next day so Bill and I stayed in Port Stanley overnight whilst the rest embarked on *Resource*. Next morning, I got hold of a Sea King and we set off on the hunt for our underslung load. The helo had a couple of tasks that required it to go via Teal Inlet, San Carlos and then Goose Green before eventually getting to Bluff Cove. As we landed at the helo pad at Bluff Cove there was the underslung load lying in the middle of the landing site. Bill and I ran across and found that it was no longer complete. The personal goods were untouched but the three sniper rifle boxes (containing 7.62mm sniper rifles) had all disappeared – another example of the army's attitude to kit. We picked up the kit, loaded it into our helicopter and then flew straight to *Resource*, arriving mid-afternoon before the ship sailed at sunset that day, 22 June.

Chapter 12

Port Stanley to Arbroath
(22 June–9 July)

I awoke on the morning of 23 June expecting to be at sea but we were at anchor in San Carlos Water. We stayed there for the next two days, during which we watched SS *Canberra* sail past us en route to the UK with 3 Cdo Bde on board.

On 25 June we sailed again but this time we turned to the southeast and headed for South Georgia! By now I was beginning to feel a little anxious that we would be down south for a lot longer than anticipated. The trip was still very interesting, and when we joined the main fleet it was a pleasure to see HMS *Hermes* with her full load of Harriers on board. Large icebergs on the approach to Gritvyken made our arrival on 27 June fascinating. I called Captain Chris Nunn RM when we arrived. The commander of M Company, he had lost his brother during the battle for Goose Green. I had written to him at the time with my condolences but I knew that he was not fully aware of the circumstances surrounding his brother's death. I felt able to give him some consolation about the event.

After 24 hours at Gritvyken, where *Resource* removed most of her stores and transferred them to a couple of other RFAs, we set sail on 28 June and headed north at last. My memory of the voyage north is rather scanty. I remember telling all the guys that we were now on a holiday cruise and I wanted them all to relax and enjoy a proper break en route to Ascension Island. I ran around the deck for what seemed like hours every day mostly to kill time but also to recover from what had been about six weeks of limited exercise interspersed with moments of tremendously hard work. Running around the decks brought a welcome relaxation that I really enjoyed. It gave me valuable solitude. I had enjoyed the company of the others but now felt that a break was needed by all of us.

When not running around the deck or attending to personal administration, I sat down and set to writing my post operation report and a series of papers in preparation for the future of both the Cadre and also the ML branch as a whole. It seemed a good time to do this following the success of our operations during the conflict.

The first paper I wrote was titled 'A future operational role of the M&AW Cadre'. This in essence encapsulated all that we had achieved on Operation Corporate with an emphasis towards our usual area of operations. It required the splitting of the Cadre into training and operational organisations. Writing the paper, I appreciated several things that would affect the future. An organisation composed solely of NCOs and officers would not work and there would be a requirement for Marines to be part of the operational team. Much like the SBS, there was a need for young Marines to provide the manpower for the sections and the potential leaders of the future. In addition I felt that an operational cadre would need to be self-sufficient in skills such as signalling, intelligence gathering and the management of intelligence data and information. An operational cadre therefore would probably need significantly more manpower. My forecast size of the brigade patrol troop as I saw it was around sixty strong, consisting of two troops of about twenty each (five teams of four men), with an HQ cell, an intelligence section and administrative support team. The conclusion of this first paper made me realise that what the ML branch needed was an 'ML3' Marine in order to achieve the early manpower for future promotion and progress through the ranks.

My second paper was 'The introduction of the ML3 rating to the Corps'. I proposed a six-week ML3 course which would produce a highly skilled climber capable of seconding most climbing routes in support of his ML2 corporal, but who was also well used to operations in OPs and in reconnaissance roles. This Marine was readily available from the Recce Tps within the Corps already and it would merely be a centralisation and standardisation of the training already carried out within the Recce Tps of the Corps.

My third paper was written to help resolve the annual problem that on every ML2 course people arrived unprepared. The majority of failures on the ML2 course occurred during the first four weeks in Cornwall. They were caused by the combination of climbing for long hours, with the daily physical exercises required to get them fit enough for the rigours of working on skis whilst carrying heavy loads in Norway. In addition, the introduction to night operational climbing towards the end of week three caused many of the students to have second thoughts about their future in the ML branch. I wanted authority to run a one-week ML course selection period. This would not be a way of excluding people whom we thought did not fit but for them to appreciate exactly what they were committing to do. An example of what can happen occurred during my first ML course in September 1980. After three weeks one of the students came to see me and asked if he could withdraw from the course. He was doing well and had plenty of civilian climbing experience but found himself freaked out by the night climbing. He asked me how I coped with it and was horrified by my response. I told him I actually enjoyed it because it removed any feelings of exposure (fear of heights), as all I had to worry about was what I had just climbed and what was immediately ahead of me. I told him it felt like climbing in black and white rather than full colour and whilst I would not have done it as my first choice of pastime I had no problem with it. He had already ascended the north face of the Eiger in Switzerland and I reminded him that a lot of that would have been in darkness. I think it was the sea below and the noise of the waves that really threw him. He had to be removed, and one place on the course was lost because we had not discovered this before the course began.

I felt strongly that because the numbers of students we could accommodate on the courses were strictly limited, we should make sure that all who arrived would be able to stay the distance and not withdraw for reasons that could have been revealed beforehand. One week of selection training would give anyone who was not entirely certain that they wanted to be an ML the opportunity to find out.

I felt the time was right to set these three plans in motion in the light of our success during Operation Corporate and the work that had been carried out within the Cadre between 1980 and 1982. I completed the three papers between South Georgia and Ascension Island and, having discussed them with my team of MLs during the writing process, I felt that they were ready to be passed to HQ 3 Cdo Bde when we returned to the UK. These tasks, along with fitness training, filled my daylight hours on the journey to Ascension Island.

Every evening, however, we drank more than was strictly necessary to promote health. I do remember drinking a different coloured drink every night. Mostly, however, I remember sleeping a lot and slowly adjusting my thinking away from the need for aggression and instant results to getting organised for work in the UK. I sent a few signals to the Cadre in the UK and ensured that we were going to be ready for the coming ML courses starting in September. We would be based at Stonehouse Barracks in Plymouth, where we had been moved during our trip down south.

After about three days I went to take coffee with Captain Seymour. I really enjoyed his company and also felt that he needed a little light-weight relaxation to escape from his enormous responsibilities, if only briefly. Whilst chatting I asked him why he had been so kind as to bend the rules to allow us to travel back with him. His reply was a surprise but truly describes the man himself. He said that I had looked so tired and washed out that it would have been churlish of him to refuse, especially as I offered to arrive with my own life-saving gear (the life rafts). I was really surprised. I had been in Stanley for six nights before calling on him and had slept really well, eaten well and generally rested well for the entire time. I had felt on top form and really thought that I looked my best when I had spoken to him. His sympathy for my predicament at the time was increased by my exhausted appearance so he felt that he could not refuse my request.

The night before our arrival at Ascension on 7 July was one of the most bizarre I have ever spent. The officers' bar generally shut at about 10pm but it was our last night on board. At about 1025 the bar telephone rang; it was one of the SNCOs who had called to say that their bar was closed and asking if they could come over for a nightcap. I spoke to the SBS commander and to the bar staff, and replied 'Come on over!' I had not realised that they had also told the corporals' and Marines' bars to make their way to the wardroom. Soon there came a call at the door and in came all the senior SNCOs from both the Cadre and SBS. This was followed by a further bang on the door accompanied by a loud chorus of 'Hi Ho!' When the door opened in came the corporals and Marines, all stark naked with their underwear on their heads! They were on their knees mimicking the seven dwarfs but without Snow White! As they marched in each was given a can of beer and the party started. What an evening it was! It just got funnier and funnier as we got rid of our lingering thoughts of the Falklands and began to prepare ourselves for the days ahead. I left at about 0600 and was not the last by a long chalk. Arriving back at my cabin, I realised that I needed a shower before going to bed as I was covered in beer from some of the liberal spraying that had been going on. I was standing, fully dressed, in the shower that I shared with some of the RFA officers when the chief officer stuck his head in and asked how I was. I replied that I was washing my clothes first and then I planned to wash myself before bed. He told me to leave all my kit in the shower and he would sort it out. I went to bed and woke at about 0900 and got up to find a parcel outside my cabin door with all my clothes, clean, dry and ironed. Once again, the RFA had come up trumps. I went to the wardroom expecting it to look like a disaster area but it was spotless and all the guys were there, mostly looking a shade worse for wear, as was I. I went up to see the captain to thank him for all his help and hospitality and to request the bar bill for the previous night. He said it was all covered by his entertainments fund and was a gift for all we had done in the Falklands. I was quite delighted by his comments and am still a fan of the RFA for their stunning professionalism and competence, as well as their wonderful joie de vivre.

That day we arrived at Ascension and were transferred ashore in order to fly back to the UK. We split up into those going to Plymouth and those going to Arbroath. As the Cadre had moved to Plymouth during Operation Corporate, most of the guys opted to go to Plymouth. Those of us who had left our cars and personal belongings in Arbroath had to go there to collect them, together with those who were to be posted to 45 Commando RM, who would be staying on there.

From Ascension, we flew via Dakar, in Senegal, to RAF Leuchars near St Andrews in Scotland. The final part of our trip had one last highlight in Dakar. We were ordered off the aircraft whilst it was being refuelled but were not permitted to enter any buildings. We all hung around just outside the terminal building awaiting orders to re-embark when an Air France aircraft came in to land and disembarked its passengers. This in itself was not particularly interesting but when they had all gone into the buildings the air crew disembarked. Suddenly about 150 Royal Marines were struck dumb at the sight of ten or so Air France air hostesses, all of whom were particularly attractive, walking through us to get into the building. We had seen women on board the various ships and of course in Stanley but we were rendered speechless by this group of very attractive and beautifully groomed women and it remains for me the final highlight of Operation Corporate.

Chapter 13

Arbroath and Post-Operational Leave

(9–23 July)

Arriving at RAF Leuchars on Friday, 9 July we were told that we were to be met by the commandant general, Lieutenant General Sir Stuart Pringle, who had been CO of 45 Commando when I was on my ML course back in 1974. The guys on board the flight comprised a mixture of 45 Commando and SBS as well as the Cadre. We, however, were by far the scruffiest of the passengers. We had lost all our personal effects and spare clothing, having left them on RFA *Sir Tristram* where they were either destroyed by enemy action or looted by the British army. We only had what we had worn throughout the campaign. I was seriously concerned that the commandant general would be offended by our appearance and told my guys to wait until the 'meet and greet' was over and then we would quietly exit the plane and head for Arbroath. About 10 minutes after the last passenger had left the plane, Captain Peter Leicester RM, an old friend and military assistant to the commandant general, came on board and asked what we were doing. I told him but he informed me that General Pringle thought we were playing at being Special Forces and avoiding publicity. This was the last thing on my mind and I explained that we were all a little embarrassed about our appearance and did not wish to cause *him* any embarrassment. Peter immediately told me there would be no photographs and we were to come ashore straight away. General Pringle was not best pleased with me as he wanted to shake the hand of every Royal Marine returning from the South Atlantic and we were holding him up! Oh well, c'est la vie!

We left the plane and I reported to General Pringle, apologising for the misunderstanding, the delay and our appearance, but he did not seem interested so I crept away and boarded the coach feeling rather foolish. The coach ride back was extraordinary. Word must have got out that the Royal Marines were returning to Arbroath and every bridge had people on it, all cheering and waving to us. Dundee should have been quiet but as soon as the bus was recognised people started clapping and cheering. I still feel a little emotional now recalling that memory, and I was not alone. None of us had any idea how the English (and Scottish) public had been following the events of the previous three months. This really brought home to us how much we had been appreciated. It was a humbling experience.

I have no real recollection of the night I spent in Arbroath or what happened to the team after we had unloaded the coach. I vaguely remember shaking hands with all the guys and wishing them a good leave and then going to the mess to find all my gear in boxes and labelled. That was a surprise as I had completely forgotten that I had packed them myself before sailing. I called the base commander's office to ask him about my car. He told me to go to his office and he would give me the keys and help me to get it going. He explained that all the cars parked in the hangar had been started and run for 15 minutes once a week to keep their batteries charged and everything in order. I got to my car to find that all the tyres were very low so I drove slowly and carefully to the nearest garage in Arbroath to top up with fuel and air and check the oil ready for my drive south the next day.

During the evening I spoke with Mike Hitchcock (operations officer of 45 Commando RM), who had to get himself, his wife Irene and his new child to Poole without any transport as his family had travelled to Arbroath to meet him by train. I was setting out for Weymouth the next morning so I offered them a lift. On the morning of 10 June we loaded my car and set off for Dorset. It is a long and tedious drive at the best of times but was now just a mere hiccup in the journey home that had already taken us almost a month.

The drive took its usual full day and Mike and Irene kindly gave me a bed for the night. The following morning I drove home to my parents in Weymouth. I had been told to report to Brigade HQ in Plymouth on the following Monday morning so, being on my route, it gave me a night with my parents. They were delighted to see me and my father particularly wanted to show me off to his friends. Immediately after dinner he told me we were off to his club to meet his pals. It proved to be another evening of note! I was not allowed to put my hand in my pocket and for the entire evening our table was covered in pints of beer bought as thanks by my father's fellow club members. The latter part of the evening is rather hazy but my overall memory is one of my father's pride and his friends' appreciation of what we had all done down south. It was a memorable evening and the bollocking I received from my mother when we got home was well worth it!

On Sunday morning, 11 June, I left home and set off for Plymouth and what an experience that was! I had my radio tuned to Radio 4 and was listening to the coverage of the arrival of the SS *Canberra* at Southampton. I was so affected by the commentaries and the band music that several times I had to stop driving as I could not see through my tears. I have never been able to explain to myself my reaction to this but can only assume it was a mixture of pride, pleasure at returning home in one piece and amazement that for the first time in thirteen years of service the British public was overtly showing their pride in the armed forces. I had been surprised in Stanley by the kindness of the telephone manager but this was even more so. Every single bridge over the road between Weymouth and Exeter and onwards to Plymouth was covered with people waving Union Flags and cheering everything that looked military. My Alfa Romeo looked neither military nor English so I was largely ignored. I am very glad I was. I do not believe that I could have coped with all that kindness and emotion in the mood I was in at that time.

The next couple of weeks were a revelation to me for many reasons. I spent a couple of days in Plymouth sorting out my accommodation in the mess and organising the preparations for the ML courses in September, as well as my own personal administration. I knew I was handing over the Cadre soon after the return from leave but I had no idea what my next job was to be and frankly I did not care. I passed on the papers I had written on my way home so that they could be processed by HQ 3 Cdo Bde and looked forward to my leave.

I took my car to a local garage on the Monday afternoon to ask for help. I explained I had been away for a while but I needed my car to be serviced as I had a fair bit of driving to do over the next month or so. The garage owner said, 'Leave it with me and we will do it tomorrow and have it ready for you by 4 o'clock.' I was in uniform but it did not occur to me that this was anything out of the ordinary until I went to pick up my car the next day. It was gleaming. It had been cleaned as if for sale, fully serviced and immaculate. I was delighted and thanked them profusely for their great job and then asked them for the bill. The garage owner asked where I had been and I said I had just returned from a long trip to sea. He responded by asking me if it had been to the southern hemisphere and I said yes. He then said 'Your money is no good here, and thank you and your colleagues for everything you have done over the last three months. This is the least we can do to say thank you to our Royal Marines for everything you do for us.' It was overwhelming and I had to leave the garage very swiftly to avoid making a fool of myself in the face of this incredibly generous gesture by a wonderful group of guys.

I was off on leave at the end of the week and told to report back to Plymouth about six weeks later in late August. I went straight to Weston-on-the-Green to my parachute club because I really wanted to have some free fall time, having missed so much of it since April. I was greeted like a returning hero which I found really embarrassing, and managed to last only one night.

I had planned to go to Cardiff the next day to attend the British Parachute Championships but I decided to stay for the day and set out in the evening along the M4. On the Saturday night I had met Matt Selfridge (a Parachute Regiment captain who had been second in command of patrol company of 3 Para during Operation Corporate). We had shared a couple of beers and talked over our difficulties in returning to normality. He was there to carry out his first parachute jump with a 'square' or ram air parachute, on his way home to his family in Edinburgh. Around mid-day as I was drinking a cup of coffee outside the clubhouse I suddenly heard a really loud noise of flapping canopy. I looked up in time to watch some poor individual completely wrapped in his main and reserve parachutes heading towards a collision with the airfield perimeter track. I immediately turned towards the clubhouse, ordered everyone inside and closed the doors. I then ran over and confirmed that the man had died in the impact, before realising that it was Matt. Obviously, all parachuting stopped and the chief instructor (Warrant Officer Ray Willis RAF), whom I had known for several years, came over to ask me who it was and his condition. I told him that it was Matt and that he hadn't made it. He went straight into the fatal accident routine and I returned to the clubhouse to drink more coffee and talk to Matt's fiancée, whom I had also met the previous night.

The young woman lived in Bulford and I told her I would get her home. Fortunately, she had Matt's car keys. I telephoned the duty officer of 3 Para in Bulford to give him the sad news and asked if he could arrange transport for me to return to Weston-on-the-Green when I arrived with Matt's car at the 3 Para Officers' Mess in Bulford. Telling Ray Willis that I would be back in about an hour or so, I set off to return the young lady to her parental home near Bulford. She was very calm and composed but I think also in a state of shock so I did not want her to be left alone. When we arrived, her parents were out shopping so I suggested she should contact them and I then sat with her and waited for their return. She insisted that she was fine and could look after herself but I was not prepared to leave her alone until her parents arrived. Once they had returned I left. At the 3 Para guardroom I asked for the duty officer to be called and gave him Matt's car and jumped into the Landrover with the driver that had been organised for me to return to Weston-on-the-Green.

By now all I really wanted to do was to head off to Cardiff but I was asked by Ray Willis if I would do him and Matt's parents one final favour. I said yes before asking what it was. Ray explained that Matt's parents were in Edinburgh and someone was needed to identify the body, as this was necessary by law following a fatal accident. As I had recently served with Matt and knew him well enough, I could make the formal identification to save his parents the experience as well as the trip from Edinburgh. As can be imagined, I was not keen but it was the least I could do so I waited for the policeman who was tasked with taking me to the mortuary in Bicester and returning me to the airfield. Had it been less tragic it would have been amusingly strange. The policeman was a kind man and I assumed him to be pretty experienced as well, but his small talk left a lot to be desired. He first questioned why I had been asked to identify the body. When I told him that I knew Matt and had recently served with him in the South Atlantic, he responded by saying 'Well that's good, so you will be well used to seeing dead bodies then.' I could have done without that! At the mortuary he explained to the man in charge there that I had just returned from the Falklands and would identify the body. The mortuary manager (I suppose) then proceeded to tell me that his son was serving on one of the carriers and had yet to come home but at least he could help out one of his colleagues. The policeman was, by now, beginning to look a bit queasy but I thought 'not my problem' and went through the identification procedure and signed the form confirming the identity of the body. Afterwards we walked back to the policeman's car. As we were getting in, he asked 'Do you fancy a drink, because I need one?' I've never been known to turn down a free drink so we stopped at a pub on the way to the airfield. I had a half of bitter and he had a very large double brandy which did not touch the sides!

I knew that I had missed the British Parachute Championships so my trip to Cardiff was one of interest and preparation for going with the free fall team to France should they be the winners. I did not have any idea if the RM free fall team would win and whether they would represent the UK in the World Championships to be held in France later in July. I arrived at Cardiff late on Sunday night to be told that the Royal Marines were well ahead in the competition and would certainly be providing the

British ten-man team to represent the UK at the World Championships, and that mine was the tenth name on the team list! I was a regular member of the competition team but apart from one parachute jump at Ascension Island I had not fallen out of an aircraft for three months so had not expected to be considered. The free fall team thought otherwise, and I was selected as second reserve for the team. I stayed at Cardiff for the entire week supporting the team and then returned to Weston-on-the-Green the following Friday for a relaxing weekend of parachuting.

My favourite pop group has always been Santana and when I returned to Weston-on-the-Green I was told by the guys that Santana would be playing live in Oxford the next night but it was sold out and no tickets were available. They then told me that the club members had got together and bought an extra ticket for me for when I returned from the Falkland Islands! This was another kindness to add to the many others shown when I returned to the world after the Falklands conflict and it fully restored my faith in humanity after the events down south. The show was superb and I found myself sitting amongst a group of skydiving friends, realising that I had returned to the real world. It was a great feeling.

The remainder of my leave was spent attending the World Parachute Championships in Vichy, France, after a six-week training period at a small parachute centre in La Palisse about 25km away. It was the first time I had parachuted in France and I thoroughly enjoyed the experience. We did rather well, gaining three bronze medals for the three different parts of the competition. After our return to the UK I spent the final couple of weeks of leave visiting family and generally relaxing before returning to work in Plymouth.

After the stress of Operation Corporate I could not have had a better break in which to return to normality. I was therefore really looking forward to returning to work even though I knew it was only to hand over the Cadre to my replacement.

Chapter 14

Return to Normality: M&AW Cadre
(September 1982)

Following a long and much-needed break from all things military, we joined or rejoined our units and the M&AW Cadre's brigade Recce Tp ceased to exist.

The papers written on the route home were sent to brigade HQ for the staff to read and forward to more senior headquarters as required. I prepared to hand over control of the Cadre to Captain Jonathan Lear, who had returned from a two-year posting to the USMC after commanding the Recce Tp of 41 Commando RM.

I had two weeks to settle into Stonehouse Barracks and to meet my new CSM, WO2 Bill Oxbery. WO2 Brian Snowdon had left during the leave period and joined 45 Commando as a CSM. Lieutenant Jon Young was to provide the continuity as he still had a further year to serve as administrative officer to the Cadre. Poor Jon had been nominated to act as the casualty reporting officer for the Commando Brigade during Operation Corporate. Whilst the rest of us had been down south, he had the dreadful job of informing next of kin of injuries and deaths that occurred among the Royal Marines. This was a difficult but very important job. I know that although he hated it, Jon had performed the task superbly well and kept the entire brigade's next of kin informed throughout the operation.

We were all glad to be back at work in the Cadre and to be preparing for the ML1 and ML2 courses that were due to start in early September 1982. I had received my new posting as a staff officer (SO3 O&D/Sy/PInfo at HQ TRSFRM) at the headquarters in Eastney near Portsmouth. As the staff officer responsible for operations and deployment, it was my job to ensure that all units under command were fully manned and equipped. In addition, I was to be responsible for the security of all specialist personnel who required higher levels of security clearance than the normal troops;

I was also the nominated controller of the public relations team (consisting of a Royal Marine SNCO and a Royal Navy photographer), the provider of defensive briefs about all relevant public relations incidents within the HQ command and also the nominated public information officer responsible for providing the commander with briefs on all matters concerning his command that came into the public eye.

It was a busy but very dull job that fully deserved its nickname as the SSLJO of the HQ (that is to say, the staff officer responsible for anything that did not clearly come under any other staff officer!). The headquarters for Training, Reserve and Special Forces Royal Marines (HQ TRSFRM) was co-located next to the Royal Marines Museum on the seafront at Eastney, about 5km east of Portsmouth Dockyard.

I was not looking forward to the posting but I knew that anything after the Cadre would be disappointing so accepted my posting with good grace. I was relieving Captain David Nicholls, whom I had replaced at the Cadre, so it was good to see him again and I knew I would receive a superb handover, just as I had two-and-a-half years previously.

After I'd had two weeks in Plymouth, Jon Lear arrived to start his two-week handover and a week into that the two ML courses started. The first week of the handover was busy and spent passing on the multiple files and plans for the coming months. The courses were already sorted up to their completion in late March 1983, leaving scope for Jon to include his planned leadership of the organisation. The arrival of the courses meant that we all decamped to west Cornwall for the first few weeks of the ML course for all participants.

The experience gained on Operation Corporate was useful for the Cadre NCOs who were now back in their instructor roles within the Cadre. Chris Stone was back with us, having recovered his fitness after being injured at Top Malo. I immediately nominated him as the course sergeant major for the next ML2 courses to keep him on his toes. The remaining senior and JNCOs were all back in place. Halfway through the second week of the handover I became surplus to requirements. Jon was now the commanding officer and I was hanging around trying not to get in the way. We (Jon and I) decided that I would leave on the Thursday, giving me a long weekend to get to Portsmouth with all my kit. Jon very kindly allowed me to use the Cadre 4-ton vehicle and driver to send all my goods and chattels to the house that I had bought in Farlington (about 10km from my new office). This was most appreciated as I had, by then, acquired a lot of domestic stuff. The official reason for the trip was to collect a large supply of ropes and other climbing kit from the main stores held in Portsmouth Dockyard, so the empty vehicle travelling to Portsmouth was most useful! In those days bachelors were not given assistance on changing postings, other than travelling expenses. Moving to a house rather than to a mess was not supported by the system, so this assistance from Jon was invaluable.

On my last day with the Cadre I was ambushed by Sergeants John Mitchell and Chris Stone and they told me they had a proper surprise for me. We were en route from St Just to Bosigran when they broke this to me and when I asked what it was, they laughed and said 'You'll find out!' Their surprise was to take me up 'Suicide Wall', which is one of the most difficult climbs on the Bosigran main cliff. It is a 210ft Mild XS (Extremely Severe) route with pitches up to 5c in individual grading. I had climbed a few HVS (Hard Very Severe) routes but this was definitely out of my league. But I couldn't let them down and it remains the highlight of my entire climbing career as I was led up this climb in farewell to the Cadre.

It was a perfect end to my time in the Cadre. Blue skies and dry, with a gentle breeze – I could not have had a better way of saying goodbye to them all than by being taken up a route that I had always felt was impossible for me. I thoroughly enjoyed both the experience and their kind farewells at the end of it.

A really good night out in the Miners Arms Inn in St Just followed and I left the Cadre the next morning after breakfast and drove back to Plymouth to prepare for my next job in the Corps.

Chapter 15

Closing Words

When the post operation reports on Operation Corporate were published in late 1982 the following comments were written by the relevant head-quarter commanders.

Brigadier J.H.A. Thompson, Commander 3 Cdo Bde Royal Marines, wrote:

> I would like to add that my brigade Recce Tp (Mountain & Arctic Warfare Cadre Royal Marines) was far more reliable than all other reconnaissance forces. They did what they were told, provided good information, did not get lost, had no 'blue on blue' situations, didn't get caught by bad soldiering, and at Top Malo House showed that they could achieve 100% success with very little preparation and no bullshit.

Major General J.J. Moore, Commander of the Divisional Headquarters/ Commander British Land Forces Falkland Islands stated in his report:

> The battle initiation of the Mountain and Arctic Warfare Cadre (M&AW) of 3 Cdo Bde was an unqualified success. Their patrolling, reporting and conduct in action were excellent. Able to deploy up to eight four-man teams and coordinated from Brigade Headquarters the Cadre was ideally suited to long-range patrolling and information gathering, in which role its performance compared most favourably with some of the Special Forces patrols.

As the very fortunate man who commanded these very competent and very capable men, I was supremely blessed during Operation Corporate. I remain incredibly proud of our achievements then and of being a member of a very special part of the Royal Marines.

Organisation

Mountain & Arctic Warfare Cadre, 1 April 1982

Officer Commanding:	Captain R. Boswell RM
Administrative Officer:	Lieutenant J. Young RM
Sergeant Major:	WO2 B. Snowdon RM
TQ (Quartermaster):	Colour Sergeant E. Young RM
Senior Instructor:	Colour Sergeant P. Montgomery RM
ML1 Instructors:	Colour Sergeant W. Wright RM (additional to complement prior to joining)
	Sergeant K. Mahon RM
	Sergeant J. Mitchell RM
	Sergeant C. Stone RM (additional to complement prior to joining)
	Sergeant D. Wassall RM
	Sergeant D. Wilson RM
	Corporal N. Devenish RM
ML2 instructors:	Corporal K. Blackmore RM
	Corporal A. Boyle RM
	Corporal G. Foster RM
	Corporal G. Heeney RM
	Corporal A. Heward RM
	Corporal T. Holleran RM
	Corporal S. Last RM (additional to complement prior to joining)
	Corporal J. MacGregor RM
	Corporal N. Meade RM
	Corporal S. Nicoll RM
Administrative staff:	Marine E. Blyton RM (Storeman)
	Marine G. Forester RM (Driver)

Appendix 2

What it Takes to be a Mountain Leader

This Appendix gives readers an insight into what makes an ML 'tick', describing what type of individual is attracted to the specialised role of a mountain leader and what a volunteer candidate for training can expect in his future employment. For a non-military reader any account of warfare replete with acronyms, abbreviations and jargon can appear daunting, almost impenetrable. However, it needs to be accessible in order to be understood without sacrificing the actual language used on the ground. To do so would lose the richness of its unique context. In order to retain the sense of reality and do so without alienating or losing the reader, it needs a helping hand. Any combination of military abbreviations and acronyms can cause disinterest, which is why there is a Glossary at the beginning of the book. In addition, the perhaps common assumption by military types that all military actions make sense, and can be easily followed by all readers, can prompt unhelpful notions of exaggeration and disbelief, leading to loss of interest.

Following are extracts from an interview given by Major General Julian Thompson in which he was asked about the attributes of mountain leaders and the work of the M&AW Cadre during Operation Corporate.

Interviewer: This is the story of one military action. From start to finish it lasted about thirty minutes. It was fought on a May afternoon in 1982 between seventeen men of Argentina's 602 Commando and nineteen men of the Royal Marines Mountain & Arctic Warfare Cadre. It was a micro-cosm of the bravery and horror of war. For the Falkland Islands read any campaign in which professional soldiers kill or are killed. Their narrow battle lines were drawn around a desolate farm called Top Malo, 65km ahead of the British lines. The man who wanted it taken was Brigadier, now Major General, Julian Thompson.

Thompson: When we made the plans for the landings, we realised that we must have reconnaissance ahead of where we wanted to go and also on the flanks of the routes we were going to use so that we didn't walk into some nasty surprises on the way. And the best way to do this was to use the Cadre and I knew that we could put these chaps out onto the tops of these mountains, they could get themselves there, they could survive whatever the weather so they wouldn't be crying for help, saying 'Come take me away because I've got frost bite', and thirdly using their expertise they would remain hidden and pass back messages to us on the radio about any enemy in the vicinity and give us the opportunity to deal with that enemy before they started dealing with us.

Interviewer: The natural habitat of the Royal Marines Mountain & Arctic Warfare unit is behind enemy lines. What kind of men are these, the invisible fighters?

Thompson: Well, I would think he's actually rather a special sort of chap; he may actually be not the sort of fellow standing in the front rank looking incredibly smart who catches everybody's eye. I think he's got to be and I've always described him as rather like a badger really. To have this ability, almost like an animal, and I don't mean this in any derogatory sense, to suborn his personal feelings of discomfort and take no notice of them and almost sort of switch off his feelings of discomfort and at the same time not switch off his other senses so that he's been dozing away and not noticing what is going on. And he must also be an absolutely first-class Marine, soldier. They are, I believe, among the best mountain troops in the world, bar none. For that's what they do and that's their special-isation. And we do teach them to use radios in the same way as the SAS and SBS are trained. But obviously there is no point putting a guy on a high hill, telling him to look out for the enemy if he can't then tell you that he has seen someone coming or wants to do something about it.

Interviewer: General Thompson had every intention of doing something about Top Malo, swiftly. But how heavily did it worry him that in one single action he was risking the loss of so many specialist men of a small elite unit?

Thompson: Yes, I was conscious of that but there were some special circumstances surrounding it. Firstly, the enemy had been spotted by a Cadre OP and therefore I wanted the people who had to go and do the job to be, as it were, familiar with the OP who had spotted the enemy because it might be that the two would have to work together and that, therefore, one didn't want to introduce a fresh element into the equation. The second point was that most of the other troops at that time were doing other things and I also wanted to make certain that the Special Forces enemy, and we knew they were Special Forces because they wore different kind of uniforms, curiously enough, from everybody else, unlike us, might be quite a hard enemy to crack and they also had to have the best people to go and take them out in a clean-cut, surgical operation. And we wanted to make certain that there were no stragglers from that lot who could cause us trouble later on. And therefore I picked what I regarded as the best people that I had to hand to go and do the job.

*   *   *

The birth of the ML branch/specialisation is very well covered by Mark Bentinck's *Vertical Assault* (Royal Marines Historical Society, Special Publication 34). This very clearly details the creation of the branch in 1942 and its history up to 2008 when the book was published. It briefly covers some aspects of Operation Corporate in 1982, but not in sufficient detail in my opinion.

What does it take to be a Mountain Leader?

Volunteers for ML training may come from any part of the Royal Marines but the majority are young corporals who may have served as Marines within the Corps' Recce Tps. There is one Recce Tp in every Commando unit. The ML role is to extend the tasks carried out by Recce Tps for their commanding officer both on exercises and on operations. The MLs, however, are far more prepared for the difficulties of terrain than any Recce Tp, in spite of the fact that most of the NCOs are MLs, as is the Recce Tp commander who is an ML officer.

In general, MLs recruit MLs. A good Marine or lance corporal or even general duties (GD) corporal serving in a Recce Tp will be approached by another ML NCO to discuss the way ahead for his career, with questions such as 'Are you interested in a future in reconnaissance work and if so, would you be interested in attending an ML course?' The course details are published regularly within daily routine orders (DROs) and any Marines up to the rank of sergeant can apply to attend. The DROs do not, however, give the full breakdown of the commitment and skills required to complete the course. A robust sense of humour is never listed in the requirements even though it is probably the most important characteristic required to get through the eight-month course.

As stated in the Introduction, the courses start in early September each year at the Commando Training Centre Royal Marines (CTCRM), which became the base for ML training courses in 2004. A week of fitness tests, military skills tests and aptitude tests are carried out to confirm the results of the ML selection tests that all candidates must pass before arrival on the course.

It should be no surprise to all candidates that the standard of fitness in the branch is very high and no quarter is given to those volunteers who do not arrive fully prepared for what is ahead. All Royal Marines recruits receive instruction and training from MLs during their basic training. All trained ranks who subsequently join any unit, or sub-unit, in 3 Cdo Bde will receive further exposure to and training from MLs. Knowing about the type of character that has already completed ML training serves as an indication of what is expected of aspiring ML students. Punishments in the course are generally press-ups, with the number of press-ups dependent upon the severity of the offence. This offers a further chance for improving upper body fitness, as well as the opportunity for mickey-taking by all involved. Unlike recruit training, all volunteers are experienced Royal Marines and thus expect the fitness standard to be high. They should arrive prepared for rigorous testing. Failure in the first week is rare!

After the initial week the course moves to west Cornwall to spend time learning to climb the numerous sea cliffs. I had climbed a little before my course but this was no excuse for slacking. All students start as *ab initio* climbers and are treated as novices for the sake of continuity and making managed progress. Established climbing routes are always named with utterly random titles and graded on difficulty. All ML students start at the lowest, easiest, rock climbing grade, following a lead climber for safety. As climbing competency improves, so will the grading and skill level until the student is leading a multi-pitch climb safely. (A pitch is defined as a rope length of safe climbing.) One of my first climbs (Black Slab at Sennen Cove) was led by Sergeant 'Prof' Harvey and I foolishly said to him that I thought I was going to fall off. He was about 3m above me at the time, and his response was 'If you do, you'll hurt yourself unless you use the correct call that we have taught you.' I had no idea what he was talking about, and as I fell off I shouted 'Ohhhh!' He held me and said 'Well done, you remembered!' Fortunately, it was a windy day and he thought I had said 'Hold', and so held me. Had I kept quiet or said something else I would definitely have hurt myself as there is little sympathy for failing to take in the relevant lessons.

At the end of the second week in Cornwall all the students are given an indication of how they are progressing with the course. Mine was given by Colour Sergeant Willie Patterson, a very experienced ML and a dour Scotsman with a superb sense of humour that showed occasionally.

I reported to him and he looked me up and down and gave me my course update which was 'Well, at least you are fit.' I waited for some more words of wisdom but was told to 'send in the next man', so I shuffled off thinking I had a long way to go!

These experiences are pretty similar for all those who attempt the ML2 course. Part of the requirement for all MLs is a healthy disregard for their own personal welfare as their priority must always be the effectiveness of those for whom they are responsible. This can be a section of eight or a company of 120 or even a unit of 650. In the mountains or in the Arctic the chain of command remains in place but the responsibility for safety always remains with the senior attending ML at whatever rank. Early realisation of the level of responsibility is built into every part of ML training. As the climbs get longer and more difficult technically, and the weather gets steadily worse, the levels of responsibility rise and the need for all the skills to be second nature to all MLs becomes more apparent.

On completion of the Cornwall phase all ML2s are capable of leading at 'Severe' level. For those climbers among the readers this may not seem very high but you should note that the MLs need to be able to lead at this level by day and by night and regardless of climatic conditions – rain or snow or whatever else is thrown at them. This ability is tested during the next phase in North Wales.

North Wales brings in the start of the mountain marches with increasing levels of kit and difficulty, and the added benefit of having to think tactically about route-finding with the ability to select sensible routes avoiding potential enemy locations as well as covering the ground at the best possible speed. The end of the Wales phase culminates with the march from east of Snowdon on a northerly course to Abergwyngregyn ('Aber') on the Gwynedd coastline. This takes in several of the sixteen Welsh 3,000ft peaks, known as 'Furths'. This demanding exercise is a genuine test of mountain craft, stamina and leadership, confirming that the first eight weeks of training have seen continual progress by all students.

In early November the emphasis switches to the specialist skill of survival and learning how to live off the land when no other food source is available. The students and instructors move from their Welsh base and home for four weeks to Scotland and its cooler climes, and the students, in teams of four, are taken to a Hebridean island where for ten days they have to live off the land and survive on what they can catch or trap. They are strip-searched prior to being deployed, to prevent any 'illegal' items being smuggled through. They are issued prisoner of war clothing and allowed a knife, a survival tin and a few tools for making shelters. They are let loose on a large estate and monitored for safety cover as well as gauging their progress in utilising survival skills. The students are expected to perform as strong individuals and contribute to a team environment. At the end of the ten-day period they are gathered together, put into a helicopter and sent back to CTCRM. At some stage during this activity they are 'captured' and subjected to a three-day prisoner of war experience, including resistance to interrogation training. On completion they are returned to CTCRM, where they are debriefed on the previous eight weeks of the course. They are then divided into Arctic Warfare-trained (AWT) students and non-AWT personnel. The non-AWT personnel are sent on a five-week ski course in Norway to ensure that they are competent skiers by the New Year when they will return to Norway for the full Arctic Warfare (AW) instructors course. The AWT personnel are put with fully trained MLs and used as additional instructors for the mountain training of the Commando Brigade as they are already competent skiers.

After Christmas leave, the course reconvenes and travels to Norway, where the students complete a modified AW course. It is modified as they are being trained to be instructors and thus they have to learn not only the skills but also to teach them. This is the most important part of the ML2 course for the Arctic novices and proof of its effectiveness is that at the end of the ML2 course all ML2s are capable of running an AWT course for novices in the Commando Brigade. When I finished my course I became OC of 40 Commando Reconnaissance Troop for two years and then was sent to be the Royal Marine officer attached to the UK battalion of the AMF(L). This was the NATO 'fire brigade' used as a tripwire force and made up from all sixteen nations within NATO at that time. This was the force that would face the Soviets first, ensuring the full involvement of NATO in any ensuing war. Despite having served only one winter in Norway, I felt fully prepared for this role and spent three happy years being the 'expert' Arctic soldier with the AMF(L) battalion.

The final part of the Norway phase for the ML course is the 200km patrol. This is a long-range ski patrol where the ML1 students lead patrols of ML2 students through a variety of military tasks, always including a long approach march on skis and, after the military tasks are completed, a long withdrawal phase, also on skis. The total distance is never less than 200km and often longer, but it is still called the 200km for convenience.

On completion of the winter phase of the ML course, the MLs gather in Norway for a concentration period of training. This has varied over the years, and has included climbing in the Norwegian Lyngen Alps as well as participating in various NATO exercises as Recce Tps. I am not aware of the current system but I am sure it will not have changed a great deal and the need for winter snow and ice-climbing training will have remained within the course.

Upon return to the UK the final phase of the course takes place: the long-range patrol exercise held in Scotland. This takes in all the military skills learnt or improved during the course. It is a complete test of military skills, fitness and stamina, and again involves the ML1 students leading ML2 students in four-man teams over very difficult terrain by both land and sea in March when the weather is never on your side.

The course for the ML2 students is in many respects a cross between teaching specialist skills and confirmation of leadership ability and aptitude. The job of an ML within the Commando Brigade is a difficult one. He must know everything about Arctic warfare and be able to pass that knowledge to his men, but he must also be able to fit in with any military requirements for long-range patrolling. It is this chameleon-like mix of skills that makes the ML specialisation unique. In my experience the MLs I had the good fortune to work with were, without exception, intelligent, committed and extremely physically fit, and as a result it was like managing a herd of cats. They did not require leading, but guiding and mentoring. They needed a firm hand to ensure that the aims of whatever activity in which we were involved were not lost in their professional enthusiasm to get the best results.

ML Experiences and Training

For the ML2 corporal, the end of his ML course is but the beginning of a long saga of additional training courses up to and including his ML1 course to produce the finished article. These courses are largely military but also include some civilian climbing and leadership courses to ensure that the ML world remains in contact with, and up to date with, all trends and techniques in climbing within the wider climbing world. An ML1 is qualified to plan, arrange and execute training up to unit level. This responsibility requires a mixture of astute professional leadership and man management. Within each Commando unit the senior ML is appointed as the experienced individual who works within unit headquarters to ensure that the commanding officers' training objectives are met.

It is worth pointing out that there has been a continual series of requests, mostly from service expeditions, for Royal Marine ML assistance in all corners of the world. As explained in Chapter 2, two of my corporals (Neal Meade and Al Heward) were on early Easter leave in 1982 before taking on the role as safety and training assistants to an army climbing expedition to the Andes mountains. I have no idea whether the expedition ever took place but I would not be surprised if it had been cancelled as the Falklands campaign took priority over all other military activities in the summer of 1982. In my time in the branch, MLs were involved in expeditions to New Zealand, the Himalayas, Borneo, Alaska, the Andes and the Alps. As far as the Cadre was concerned, if the expeditions took place during the summer months (May to August) then it was perfectly acceptable to release people to participate as it was continuation training of good value.

The primary military courses for MLs included initially the parachute course and, for several of the corporals, specialist signals courses, the former for additional insertion skills and the latter to ensure that we were always able to pass on information gained on patrols to the higher HQs that needed the information. Occasional specialist skills required for certain tasks involved self-organised attachments to specialist units where the necessary professional skills were to be found.

Thus by the time an ML1 SNCO completes his ML1 course he will have spent a minimum of two years undergoing ML and specialist courses, as well as promotion courses. Each ML was, and is, a very highly trained soldier who can fit into any specialised intelligence-gathering organisation within the armed forces – and often does.

The advent of the specialised operational role of the Cadre, and the ML branch as a whole, in 1992 has meant that the inherent competence and professionalism of the ML branch is now recognised and well respected throughout the Royal Marines and the military world in general. MLs are now stationed with many foreign armed forces, as well as with the army in the UK. The ML course is acknowledged worldwide, and every year a number of non-UK troops participate on the ML2 course, thus adding to the scope of the training provided.

The ML Character

It is my belief that the ML character has not changed one iota since the misguided belief held by many within the Corps that it was a 'climbing club'. Throughout the time that this epithet was used by non-MLs to describe an organisation that they neither understood nor wished to join, the Cadre was training the Commando Brigade for operations in the Arctic and the mountains. ML NCOs were providing leaders for all the Recce Tps of Commando units, and various SNCOs and ML officers were being sent on secondments all over the world to share their skills with the mountain troops of many other nations. The fact that a few were able to participate in mountaineering expeditions was but a minor side skill that was jumped upon by the misinformed, who neither understood nor wanted anything to do with a branch with such high standards and skills.

I remain (quite obviously) very proud of my ML history and experience, and I was not at all surprised by the success of the Cadre in 1982 and by its many successes ever since. Being an ML within the Royal Marines is now one of the important ambitions of both new recruits and new young officers to the Corps. As an ML this, I believe, is something of which to be proud.

Order of Battle

M&AW Cadre, Operation Corporate, 21–31 May 1982

Headquarters Section

Capt R. Boswell OC
CSgt W. Wright CSM/TQ

Sgt M. Mclean
Cpl S. Groves

1 Section

Lt F. Haddow
Cpl Foster (M79)
Cpl G. Heeney (Radio)
Cpl N. West

2 Section

CSgt E. Young
Sgt J. Martin
Cpl J. White (Radio)
Cpl J. O'Connor (M79)

3 Section

Sgt D. Wassall
Cpl N. Meade
Cpl S. Last (Radio)
Cpl A. Heward (M79)

4 Section

Sgt K. Mahon
Sgt J. Mitchell (Radio)
Cpl M. O'Donnell
Cpl G. Bickett (M79)

5 Section

Lt C. Murray
Cpl N. Devenish
Cpl S. Nicoll (Radio)
Cpl R. Sharp (M79)

6 Section

CSgt P. Montgomery
Sgt D. Wilson (M79)
Cpl K. Blackmore (Radio)
Cpl R. Sey

7 Section

Sgt C. Stone
Sgt J. Rowe
Cpl A. Boyle (Radio)
Cpl M. Barnacle (M79)

8 Section

Sgt T. Doyle
Cpl T. Holleran (Radio)
Cpl J. McGregor (M79)
Cpl S. Healey

Notes: If required we had two Troops: 1 (Sections 1–4) and 2 (Sections 5–8). Any operations requiring more than a troop to be commanded by the OC. The majority of operations were by sections acting alone.

* * *

From 1 June 1982

After injuries suffered at Top Malo and elsewhere*, the Cadre was reorganised into seven sections as follows:

Headquarters Section

Capt R. Boswell (OC)   Cpl T. Holleran
CSgt W. Wright (CSM/TQ)   Cpl N. West
Sgt M. Mclean

1 Section	2 Section	3 Section
Lt F. Haddow	CSgt E. Young	Sgt D. Wassall
Cpl Foster (M79)	Sgt J. Martin	Cpl N. Meade
Cpl G. Heeney (Radio)	Cpl J. White (Radio)	Cpl S. Last (Radio)
Cpl J. McGregor	Cpl J. O'Connor (M79)	Cpl A. Heward (M79)

4 Section	5 Section	6 Section
Sgt K. Mahon	Lt C. Murray	CSgt P. Montgomery
Sgt J. Mitchell (Radio)	Cpl N. Devenish	Sgt D. Wilson (M79)
Cpl M. O'Donnell	Cpl S. Nicoll (Radio)	Cpl K. Blackmore (Radio)
Cpl G. Bickett (M79)	Cpl R. Sharp (M79)	Cpl R. Sey

7 Section

Sgt J. Rowe
Cpl A. Boyle (Radio)
Cpl A.M. Barnacle (M79)
Cpl S. Healey

* Sgt Stone, Sgt Doyle and Cpl Groves were all injured at Top Malo. Cpl West was injured on patrol and moved to HQ Section.

Index